Credit and the Australian Department Store Since 1900

Jackie Dickenson

Credit and the Australian Department Store Since 1900

palgrave
macmillan

Jackie Dickenson
School of Historical and Philosophical Studies
University of Melbourne
Melbourne, Australia

ISBN 978-3-032-16611-1 ISBN 978-3-032-16612-8 (eBook)
https://doi.org/10.1007/978-3-032-16612-8

This Palgrave Macmillan imprint is published by the registered company Springer Nature Switzerland AG.
The registered company address is: Gewerbestrasse 11, 6330 Cham, Switzerland

To Moira, my mum, who loathed inequality.

Acknowledgements

This book grew out of research work for the Australian Research Council-funded project, 'Shop Talk: Department Stores, Shoppers and Consumer Capitalism, 1945–2025' (DP220100943). My heartfelt thanks go to Robert Crawford for giving me the opportunity to work on this terrific project and for his guidance and generosity, especially in allowing me to use his interview material. Besides being an exemplary historian, Robert is the epitome of collegiality. I also wish to thank Kate Darian-Smith, Catherine Kovesi, and Sean Scalmer for their insightful comments on an earlier draft of this manuscript and for their continuing friendship and support.

Ethics Approval RMIT University, no. 25587 Shop Talk: Department Stores, Shoppers and Consumer Capitalism, 1945–2025. Approved 26 July 2022.

Competing Interests The author has no competing interests to declare that are relevant to the content of this manuscript.

About the Author

Jackie Dickenson is an Honorary Fellow in the School of Historical and Philosophical Studies at the University of Melbourne, Australia. She has published widely on Australian history, labour history, and advertising history, including *Australian Women in Advertising in the Twentieth Century* (2016) and *Behind Glass Doors: The World of Australian Advertising Agencies 1959–1989* (co-written with Robert Crawford, 2016). Her recent publications include *The Routledge Companion to the History of Advertising* (2025), as co-editor and contributor. She is currently editing Volume 6 (1920s to the present) of Bloomsbury's forthcoming *A Cultural History of Luxury*, as well as developing (with Professor Crawford) a study of J. Walter Thompson's expansion into the Asia Pacific region after the Second World War and researching a cultural history of luxury in Australia.

Contents

List of Abbreviations

ACA	Australian Consumers Association
AEU	Amalgamated Engineering Union
AICM	Australian Institute for Credit Management
ALP	Australian Labor Party
ALS	Australian Loyalty Association
AMA	American Marketing Association
ARFN	Australian Retail Financial Network Ltd
CM	Records of Coles-Myer Ltd
CRC	Commonwealth Rationing Commission
DAV	Drapers' Association of Victoria
DPS	Deposit-Purchase System
GFC	Global Financial Crisis
ME	Myer Emporium
MSL	The Mutual Store Limited
NAB	National Australia Bank
NRCA	National Retail Credit Association
NRMA	National Retail Merchants Association
NSW	New South Wales
OPA	Optional Payment Account
PBA	Permanent Budget Account
RBA	Reserve Bank of Australia
RCMA	Retail Credit Men's Association
RCMNA	Retail Credit Men's National Association
RTA	Retail Traders' Association of NSW
SLV	State Library of Victoria

UMA	University of Melbourne Archives
VSS	Victorian Shopping Service
VURC	Victorian United Retailers' Council

List of Figures

CHAPTER 1

Introduction

Abstract Histories of consumer credit in the Australian context are limited. Recent shifts away from interest-bearing credit and towards Buy Now Pay Later (BNPL) platforms make its history in Australia deserving of reassessment. Focusing on retail credit in Australian department stores, the book explores the social distinctions, technological innovations, and marketing activities that have influenced the expansion of this form of credit in Australia since 1900, placing them in their economic, social, cultural, and political contexts. The book asks two key questions. Was the entanglement of Australian consumers in credit culture 'inevitable'? And was access to credit 'democratised' after the Second World War?

Keywords Credit • Retail • Class • Status anxiety • Marketing • Technology • Australian history

Australians have relied on credit since the European invasion. They have borrowed money to buy land, build businesses, establish homes, and indulge all manner of personal desires. They have used credit to make it through to payday, to feed their families, heat their homes, and manage an unforeseen expense. In the second half of the twentieth century, however, more Australians were drawn into using credit than ever before. By 2008, the massive growth in the acceptance of credit as a consumer product

J. Dickenson, *Credit and the Australian Department Store Since 1900*, https://doi.org/10.1007/978-3-032-16612-8_1

meant that 'people now literally borrow for anything and everything'.[1] Now, in 2025, as interest-bearing credit gives way to new forms of payment such as Buy Now Pay Later (BNPL) platforms that, on the face of it, incur no interest, its history in Australia deserves reassessment. This book addresses two aspects of that history: the 'inevitability' of the entanglement of the Australian 'masses' in credit culture and the 'democratisation' of access to credit after the Second World War.

There has been significant academic attention to credit history, especially in a Judaeo-Christian context, but histories of consumer credit in the modern, and particularly the Australian context, are limited. Explanations for this include that examining credit has been the work of economists, that credit is less glamorous than other aspects of consumption, and that the confidential nature of credit means material culture and other primary sources are relatively sparse.[2] What histories there are approach the topic from a range of perspectives. Historians have examined emerging forms of credit in the early modern era. Craig Muldrew, for example, has argued that credit provided a 'cultural currency' of trust, which was used to transact most business until the late sixteenth century.[3] Marieke de Goede has revealed the links between morality, slavery, and the new credit money of the sixteenth century, also revealing that the feminisation of credit has a long history, its sexualised personification as a fickle woman linking back to the ancient goddess Fortuna, the 'mistress of chance and luck'.[4]

With regards to the modern era, historians have emphasised the long history of consumer credit, showing that 'modern' forms of credit (credit introduced after the Second World War) evolved from earlier forms. In particular, Rowena Olegario has argued that this longer history challenges anxieties about present-day indebtedness, showing how Americans have used credit since the time of the Revolution, to increase assets and conduct commerce.[5] Also for the United States, Louis Hyman has shown how credit could be used to stimulate a sluggish economy and explored the emergence of revolving credit (rather than fixed-term credit forms, such as hire purchase) in the United States in the 1940s, which laid the groundwork for the modern credit card.[6]

Historians have also attempted sweeping histories of credit, works that range across time and space. The most ambitious of these is David Graeber's *Debt: The First 5000 years*, which shows that humans used elaborate credit systems far earlier than is usually acknowledged, with societies divided into debtors and creditors long before the emergence of cash or organised barter. Graeber provides valuable insights into the impact of

European-style financial systems on First Nations people, including in Australia, examining debt as a tool of colonialism and highlighting how it has been used historically to create and maintain social hierarchies and power imbalances, often leading to dispossession and economic hardship. Graeber's analysis of debt can also be applied to understanding colonialism's impact on Indigenous economies, with existing systems of resource management and exchange disrupted and replaced by debt-based systems that favoured the colonisers.[7]

Rosa-Maria Gelpi and François Julien-Labruyer also reach back to ancient forms of credit to shed light on consumer credit in contemporary US and European economies.[8] Jan Logemann's collection of essays on the history of consumer credit in developed countries such as France, Germany, Britain, Japan, and the United States, shows how the debates that occurred over the institution of consumer credit were frequently cast in comparative, international, and transnational terms.[9] Further to this, Logemann has complicated the theory that the spread of credit after the Second World War helped 'Americanise' European economies by drawing attention to a longer, previously over-looked history of credit in Germany.[10] In his cultural history of consumer credit in the United States, Lendol Calder also emphasises the long history of borrowing and lending, pinning the invention of consumer credit to the early twentieth century.[11] Orsi Husz's recent study of the 'bankification' of Swedish economic life draws attention to a longer history of consumer credit (specifically the credit card) in Sweden, again bringing the 'Americanisation' thesis into question.[12] In the Canadian context, Sylvie Taschereau and Yvan Rousseau have examined working-class consumers' growing use of consumer credit in the interwar years, decades earlier than is usually asserted.[13]

Victoria de Grazia's work on the gendered and class dimensions of consumer credit underpins this study, in particular the observation that working-class families had little choice but to resort to credit for everyday necessities despite the fact that society considered it 'bad' to use credit for such basic items.[14] This aspect of credit is also explored by British historians who have tended to concentrate on the way credit worked in the context of working-class communities, emphasising the significance of neighbourhood networks and the importance of women to these networks.[15] Also valuable has been work on the moral dimension of the debtor-creditor relationship, as Karl Marx observed in 1844, 'credit is the economic judgment on the morality of a man'.[16] Friedrich Nietzsche's idea of 'infinite debt' posited that human notions of morality emerged from the relationship between creditor and debtor, and this idea has since been applied to relations under contemporary capitalism.[17] Particularly significant for the discussion that follows is Graeber's contention that the debtor/creditor relationship is contingent and not fixed, and Brett Williams' formulation of the relationship as 'embodied domination'.[18]

Linked to this is the work of historians who have examined governments' ambivalence towards consumer credit and their citizens' growing indebtedness. As Christopher Payne notes, policy-makers in Britain and the United States have done little to stem rising consumer and household indebtedness, instead choosing to encourage the endless rise in house prices.[19] Again Husz's study is useful here. Asking how banks and banking became an integral part of everyday life in Sweden despite that country's extensive welfare state, her study contends that 'At least in the North American setting, credit cards ensured financial independence from both state and community, and were described as a substitute for welfare policies'.[20] This raises the issue of tolerance for excessive indebtedness in Australia and elsewhere, suggesting that governments may be slow to address rising indebtedness because it enables them to restrict public spending, as payday and fast loans with their excessive interest rates fill gaps in inadequate welfare systems.[21]

Historians of post-war Australia have paid limited attention to consumer credit, with the notable exception of hire purchase, the instalment plan used for significant purchases such as motor cars, furniture, and large white goods.[22] Greg Whitwell's influential *Making the Market* includes a brief discussion of the increased respectability of hire purchase in the years immediately after the Second World War, linking the willingness to take on debt to the mood of optimism that prevailed in those years of full employment.[23] Pierre van der Eng surveyed the growth of consumer credit (particularly hire purchase and personal loans) in Australia across the twentieth century, with an emphasis on the decades following the Second World War. Eng's survey revealed the impact of the deregulation of the financial market from the 1960s on the shift from finance companies to the banks as the major source of personal loans.[24] Reporting on a study about the use of credit by Australian consumers between 1980 and 1996, Margaret Griffiths shows considerable growth in this period 'coupled with an increasing reliance on credit to finance purchase transactions as other sources of purchase finance' (such as income and savings) became depleted.[25] An increasing number of consumers were found to be experiencing difficulty meeting their debt-servicing commitments, and Griffiths discusses the implications of this for the consumer and the Australian economy.[26]

This book differs from these earlier studies in three ways. First, it takes a longer view of credit in Australia, beginning at the start of the twentieth century as department stores consolidated their grip on the imagination of the Australian consumer and ending in the present day, in the wake of the introduction of smartphones and the BNPL schemes that have launched consumer credit into a new technological era.

Second, it focuses on retail credit. In contrast to the common usage of that term today—the credit that banks lend to individuals, such as mortgage banking, residential lending, and unsecured loans—the book uses the term 'retail credit' to mean the credit used by consumers to purchase goods and services in retail stores, which was the more common usage in the first half of the twentieth century.[27] In particular, it focuses on the retail credit provided by the department store, which, as the premier form of retail organisation throughout the twentieth century, provides a valuable prism through which to trace the expansion of retail credit. This focus means that hire purchase—the means by which consumers bought motor vehicles and large durable goods such as furniture and television sets—receives limited attention in this study: in 1955, it represented less than 10% of all Australian department stores' credit transactions.[28]

Finally, the book is concerned with the impact of economic, social, and cultural hierarchies on access to retail credit. Griffiths has argued that the use of credit no longer attracts social stigma and that, conversely, being able to access credit now confers status on the consumer.[29] This study picks up on this by examining the part played by class (the consumer's position in the capital/labour relationship) and social status (their family background, occupational prestige, and cultural standing) in the rapid expansion of retail credit, during the twentieth century and the first quarter of the twenty-first century. It aims to shed light on how retail credit became entrenched in Australian economic life by unpicking the ways in which its operations might have reflected and shaped various hierarchies.[30]

Understandings of class and status shifted significantly in the period covered by this book. Marx's earlier proposition—that an individual's position in society, their class or social class, derived from their relationship to the means of production, that is, whether they owned capital (including land) or sold their labour to those who owned capital—was challenged by the sociologist Max Weber.[31] Weber argued that an individual's status in society, which derived from a range of factors such as family background, occupation, and cultural power, was at least as important as class in Marx's formulation.[32] The book's discussion of relations between consumers and sales staff is informed by Thorstein Veblen's insight that class belonging is relational, defined by the way an individual is perceived by others, as well as by themselves, and E.P. Thompson's further observation that class relationships are constantly made and remade through everyday interactions.[33] Pierre Bourdieu extended Veblen's analysis (finding that individual tastes were socially conditioned) and the definition of class, arguing that indices such as sex ratio and geographical space should also be taken into account.[34] Finally, in recent decades, Kimberlé Crenshaw's ground-breaking conceptualisation of intersectionality called for analysis to take into account an individual's multiple, overlapping identities.[35] Since the 1970s, class has increasingly been perceived as just one of the many identities to which an individual might lay claim and has been somewhat lost from view in the process, often subsumed by identities such as race or gender.

Using the records of Coles-Myer Ltd., which are held at the State Library of Victoria (SLV) and include Myer's acquisitions Farmer & Co. and Grace Bros, as well as the records of the Myer Emporium and the Mutual Stores Ltd held at the University of Melbourne Archives (UMA); trade and organisational press; newspaper coverage; interviews; and government documents, the book investigates the relationship between class, social status, and retail credit within the social, cultural, and economic contexts that impacted the operations of retail credit across the course of the twentieth and early twenty-first centuries. By doing so, it recognises that economic activity does not sit outside the culture in which it takes place but is, in fact, deeply embedded in cultural practices, thus taking what Liz McFall has called a 'cultural economy' approach to this topic.[36]

Broadly chronological in its structure, the book draws out the key factors that have influenced the history of retail credit in Australian department stores—social distinctions, technological innovations, and marketing activities—placing them in their economic, social, cultural, and political contexts. Chapter 2 discusses women as the default consumer, shopping as a classed activity, and the expansion of credit in the early years of the twentieth century. It shows that the intersections between class, status, and desire were inextricable from issues of gender. Women's credit use (particularly that of working-class women) has long been policed by regulators, the media, and popular opinion, with women occupying an ambiguous position in relation to credit of all types, but especially retail credit. While they were to be encouraged to use credit (to maximise profits for retailers), could they be trusted to use it wisely? Lara Swartz has examined the targeting of women by US marketers from the 1960s, showing how the promotion of a young woman's use of a credit card 'for pleasurable expenses that she ultimately could not afford' helped normalise and romanticise working women's previously hidden use of payment cards: a similar discourse occurred in Australia.[37]

Despite such deliberate targeting and normalisation, Australian women were only begrudgingly included in the expansion of consumption. From the turn of the twentieth century, their use of credit sent politicians and the media into fits of moral outrage, as women were not trusted to behave sensibly around credit without the guidance of a husband, father, or brother. As we will see, many women absorbed this discourse, often feeling shame and embarrassment about their use of retail credit. These feelings persist: women today report higher stress levels than men for all types of debt with levels significantly higher for credit card debt (55.8% women; 45.9% men).[38] That said, the fact that Australian women earn an average of 11.5% less than men for doing the same job might also make them more anxious than men about accumulating debt.[39]

Chapter 3 moves to the technological innovations in credit management that reached Australia from the United States, tracing the ways in which department stores, governments, and financial institutions responded to these innovations. It pays particular attention to the links between technological change and the increasing desire to consume. Rather than rationalising and reducing passion, as some contend, technology has been found to increase the passion to consume, drawing consumers into 'networks of desire' that create 'a passionate new universe of technologically enhanced desire'.[40]

The chapter continues with a discussion of the broader context in which the expansion of credit occurred, in particular, the prevailing religious and political attitudes towards money-lending. Improved access to retail credit might have made it easier for consumers to indulge in the pleasures of impulse buying but that did not mean they were always comfortable with this change.[41] Because of the social stigma attached to the use of credit, consumers often experienced shame and embarrassment about its use.[42] Moreover, media representations helped shape attitudes to credit by promoting what Amy Hanser has called the 'structure of entitlement', that is, notions about who was and who was not entitled to consume conspicuously, as well as who should or should not be able to purchase certain goods.[43] The entitled (those consumers with sufficient disposable income) judged those on more limited incomes harshly for using credit, whether it was to purchase 'luxuries', which they had no right to aspire to, or 'necessities', which reinforced the prejudice that they were profligate and irresponsible. Media representations of those using credit to survive targeted the vulnerable individual or family rather than the system that had put them into such a position. The book recognises these tensions: between the demand that consumers took personal responsibility for their lack of funds and the need for government help through the redistribution of wealth that would render it unnecessary for families to depend on credit to make it through to the next pay. Chapter 4 continues this theme of credit and hierarchies of consumption with a discussion of working women's use of credit in the form of the cash order in the decade after the First World War, showing how the cash-order system provided a bridge between working-class forms of credit such as the 'tick' and the 'slate' and the introduction of revolving credit in the 1950s.

Chapters 5 and 6 trace department stores' responses to innovations such as revolving credit, cycle-billing, and data processing, as well as the launch of Bankcard, Australia's first credit card, in 1974. These developments enabled increasing numbers of Australian customers to access retail credit, including those who had previously been excluded because of class or status anxieties, and these new users joined an exciting, modern culture of consumption. Marketers and advertising professionals who prepared campaigns to promote credit and charge cards employed strategies and techniques aimed at encouraging Australians to indulge their desire for instant gratification. While advertising appeals and target audiences changed over time, in particular, with the growth of direct mail and relationship marketing from the 1960s to 1980s, marketers consciously maintained a hierarchy of credit access and reward through stratification. Chapter 7 continues this discussion of distinction, status, and hierarchies, looking at the ways these tools were employed in Australian loyalty programmes, particularly those launched in the 1980s.

The final chapter outlines developments in retail credit and department stores in the past two decades. Once the leviathans of the high street, department stores have been losing ground to competitors since the early 1980s. Their slow decline has only accelerated since the turn of the millennium, with closures and contractions because of discount chains, specialty stores, and the gradual shift to online shopping.[44] Department stores have tried to navigate these changes in part by improving their credit offerings and introducing loyalty programmes, but change and the challenges it presents have been relentless. As the chapter shows, the growth of digital credit, including virtual and single-use credit cards, and the increasingly popular BNPL schemes that charge late fees rather than interest, have made spending without having the ready cash easier than ever and department stores have moved to exploit this.[45]

Australians of all classes have used retail credit since before federation, but in the past half century, its use has become commonplace. However, its ubiquity was never inevitable. As we will see, department stores repeatedly employed technological innovations and marketing techniques to ensure their consumers remained in thrall to a culture of aspiration, helping to entrench distinctions between consumers based on income and social status in order to sustain profits. Given this context, claims of the democratisation of credit since the Second World War have been overplayed. Those Australians least able to afford it still pay more in interest charges and late fees, and are judged harshly for their lack of thrift. Those who can afford to spend up big still have the satisfaction of knowing that the more money they lay out, the more services, benefits, and rewards they can expect to receive.[46] In short, the hierarchies of retail credit are as entrenched in Australia now as they ever were.

Notes

1. Margaret Griffiths, 'Consumer Issues in Credit and Debt', *International Journal of Consumer Studies* 32, no. 3 (2008):187.
2. Dawn Burton, *Credit and Consumer Society* (New York: Routledge, 2008), 30–31.
3. Craig Muldrew, *The Economy of Obligation: The Culture of Credit and Social Relations in Early Modern England* (New York: Palgrave, 1998).
4. Marieke de Goede, *Virtue, Fortune, and Faith: A Genealogy of Finance* (Minneapolis: University of Minnesota Press, 2005), 21–46. See also Klas Nyberg and Håkan Jakobsson, eds, *Luxury, Fashion and the Early Modern Idea of Credit*, Perspectives in Economic and Social History 62. Abingdon: Routledge, 2021.
5. Rowena Olegario, *The Engine of Enterprise: Credit in America* (Cambridge, Mass.: Harvard University Press, 2016).
6. Louis Hyman, *Debtor Nation: The History of America in Red Ink* (Princeton, NJ: Princeton University Press, 2011), 10–16, 105, 117.
7. David Graeber, *Debt: The First 5000 Years* (Brooklyn, N.Y.: Melville House 2011).

8. Rosa-Maria Gelpi and Francois Julien-Labruyer, *The History of Consumer Credit: Doctrines and Practices* (Houndsmills, Basingstoke, UK: Macmillan, 2000).
9. Jan Logemann, *The Development of Consumer Credit in Global Perspective: Business, Regulation and Culture* (New York: Palgrave Macmillan, 2012).
10. Jan Logemann, 'Americanization through Credit? Consumer Credit in Germany, 1860s–1960s', *Business History Review* 85, no. 3, Consumer Finance (2011): 529–50.
11. Lendol Calder, *Financing the American Dream: A Cultural History of Consumer Credit* (Princeton: Princeton University Press, 2001), 37.
12. Orsi Husz, *Bankminded: Banks As Intimate Agents of Everyday Life in Welfare State Sweden* (Palgrave Studies in Economic History, 2025).
13. Sylvie Taschereau and Yvan Rousseau, 'The Hidden Face of Consumption: Extending Credit to the Urban Masses in Montreal (1920s–40s)', *The Canadian Historical Review* 100, no. 4 (December 2019), 509.
14. Victoria de Grazia, 'Introduction', in *The Sex of Things, Gender and Consumption in Historical Perspective*, ed. Victoria de Grazia and Ellen Furlough (California: University of California Press, 1996) 1–10.
15. Paul Johnson, *Saving and Spending: The Working-class Economy in Britain 1870–1939* (Oxford: Clarendon Press, 1985; Avram Taylor, *Working Class Credit and Community* (Basingstoke: Palgrave Macmillan, 2002); Sean O'Connell, *Credit and Community: Working-Class Debt in the UK since 1880* (Oxford: OUP, 2009).
16. Karl Marx, 'Comments On James Mill' (1844), https://www.marxists.org/archive/marx/works/1844/james-mill.
17. Friedrich Nietzsche, *On the Genealogy of Morals* (1887, 111), in Michael D. Sousa, 'Consumer Bankruptcy in the Neoliberal State', *Emory Bankruptcy Developments Journal* 39 (2023): 206; Maurizio Lazaretto, *The Making of the Indebted Man: An Essay on the Neoliberal Condition* (Los Angeles: Semiotexte: 2012), 10–11, 23, 30–31, 33, 55, 72–73, 76, 79, 90–91; Gilles Deleuze and Félix Guattari, *Anti-Oedipus: Capitalism and Schizophrenia*, trans. Robert Hurley, Mark Seem and Helen R. Lane (Minneapolis: University of Minnesota Press. 1983), 180, 197, 216–17, 229–30, 237, 254.
18. David Graeber, *Debt: The First 50000 Years*, 'On the Experience of Moral Confusion', 2011, https://theanarchistlibrary.org/library/david-graeber-debt, accessed 8 August 2025; Brett Williams, *Debt For Sale: A Social History of the Credit Trap* (Philadelphia: University of Pennsylvania, 2004), 6.
19. Christopher Payne, *The Consumer, Credit and Neoliberalism: Governing the Modern Economy* (London, New York: Routledge, 2012).

20. Orsi Husz, *Bankminded: Banks As Intimate Agents of Everyday Life in Welfare State Sweden* (Palgrave Studies in Economic History, 2025)
21. ACOSS, 'Raise the Rate Survey', September 2024, https://www.acoss.org.au/wp-content/uploads/2024/09/ACOSS-COL-Report-Sept-2024_v03.pdf, accessed 29 July 2025.
22. Roy E. Maskell, *The Hire Purchase and Instalment Habits: Trends in Australia, New Zealand, Great Britain and the United States of America* (Sydney: Law Book Company of Australasia, 1964), 340; Neil Runcie, ed. *The Management of Instalment Credit: the Australian Experience* (London: University of London Press, 1969); Richard White, *Inventing Australia: Images and Identity, 1688–1980* (Sydney: Allen & Unwin, 1981), 164–65; John Murphy, *Imagining the Fifties: Private Sentiment and Political Culture in Menzies' Australia* (Sydney: Pluto Press, 2000), 186–87.
23. Greg Whitwell, *Making the Market: The Rise of Consumer Society* (Fitzroy, Vic.: McPhee Gribble, 1989), 34.
24. Pierre van der Eng, 'Consumer Credit in Australia during the Twentieth Century'. *Accounting, Business & Financial History* 18, no. 2 (2008): 258–59.
25. Margaret Griffiths, 'The Sustainability of Consumer Credit Growth in Late Twentieth Century Australia', *Journal of Consumer Studies and Home Economics* 24, no.1 (March 2000): 24.
26. Griffiths, 'The Sustainability of Consumer Credit Growth', 24.
27. 'Retail Credit', *Office of the Comptroller of the Currency*, https://occ.gov/topics/supervision-and-examination/credit/retail-credit/index-retail-credit.html, accessed 7 August 2025; 'Clyde W. Phelps, *Retail Credit Fundamentals* (National Retail Credit Association, St Louis, 1938), 1, 8; Elizabeth Redford, 'History of the National Retail Credit Association', *Honors Theses* (1941), https://scholar.utc.edu/honors-theses/283.
28. 'Spotlight on Hire Purchase', *Retail Merchandiser*, August 1955, 28; 'Hire Purchase on the News', *Retail Merchandiser*, May 1956, 24.
29. Griffiths, 'Consumer Issues in Credit and Debt'; Sousa, 'Consumer Bankruptcy in the Neoliberal State', 204.
30. Griffiths, 'Consumer Issues in Credit and Debt'.
31. Karl Marx, *Wage Labour and Capital*, 1849, https://www.marxists.org/archive/marx/works/1847/wage-labour/index.htm, accessed 22 May 2023.
32. Max Weber, 'The Distribution of Power Within the Community: Classes, Stande, Parties', trans., Dagmar Waters et al., *Journal of Classical Sociology* 10, no. 2 (2010 [1921]): 137–52.
33. Thorstein Veblen, *The Theory of the Leisure Class* (London: Macmillan, 1899); E.P. Thompson, *The Making of the English Working Class* (London: Penguin, 1963), 8. For critiques of Veblen's thesis, see Rick Tilman,

Thorstein Veblen and His Critics, 1891-1936: Conservative, Liberal and Radical Perspectives. Princeton NJ: Princeton University Press, 1992, 12 and Colin Campbell, 'Conspicuous Confusion? A Critique of Veblen's Theory of Conspicuous Consumption, *Sociological Theory* 13, no. 1 (1995): 37–47.

34. Pierre Bourdieu, *Distinction: A Social Critique of the Judgement of Taste*, Trans. R. Nice (London: Routledge, 1984 [1979]), 102.
35. Kimberlé Crenshaw, 'Mapping the Margins: Intersectionality, Identity Politics, and Violence against Women of Color', *Stanford Law Review*, 43, no. 6 (July 1991): 1241–299. See also, Thomas Kuehn, 'Understanding Gender Inequality in Renaissance Florence', *Journal of Women's History* 8, no. 2 (1996): 58–80 and Judith Butler, *Gender Trouble: Feminism and the Subversion of identity* 1999, 162–65.
36. For the economy as a cultural activity, see Liz McFall, *Advertising: A Cultural Economy* (London: Sage, 2004), 1–8; Hannah Forsyth and Sophie Loy-Wilson, 'Seeking a New Materialism in Australian History', *Australian Historical Studies* 48, no. 2 (2017): 169–88; Abigail Marks and Esme Terry. 'Using a Moral Economy Perspective to Understand Working class Finance and the Decline of Home Credit in the United Kingdom *Economic and Industrial Democracy* 46, no. 1(2025): 90.
37. Lana Swartz, 'Gendered Transactions: Identity and Payment at Mid-century', *WSQ: Women's Studies Quarterly* 42, 1 & 2 (Spring/Summer 2014): 140.
38. In mid-2024, women were more stressed than men about home loans (63.3% vs 53.8%) and personal loans (66.4% vs 58.6%). The exception was stress levels over BNPL (49.1% women vs 50.2% men), *NAB Australian WellBeing Survey* Q2, 2024, 4, https://business.nab.com.au/wp-content/uploads/2024/07/NAB-Australian-Wellbeing-Survey-Q2-2024.pdf, accessed 26 July 2025.
39. 'The ABS Data Gender Pay Gap', May 2024, wgea.gov.au, accessed 6 October 2024.
40. Robert Kozinets, Anthony Patterson, and Rachel Ashman, 'Networks of Desire: How Technology Increases Our Passion to Consume', *Journal of Consumer Research* 43 (2017): 659–82.
41. Yi Sunghwan and Hans Baumgartner, 'Coping with Guilt and Shame in the Impulse Buying Context', *Journal of Economic Psychology* 32 (2011): 458–67.
42. Sousa, 'Consumer Bankruptcy in the Neoliberal State', 206; Maurizio Lazaretto, *The Making of the Indebted Man: An Essay on the Neoliberal Condition* (Los Angeles: Semiotexte: 2012), 30–31.

43. Amy Hanser, *Service Encounters: Class, Gender, and the Market for Social Distinction in Urban China* (Stanford: Stanford University Press, 2008), 3, 8.
44. Peter Spearitt, 'Suburban Cathedrals: The Rise of the Drive-In Shopping Centre', in *The Cream Brick Frontier*, 88–107.
45. 'What is Buy Now Pay, Later for Business', https://gocardless.com/en-au/guides/posts/what-is-buy-now-pay-later-for-business/, accessed 6 October 2024.
46. Fiona Guthrie, 'Debt Is Our Drug and Credit Pushers Are To Blame', *Courier Mail*, 5 July 2004, 13.

References

Bourdieu, Pierre. *Distinction: A Social Critique of the Judgement of Taste*, trans. R. Nice. London: Routledge, 1984[1979].

Brett, Judith. *The Moral Middle Class: From Alfred Deakin to John Howard*. Cambridge, Cambridge University Press, 2003.

Burton, Dawn. *Credit and Consumer Society*. New York: Routledge, 2008.

Calder, Lendol. *Financing the American Dream: A Cultural History of Consumer Credit*. Princeton: Princeton University Press, 2001.

Crenshaw, Kimberlé. 'Mapping the Margins: Intersectionality, Identity Politics, and Violence against Women of Color.' *Stanford Law Review*, 43, no. 6 (July 1991): 1241–299. https://doi.org/10.2307/1229039

Davison, Graeme, Tony Dingle and Seamus O'Hanlon, eds. *The Cream Brick Frontier: Histories of Australian Suburbia*. Melbourne: Monash Publications in History, 1995.

De Goede, Marieke. *Virtue, Fortune, and Faith: A Genealogy of Finance*. Minneapolis: University of Minnesota Press, 2005.

De Grazia, Victoria and Ellen Furlough, ed. *The Sex of Things, Gender and Consumption in Historical Perspective*. California: University of California Press, 1996.

Deleuze, Gilles and Félix Guattari. *Anti-Oedipus: Capitalism and Schizophrenia*. Minneapolis: University of Minnesota Press, 1983.

Forsyth, Hannah and Sophie Loy-Wilson. 'Seeking a New Materialism in Australian History'. *Australian Historical Studies* 48, no. 2 (2017): 169–88.

Gelpi, Rosa-Maria and François Julien-Labruyer. *The History of Consumer Credit: Doctrines and Practices*. Houndsmills, Basingstoke, UK: Macmillan, 2000.

Graeber, David. *Debt: The First 5,000 Years*. Brooklyn, New York: Melville House, 2011.

Griffiths, Margaret. 'The Sustainability of Consumer Credit Growth in Late Twentieth Century Australia'. *Journal of Consumer Studies and Home Economics* 24, no.1 (March 2000): 23–33.

Griffiths, Margaret. 'Consumer Debt in Australia: Why Banks Will Not Turn Their Backs on Profits'. *International Journal of Consumer Studies* 31, no. 3 (2007): 230–36.

Griffiths, Margaret. 'Guest Editorial: Consumer Issues in Credit and Debt'. *International Journal of Consumer Studies* 32, no. 3 (2008): 187.

Hanser, Amy. *Service Encounters: Class, Gender, and the Market for Social Distinction in Urban China*. Stanford: Stanford University Press, 2008.

Hyman, Louis. *Debtor Nation: The History of America in Red Ink*. Princeton, NJ: Princeton University Press, 2011.

Husz, Orsi. *Bankminded: Banks As Intimate Agents of Everyday Life in Welfare State Sweden*. London: Palgrave Macmillan, 2025.

Johnson, Paul. *Saving and Spending: The Working-class Economy in Britain 1870–1939*. Oxford: Clarendon Press, 1985.

Kozinets, Robert, Anthony Patterson and Rachel Ashman. 'Networks of Desire: How Technology Increases Our Passion to Consume'. *Journal of Consumer Research* 43 (2017): 659–82. https://doi.org/10.1093/jcr/ucw061

Lazaretto, Maurizio. *The Making of the Indebted Man: An Essay on the Neoliberal Condition*. Los Angeles: Semiotexte: 2012.

Logemann, Jan, ed. *The Development of Consumer Credit in Global Perspective: Business, Regulation and Culture*. New York: Palgrave Macmillan, 2012.

Logemann, Jan. 'Americanization through Credit? Consumer Credit in Germany, 1860s–1960s'. *Business History Review* 85, no. 3 (2011): 529–50. https://www.jstor.org/stable/41301433

Marx, Karl. 'Comments on James Mill' (1844), https://www.marxists.org/archive/marx/works/1844/james-mill/, accessed 6 August 2025.

Marx, Karl. *Wage Labour and Capital* (1849), https://www.marxists.org/archive/marx/works/1847/wage-labour/index.htm, accessed 22 May 2023.

Maskell, Roy E. *The Hire Purchase and Instalment Habits: Trends in Australia, New Zealand, Great Britain and the United States of America*. Sydney: Law Book Company of Australasia, 1964.

McFall, Liz. *Advertising: A Cultural Economy*. London: Sage, 2004.

Muldrew, Craig. *The Economy of Obligation: The Culture of Credit and Social Relations in Early Modern England*. New York: Palgrave, 1998.

Murphy, John. *Imagining the Fifties: Private Sentiment and Political Culture in Menzies' Australia*. Sydney: Pluto Press, 2000.

O'Connell, Sean. *Credit and Community: Working-Class Debt in the UK since 1880*. Oxford: OUP, 2009.

Olegario, Rowena. *The Engine of Enterprise: Credit in America*. Cambridge, Mass.: Harvard University Press, 2016.

Payne, Christopher. *The Consumer, Credit and Neoliberalism: Governing the Modern Economy*. London, New York: Routledge, 2012.

Phelps, Clyde W. *Retail Credit Fundamentals.* St Louis, National Retail Credit Association, 1938. https://babel.hathitrust.org/cgi/pt?id=uc1.$b39011&seq=28

Redford, Elizabeth. 'History of the National Retail Credit Association'. *Honors Thesis* (1941). https://scholar.utc.edu/honors-theses/283/

Sousa, Michael D. 'Consumer Bankruptcy in the Neoliberal State.' *Emory Bankruptcy Developments Journal* 39 (2023) 199–284. https://scholarlycommons.law.emory.edu/ebdj/vol39/iss2/1

Swartz, Lara. 'Gendered Transactions: Identity and Payment at Mid-century'. *WSQ: Women's Studies Quarterly* 42, 1 & 2 (Spring/Summer 2014): 137–53. https://doi.org/10.1353/wsq.2014.0029

Taschereau, Sylvie and Yvan Rousseau. 'The Hidden Face of Consumption: Extending Credit to the Urban Masses in Montreal (1920s–40s)'. *The Canadian Historical Review* 100, no. 4 (December 2019), 509.

Taylor, Avram. *Working Class Credit and Community.* Basingstoke: Palgrave Macmillan, 2002.

Marks, Abigail and Esme Terry. 'Using a Moral Economy Perspective to Understand Working class Finance and the Decline of Home Credit in the United Kingdom *Economic and Industrial Democracy* 46, no. 1(2025) 75–95.

Tharpe, Barbara. 'The National Retail Credit Association: An Experiment in Cooperation for Retail Credit Control'. *Honors Theses* 1946. https://scholar.utc.edu/honors-theses/284

Thompson, E.P. *The Making of the English Working Class.* London: Penguin, 1963.

Van Der Eng, Pierre. 'Consumer Credit in Australia during the Twentieth Century'. *Accounting, Business & Financial History* 18, no. 2 (2008) 243–65, https://doi.org/10.1080/09585200802058917

Veblen, Thorstein. *The Theory of the Leisure Class.* London: Macmillan, 1899.

Weber, Max. 'The Distribution of Power Within the Community: Classes, Stande, Parties', trans., Dagmar Waters et al., *Journal of Classical Sociology* 10, no. 2 (2010 [1921]): 137–52. https://doi.org/10.1177/1468795X10361

White, Richard. *Inventing Australia: Images and Identity, 1688–1980.* Sydney: Allen & Unwin, 1981.

Whitwell, Greg. *Making the Market: The Rise of Consumer Society.* Fitzroy, Vic.: McPhee Gribble, 1989.

Williams, Brett. *Debt For Sale: A Social History of the Credit Trap.* Philadelphia: University of Pennsylvania, 2004.

CHAPTER 2

A Woman's Paradise

Abstract From the mid-nineteenth century, department stores captured the consumer imagination in Australia and around the world. In the early twentieth century, media depictions of the relationship between women—the default consumer—and department stores were ambiguous. Newspapers classified most women shoppers as naïve and vulnerable, and compared them unfavourably to 'rational' men shoppers, at the same time as their popular serials portrayed the department store as a glamourous site of potential transformation for women. The operation of class hierarchies in Australia included debates around whether those on limited incomes were entitled to consume beyond the 'necessities' of life. However, as production increased and more consumers were needed to support it, manufacturers and retailers encouraged low-income workers to use credit.

Keywords Credit • Retail • Consumer • Women • Class • Australian history

In the mid-nineteenth century, department stores emerged in markets around the world.[1] Most of these new institutions began as smaller drapery stores, including in Australia. From the 1870s, as mass consumption expanded in Australia (as it did elsewhere), fuelled by more efficient production technologies and workers' growing purchasing power, these

J. Dickenson, *Credit and the Australian Department Store Since 1900*, https://doi.org/10.1007/978-3-032-16612-8_2

drapery stores evolved into monumental department stores, or 'big stores', as they were called colloquially.[2] Drapers such as Sydney's Anthony Hordern (1832), David Jones (1838), and Farmer & Co. (1840), for example, expanded their retail space throughout the city, adding household items such as furniture, napery, and bedding to their offerings.[3]

Despite the cataclysmic economic depression of the early 1890s, Australians experienced a general rise in their standard of living in the final quarter of the nineteenth century and, combined with an improvement in women's economic status facilitated in part by the Married Women's Property Acts of 1879 and 1893, the desire to consume became easier to satisfy than ever before.[4] The big store's selling point was choice. In Melbourne, the upmarket emporium George and George Limited (Georges) of Collins Street promoted itself as 'the Universal Provider'.[5] Besides offering drapery 'with all its departments (dress goods, costumes, mantles, millinery, laces, underclothing, manchester [sic], tailoring, dress making, &c.)', it sold grocery, ironmongery, carpets, furniture, boots and shoes, stationery, confectionery, drugs and perfumery, tobaccoes [sic], cigars, wines and spirits, produce, wood and coal.[6] The Myer Emporium—opened in 1911—was touted as 'a women's paradise', where 'everything is to be had', including hosiery, neckwear, boots and shoes, silken, woollen and cotton goods, underclothing, carpets, crockery, Manchester goods, ironmongery, laces and trimmings, 'toilettes', and 'exquisite creations'.[7]

The Default Consumer

By the time Sidney Myer opened his emporium in Melbourne's Bourke Street, women were well on the way to becoming Australia's default consumer.[8] Those women with money to spare had long patronised Australia's drapery stores, tempted by the fashionable goods on display. Now they patronised the big stores, where they could spend hours browsing an ever-expanding range of goods. However, at the Myer Emporium, as with other big stores, there was more to enjoy than an enticing array of merchandise.

With the gradual exodus of Australian working women from domestic service to factory work in search of more autonomy and better pay, middle-class housewives were now increasingly responsible for the family's shopping: shopping had become 'unambiguously women's work'.[9] Shopping did indeed become 'women's work' when reports came in from New York and London of 'women employed as professional shoppers'.[10] Suitable work for 'a young and well-educated lady of keen commercial instincts', this new form of 'expertise' was particularly useful for businesses with country clients who paid a 5% charge for the service.[11]

However, most women were not paid to go shopping and setting them loose in a city's high street made sectors of society anxious.[12] Commentators resorted to stereotypes and unscientific hierarchies to try and manage their behaviour, pitching women shoppers against men shoppers. When Melbourne's *Age* newspaper asked a rhetorical 'Can Women Shop?' in 1906, the answer was a predictable 'yes' and 'no'.[13] Women could certainly shop but, of course, they did not shop as well as men. Depicted as more naturally inclined to enjoy shopping than men, some women were idealised as 'clever housewives'—those who made a list and stuck to it—but most were dismissed as naïve and vulnerable to the slick sales pitch. According to this way of thinking, a man entered a shop knowing what he wanted and—recalling how hard it had been to earn his money—could not be swayed by the salesman's patter. Women on the other hand—being 'happily ignorant of the art of making money'—were prone to throwing it away and trying to make 'a pleasant pastime out of a plain business transaction'.[14] Women enjoyed taking their time to decide on a purchase, whereas men 'rushed in'.[15] A snippet in Australian newspapers reported an observation by an anonymous 'Tailor and Cutter': 'men were "funny" to cater for, as they only bought what they needed, while women bought 'what takes their fancy for the time being.'[16] Reflecting on this, a correspondent to Sydney's *Sunday Times* claimed that shopping was 'a religion or second nature to most women':

> They will buy as long as money or credit lasts, and then not be satisfied. Those who have no money and no credit will content themselves with watching their more fortunate sisters accumulating bargains, or, rather, they will worry the poor shop assistants to death looking through articles which they never had any thoughts of buying.
>
> Men, on the other hand, except the few dandies who live for dress, and are not really worthy of the masculine appellation, mostly hate the shop like poison. Many of them would sooner go to a dentist's to have a tooth pulled than spend half an hour in a clothes shop, and they leave their better halves to do almost all their shopping.[17]

Commentators also looked to the emerging discipline of psychology for ways of ranking and managing these annoying women shoppers. They identified three predominant types of woman shopper—the intellectual, 'the woman who thinks'; the emotional, 'the woman who feels'; and the volitional, 'the woman who decides':

> If the woman belongs to the intellectual class, she must be shown the advantage of the purchase. She must be convinced by reason. If she belongs to the emotional class, she is a 'sure sale', as things which appeal to the eye and the emotions catch her. All the talking in the world and all the winning smiles in the universe won't make the volitional woman buy a penny's-worth more than she wants. Her mind is made up, and the shopman will employ his time better by devoting his attention to the next customer.[18]

Another report also grouped women shoppers into three classes: the first-class woman shopper was the 'Good Manager'; the third class was the 'lady of leisure' who wandered around the store buying nothing, also known as the professional shopper (before there was a profession of the same name): 'Professional shopper. What is that? It is a lady who shops. She never buys'.[19] But it was the second-class shopper who came in for the sharpest criticism: 'She goes to a sale "Just to have, a look round," and, being a weak mortal, is easily persuaded to make a number of useless purchases'. She was 'generally a woman with little decision of character', and even when she started out with a definite idea of her requirements, she was 'prevailed on to alter it', and returned home to find that her purchase did not 'go' with anything else in her wardrobe, and the money spent on it was 'practically wasted'.[20]

The stereotypes came from all directions with women shoppers also portrayed as lazy and ignorant. According to one 'fashionable dressmaker', most women were 'absolutely helpless' when they visited her salon and seemed to know 'no more than a child about what they want'. 'Woman' was 'the most conventional creature that lives', she claimed, 'and must have the correct thing, according as someone else has determined for her. ... As to what is most becoming to them and fitting under the circumstances, as a rule, they haven't the remotest idea. Most of them would be absolute frights if it wasn't for us'. [21]

Women shoppers were also accused of being deceitful time wasters. In 1904, an association formed in London to protect shopkeepers from 'Lady Shoppers', demanding an amendment to the law 'relating to the liability of married women', prompted by the 'many cases ... where lady customers had obtained goods for nothing by pledging their husbands' credit without their knowledge or consent'.[22] One Australian writer suggested legislation to improve shoppers' behaviour. She described shopping with her aunt on a sweltering summer's day. Unable to make up her mind about a trivial purchase, the aunt's chatter tried the patience of the exhausted shop assistant. The writer's 'strongest, political friend' promised to introduce a bill to parliament 'to protect the girl behind the counter from unnecessary conversation' by legislating fines for verbose shoppers.[23] Women's reputed shoplifting activities meant both shoppers and sales staff were under increased surveillance in-store.[24]

The Glamour of Shopping

The press might have frowned on women's alleged profligacy and their penchant for in-store pleasure, but both characteristics were good news for department stores. Reports from London described 'the convenience and luxury of the modern shop'.[25] Debenham's new store was 'a club for shoppers on a magnificent scale', aimed at 'the woman who lives in the country or even in a distant suburb, and, of course, to the motoring woman...':

> Dressing-rooms, fitting-rooms, writing rooms, restaurant, and lounges open out of the central clubroom—the Rendezvous is its official designation. This is a magnificent apartment and luxuriously furnished. Here ladies can write their letters, read the English and American newspapers and the illustrated weeklies. Adjacent is another room where letters may be dictated to a staff of typists.[26]

The Australian press outlined the ways in which New York's retailers understood women and were giving them the glamour they desired. This included 'Seductive Restrooms', which could be found in 'every American shop', 'beautifully furnished' with 'thousands' of fresh hand towels, fresh soap, and face powder ('All free, all free'); 'seductive music' from 'a hundred gramophones, pianos and music boxes'; and a free tearoom with 'delicious cakes and fluffy little biscuits' served on 'a pretty inlaid table' to the shopper ensconced in a 'luxuriously upholstered' chair.[27] It took a decade, but by 1916 the Myer Emporium had also been re-configured to ensure shopping was a pleasurable experience, with the store providing what it called 'congenial circumstances' for its clientele: a spacious tea-room and adjacent roof-garden; a public lounge and creche for children 'whose mothers were shopping in the store'; and 'the services of a certificated nurse for emergency cases amongst the employees or patrons'.[28] Department stores such as Farmer's and David Jones began similar programmes of renovation in this period.[29]

The magic and glamour surrounding the brightly lit windows of the department store and the excited crowds they attracted led writers to use them as the *mise en scène* for their stories of romance and adventure. The department store and its shopfront became the setting for the modern woman's arrival on the public stage, as well as a new way for her to meet a romantic partner. Examples of this were the musical works 'The Shop Girl' (1895), which was performed in Australia for the first time in 1906, and 'The Girl Behind the Counter' (1906), which arrived in Australia in 1909.[30] Both comedies would become staples of Australian musical theatre.[31]

The department store was a locus for change in a young woman's social class, personal relationships, and self-knowledge. Also called 'The Girl Behind the Counter', a serial by the prolific writer Lillian Quiller Couch ran in *The Journal* for two months in 1913.[32] It tells the story of Mary, a young, modest, and (of course) beautiful country girl, who leaves her job at a small drapery store in a Cornish town to work in the drapery department at Denton's, a large London store. Arriving at the store for the first time, Mary is entranced by the 'Bold, lavish decoration of the great windows that flashed before her eyes'.[33] She is less enamoured of the store's manager whose unwanted attention she finds unsettling.[34] The rest of the story follows a familiar path. After numerous misunderstandings, trials, and tribulations—including a fire that destroys Denton's as well as the lascivious manager—Mary is lifted from the drudgery of shop work to marry the nephew of a lord. The promise of the good life offered up by those entrancing shop windows has been fulfilled.

In the 'Open Door', the strict rules for sales staff help a lover beat off his rival for the hand of another 'pretty' shopgirl.[35] In 'A Cheserby Sensation', a hard-hearted businessman discovers his long lost daughter. When the daughter, who is 'perfect with an almost rare loveliness', asks for a job at the large store that has forced her family's small store out of business, the relationship is revealed.[36] In 'More Than Money', Lydia, 'a shrewd shopper', discovers that the joys of shopping cannot compete with true love.[37]

The stories also showed the behind the scenes experience of the shop worker, which was much less romantic than some of the stories implied. One example was 'The Little Girl Who Stayed', the story of 'lame' Dorry Cayle who worked in the basement of the Bon Ton department store, wrapping packages.

> Her business hours were spent in an open-top, imitation mahogany cupboard, high up behind the bargain-notion counter, crawled into it and out of it by means of a hole about the size of a hat-box. Her duties were to receive from the sales girls each small article that was sold, with the sale check and the purchaser's money; to wrap up the article; to send the check and the money through the pneumatic tube to the cashier, and to return to the proper clerk the package and the change. [38]

Trapped in a store fire caused by the penny-pinching store owners, Dorry proves to be an unlikely heroine. In 'The Tempter and Maria', the protagonist works in a store 'that swarmed every day with shoppers who couldn't afford to buy elsewhere': 'At Sneddenfeld's, economy was the watchword; even the air was used over and over again'. At night, the heroine Maria wondered why 'she had so continuing a headache'.[39]

Sometimes these stories drew attention to the class implications of the department store's allure, warning women against becoming too enamoured of shopping and the department store at the cost of forgetting their class origins and their obligations to the poor. These moralising stories were particularly favoured by the Australian Catholic press, which used them as an opportunity to remind the well-off of their obligations to the poor and to the Church. Reprinted from *The Rosary*, a US Dominican magazine, 'The Lesson of the Day' tells the story of Mrs Morrison who is nervous as she enters the city's 'largest and most fashionably equipped dry goods store'. Born into a poor farming community, Mrs Morrison has married money. Now, as she browses the store's beautiful wares, she recalls how she felt at first in the swanky store, concerned about the judgement of the sales staff and the other customers:

> There was a fascination in lingering over those bolts of soft, filmy goods, hanging the brink of purchase over one piece, then passing easily on to examine something of a richer texture, without experiencing that hunting nervous fear of living beyond her means. She had hung in the background often, enviously watching others at this fascinating task of selection. The

dallying ways of these more fortunate women had seemed to her trivial and foolish then.

Now she is one of those fortunate women, the beneficiary of upward mobility. She had come into 'the class of leisure and wealth, she regarded it as her province to dally, to harass busy clerks, to linger on the brink of purchase, and then, if she choose purchase nothing at all'.

Returning home she is greeted by her young niece who is visiting from the family's hometown. Mrs Morrison notes the poverty evident in her niece's attire: 'The very atmosphere of [the hometown] clung to her; it was evident in the ill-fitting dress, the coarse heavy shoes, and the tired drooping nose'. Later, Mrs Morrison reflects on how, caught up in her privileged life, she forgot the grinding poverty of her upbringing. With her husband, she vows to donate money to the church in her hometown: 'The spirit of the old days of poverty had comeback to reside in Mrs. Morrison's heart, and she was grateful for the lesson that "the day had taught"'.[40]

A Classed Activity

The 'Lesson of the Day' reminded readers that not all Australian woman had access to the 'paradise' of the department store. In the mid-nineteenth century, Friedrich Engels noted how long boulevards of well-kept shops reflected and deepened class difference in England, as they shielded middle-class shoppers from the conditions endured by workers living in surrounding districts.[41] A century later, the historian William Leach drew attention to 'the misery many poor women must have felt as they passed the windows of city retail stores, which revealed to them an unobtainable world of luxury'.[42]

Poor women might have been excluded from Émile Zola's 'Ladies' Paradise', but, as Melita Schaum has pointed out for the United Kingdom, that did not stop critics of the department store using class to express their fears about its impact on society. Some critics saw the accessibility offered by the department store as escalating the levelling out of social and class distinctions.[43] Others feared that workers would be unable to resist the temptations offered by the department store: the writer H.G. Wells, for example, described the stores as 'low-class' jumbles of merchandise designed to dupe and entertain the masses.[44] Though the makeup of class relations in Australia differed from those in the United States and the United Kingdom,[45] shopping in Australian cities was also a classed activity.

In the decades before the introduction of market research in Australia, establishing who shopped in which department store is challenging, but the appeals that stores made in their promotional campaigns offer some clues.[46] Location was clearly a factor and Engels' observation can be applied to the city of Melbourne, at least to some extent. Those who lived in the working-class suburbs that ringed the city centre—Fitzroy, Collingwood, Richmond, Footscray, North Melbourne, South Melbourne, and Port Melbourne—began to shop at the so-called big stores in Bourke Street in the city centre and in suburbs such as Prahran, with their broader range of goods and price points, as well as bargain basements and budget prices. Others stuck to the local shops, in part for the convenience, but also to access credit terms (in traditional ways) that city stores denied to those of modest means.[47] Those residing in the new bay-side and eastern suburbs, away from the inner-city factories, shopped along Collins Street in the city, which was 'lined with some fine emporiums' and where 'the workman' was 'distinctly out of place'.[48] At the finest of the Collins Street emporiums—'the towering house of Messrs. George and George Limited'—the 'elite of Melbourne gathered', away from the dust and noise of the more prosaic Bourke Street.[49]

Location was just one component in a store's aura: others included a store's architecture, interior design, window dressing, colours, sounds, odours, textures, and the demeanour of its staff.[50] The scholarship on 'aura' and 'authenticity' in mass consumption is underpinned by Walter Benjamin's 1935 essay 'The Work of Art in an Age of Mechanical Reproduction', in which he argued that the aura of an original work of art did not survive replication.[51] For example, in her study of the ways in which Selfridges, the London department store, negotiated modernity, Elizabeth Outka interrogated the notion of a binary between the 'authentic' and the mass market.[52] More recently, Catherine Kovesi has explored the relationship between objects of holy veneration in the past and the modern-day veneration of luxury brands, drawing attention to the use of Benjamin's theory by lawyers representing luxury brands at the European Court of Justice.[53] Kovesi identifies the meshing of three factors—the original object, the brand, and the location—required to create and maintain the aura of an object and to generate its cult following, whether it is a religious relic of the fourteenth century or twenty-first-century brands such as Moët et Chandon and Dior.[54] Alexander and Doherty have also used Benjamin's essay to conceptualise the antecedents of brand aura, finding that, rather than being a core component of a brand, brand aura is 'the culmination of consumers' experiential engagement with the brand'.[55]

In 1959, Melbourne's *Retail Merchandiser* described a store's aura or personality as 'the curious intangible that unites the whole store and holds up the image that is so important in the mind of the consumer'.[56] Personality was not 'an ephemeral characteristic' that 'you can put on for a day'; there was no short cut to developing a store personality and no infallible formula for its development.[57] For store management, it presented 'a continuing long-range problem'. Although the real difference between stores may be slight, there were important differences in the minds of shoppers: 'All shoppers have their likes and dislikes' based on 'intuitive judgments'.[58] Unsurprisingly, the analysis was lazily gendered: 'As the majority of shoppers are women, some of these likes and dislikes are not necessarily logical'.[59]

According to the US social researcher Pierre Martineau, 'the upper-status woman' could not 'conceive of herself' shopping in the 'subway' ('the bargain basement' in Australia) of a large department store. Regardless of the bargains she might find there, this woman was 'repelled by the thought of odours, milling crowds, poorly educated clerks'. On the other hand, 'the wage earner's wife' was 'not going to expose herself to the humiliation of shopping in a quality store' … even if she could afford to buy something there.[60]

As E.P. Thompson showed, class is something that happens in human relationships, 'defined by men [sic] as they live their own history'.[61] Class distinctions are not automatic but have to be constantly reproduced in practice and are recognised, performed, legitimised, and reinforced through daily social interactions. The exchanges between customers and department store sales staff fit into this category and the tenor of these exchanges—or 'service encounters'—is important because, over time, they helped to construct a department store's aura, which, in its turn, became crucial to building store loyalty. Delphine Dion and Stéphane Borraz have drawn attention to the ways in which brands manage status through service encounters, making 'consumers behave as class subjects who have a specific understanding of their position in the social hierarchy'.[62] They are particularly interested in luxury brands, but department stores, especially upmarket stores, also managed their customers' status subjectivities 'through the material and social cues of the servicescape'.[63]

Studies of service work offer valuable insights into the ways in which class operates in service encounters. Echoing Thompson, Dion and Borraz conceptualise class as a practice that is socially constituted through everyday interactions such as service encounters. They also place the interactional dynamics of class at the centre of the analysis of service interactions and reconceptualise the service encounter as an important locus for the class struggle, in which class-based entitlements are created and social hierarchies are expressed, reproduced, and reconfigured. Finally, they perceive service workers as embodying the values of a brand to achieve the aesthetic and interactional styles demanded by the social context. The process of internalisation means that working in a luxury store conveys the status of a social elite. As representatives of a luxury brand, service employees need to embody a certain style, taste, and class.[64]

The context in which service encounters take place affects both parties as it usually involves unspoken information beyond the event, most of which reflects existing hierarchies of class: for example, the cultural setting, language proficiency, and shared background assumptions.[65] As Hanser points out for contemporary China, what she calls 'structures of entitlement' find expression in service encounters, with the social distinctions made in these settings part of a larger story about inequality and social change in urban China.[66] The same can be said for Australia at the start of the twentieth century.

On the floor of the department store, class 'happened' every day in the 'human relationship' between middle- and upper-middle-class shoppers and sales personnel, who were usually (but not always) from the working class. In the United States, 'The low wages and mixed feelings of salesclerks were hidden behind courteous smiles and fashionable clothes or uniforms', according to Leach.[67] In a supposedly egalitarian Australia, too, the sales encounter was fraught and hitting the right note became a delicate balancing act for both parties but especially for the salesgirl:

> Something between the empress and the indifferent is required in the manner of an Australian shop assistant. Too much deference offends a democratic taste, as it seems to border on servility. But the constant shopper likes a salesman [sic] to share some of the interest she feels in her occupation.[68]

Despite these delusions of democracy, money bought privilege. As Susan Porter Benson has noted for the United States, staff were expected to provide the 'freest spenders' with a superior level of service and the granting of a charge account was the key tool for identifying who these select customers were. Only the wives of 'substantial citizens' were granted charge cards and managers favoured these women, treating them better than other customers. Perceived as more financially stable (because they were more prosperous), they also spent more with the store. The store cultivated their loyalty with a range of privileges, including complimentary services, although, as Benson points out, offering these services could be a costly business for stores: customers soon took these privileges for granted and what had been a 'luxury' at first became in time a 'necessity' that they could not do without. Another problem with cultivating this special class of customer was their response when the store tried to expand its target audience and the customer felt that their privileges were being undermined.[69]

A story serialised in Sydney's *Telegraph* newspaper in 1912–1913 drew attention to the ambiguities at work in the big stores. Written by the Australian radical nationalist Vance Palmer while living in the United Kingdom, 'The Shop Assistant' follows the romantic adventures of Millie, a young middle-class woman who takes a job as a sales assistant at a leading department store to escape an arranged marriage. Palmer describes Millie's first impressions of the 'big emporium' whose 'name was known all over England', and which 'to some girls … had the attraction of the footlights'.

> The firm of Dobbin and Carter's, with its dozens of glittering windows, fronted one of the principal streets of South London, and on spring afternoons fashionably dressed women fluttered round it like butterflies round a flower-bed. Everything about it seemed spacious and ideal, from its neat front to its airy show rooms. Leisurely ladies, sauntering from counter to counter, looked at the trim assistants through their lorgnettes, and thought how lucky they were to be serving in so palatial a place, where the wheels of business seemed to be oiled with courtesy and kindliness.

Millie's co-workers immediately recognise her middle-class origins and question her presence on the shopfloor at Dobbin and Carter's. In her turn, Millie is appalled by the conditions she is expected to endure as an employee of the store, sharing a bed in 'a dingy basement with its bare walls and its stained table covers'. She contrasts this with her own room at home, but also with the store's outward appearance: 'Was it all a lie, that gaudy shop front with its glittering windows and its airy show rooms? Was it merely the showy covering that hid all this?' It turns out that everything is a mirage at Dobbin and Carter's:

> 'Such a nice place', Millie heard one lady say. 'What an easy time the girls in here must have.' [Millie] was nearly dropping with fatigue, and her fingers fumbled as she tied up the parcels. It seemed as if the end of the day would never come. Her feet ached with continual standing....

It was not just the shop assistant who felt ambivalent towards the 'glamour' of the department store. As we will see, when credit entered the frame, service encounters could be the scene of deep shame and embarrassment for the shopper—for example, the public humiliation of the woman who does not know her husband has failed to pay the monthly account—and sales staff needed to know how to handle these scenarios sensitively in order to retain the customer's business.[70] Myer's later decision (in 1941) to provide staff with weekly 'cultural training' classes served to highlight the importance of the service encounter to long-term profitability and indicated that Myer had concerns about its staff's abilities in this endeavour.[71]

For its part, Georges fought a battle between profit and brand image, at least at Christmas time when it was crucial for the year's profits to make the most of the annual buying frenzy. 'Messrs George and George consider every class', they reassured the wage-earner's wife who might feel uncomfortable browsing in its store.[72] 'Scores of assistants' were busy 'disposing of toys for cottage and mansion at a bewildering rate'.[73] Depictions of excited crowds inundating Georges belie the more common portrayal of upper-middle-class shopping as well-mannered and serene in contrast to the supposed violence of the bargain counter, although some contended that women of all classes grew 'ugly looking' while shopping at sales.[74] Shopping in department stores, particularly at sales time, was depicted as a competitive sport, with good shoppers (the thrifty 'good manager') versus bad shoppers (the weak, the vulnerable, and those with more money than sense).[75] From the United States, came reports of the deaths of customers in the rush for a bargain.[76] Australian women were equally excited at the prospect of a bargain, summed up by this doggerel published in a Sydney newspaper:

We've got to buy,
Oh, don't ask why,
You know we can't explain it.
Things are so sweet.
It's quite a treat.
To buy and, try to make them fit
And somehow, when, they're in a heap,
We have to buy, they seem so cheap![77]

Newspapers reported injured shoppers and broken plate-glass windows, using words such as 'battle' and 'crush' to describe the frenzied scenes.[78] Five children were 'forgotten' by their mothers in the excitement of a half-price sale at Finney's in Brisbane.[79] As we will see in Chap. 4, criticism of women shoppers, whether 'weak', 'vulnerable', or excitable, would reach new heights as credit became easier to attain, with a new emphasis on working-class women.

Credit Expands

Towards the end of the nineteenth century, women were increasingly able to open their own charge accounts at US department stores and by 1902 these accounts had wide acceptance.[80] In New York, cash had become unfashionable. The cash customer might be more profitable, but 'fashion' had deserted 'those stores where cash payments were the rule'.[81] There were benefits in this for the shopkeeper and the customer. It took more staff to handle cash purchases, so the shopkeeper saved on staffing costs. The customer saved time because they did not have to wait around for change, which was important in large cities, where 'time has a value not attached to it in smaller places'.[82]

This expansion took a little longer to reach Australia. Australians were used to using credit in specialist retailers, with the middle class charging purchases to an approved account and the working class buying goods on 'the slate'. Society's opinion on this situation was clear and influenced by class hierarchies: it was perfectly acceptable for the middle class to make use of credit but, when the workers did the same, it was irresponsible behaviour and evidence of poor budget management. This commentary from 1883 demonstrates the type of class-based judgements around working people using credit to make it through to pay day that circulated:

> Men, and women too, who perhaps cannot raise a five pound note in the world, can get credit at almost any business house they go into, and run up accounts very far beyond anything to which their position in life entitles them, and very frequently very far beyond what they have the most remote idea of paying.[83]

Besides the obvious slur of suggesting that working people 'frequently' accessed credit with no intention of repaying the debt, the notion of people using credit to buy goods 'beyond anything to which their position in life entitles them' reflected the deep ambiguity surrounding the kinds of goods workers were or were not entitled to enjoy. This critique extended to store employees, especially young women. Asking 'Should employers give credit to their staff?', one columnist argued that 'in young people' this might have 'very bad after-effects' because it encouraged 'an entirely unnecessary extravagance, and not infrequently leads to temptation'.[84]

Credit was an 'enervating luxury', argued another writer, in the context of the push by trade unions to shift the frequency of public servants' pay from monthly to fortnightly. Those on 'small wages' who were paid monthly were often forced to turn to credit to get through to the next pay day; railwaymen, for example, complained of having to resort to 'too much tick'.[85] Some public servants even ended up in the Insolvency Court.[86] Fortnightly pay might help them manage better, but it would also make credit easier to get.[87] Nevertheless, the switch to fortnightly payments was granted in Victoria in 1905 and federally in 1906.

As mass production took hold in Australia, such judgements about what a worker and his family deserved from life were in the process of changing significantly, a shift made clear in the appeals that manufacturers made in their advertising campaigns. With more products than ever rolling off production lines, Australian manufacturers needed more consumers to sell them to. More efficient production meant lower prices, so one solution was to give those with limited incomes permission to buy goods previously unavailable to them. By the 1920s, retail credit had become widespread. Retailers began to target women wage-earners, and women's ability to consume was further enhanced by the extension of credit facilities.[88] But, as Chap. 4 shows, working-class women still struggled to open charge accounts and sought out other means of accessing retail credit. The expansion of credit attracted the attention of legislators, as we will see in the following chapter.

Many low to mid-market department stores had a preference for cash, in part to appeal to a working-class trade who were unable to access credit, but also to save on employing a credit-reporting agency, credit bureau, or debt collection agency; smaller retailers with fewer customers to investigate were better able to manage these costs.[89] Upmarket department stores such as Farmer's and David Jones ran credit schemes, restricting access to those account customers whose creditworthiness had been investigated. As credit expanded over the coming decades, some department stores set up their own credit bureaus to collect and store information about customers' credit histories. Like most of the innovations around the expansion of credit, credit bureaus were an idea picked up from overseas and adapted to suit Australia's circumstances.[90] The following chapter will examine this international influence in more detail to better understand how it helped smooth the expansion of retail credit in Australia, before turning to the context in which these innovations were introduced, in particular, society's attitudes towards money-lending.

Notes

1. The relevant histories include R.S. Lambert, *The Universal Provider: A Study of William Whitely and the Rise of the London Department Store* (London: Harrap, 1938); Ralph M. Hower, *History of Macy's of New York 1858–1919: Chapters in the Evolution of a Department Store* (Cambridge, Massachusetts: Harvard University Press, 1946); Reginald Pound, *Selfridge: A Biography* (London: Heinemann, 1960); Michael Miller, *The Bon Marché: Bourgeois Culture and the Department Store 1869–1920* (New Jersey: Princeton UP, 1981); and Vicki Howard, *From Main Street to Mall: The Rise and Fall of the American Department Store* (Philadelphia: University of Pennsylvania Press, 2015).
2. See Rosalind Williams, *Dream Worlds: Mass Consumption in Late Nineteenth-Century France* (California: University of California Press, 1982); Robert Crawford, Kim Humphery, and Judith Smart, eds., 'Introduction', *Consumer Australia: Historical Perspectives* (Newcastle: Oxford Scholar, 2010), 2; Frank Trentmann, *Empire of Things: How We Became a World of Consumers, from the Fifteenth Century to the Twenty-First* (UK: Penguin, 2016); Alan Marshall, *The Gay Provider: The Myer Story* (Melbourne: F.W. Cheshire, 1961); Stella Barber, *Your Store Myer* (Woolloomooloo, NSW: Focus, 2006).

3. *Hordernian Monthly: Australia's 150th Anniversary Number 15*, no. 5 (January 1938): 16, 37; Helen O'Neill, *David Jones: 175 Years* (Sydney: NewSouth Publishing, 2013); 'David Jones', https://mhnsw.au/stories/sydneys-home-furnishing-stores/david-jones/, accessed 7 August 2025; E.A., 'Century of Progress', *Sydney Morning Herald*, 14 September 1940, 11.
4. David T. Merrett, 'Capital Markets and Capital Formation in Australia, 1890–1945', *Australian Economic History Review* 37 (1997): 184; Reekie, *Temptations*, 28.
5. 'George and George Limited', *Leader*, 1 January 1901, 98.
6. 'George and George Limited'.
7. 'Trade and Finance', *Age*, 30 March 1925, 12; 'Myer Australia Limited', *News*, 30 March 1925, 9; 'Myer Emporium Limited. New Company Registered', *Register*, 9 May 1925, 12; 'The Myer Emporium Ltd.', *Sydney Morning Herald*, 24 September 1924, 13.
8. In the United States, women were doing between 80 and 85% of the consumer buying by 1915; William Leach, 'Transformations in a Culture of Consumption', *The Journal of American History* 71, no. 2 (1984): 319–42, 333; Beverley Kingston, *Basket, Bag and Trolley: A History of Shopping in Australia* (Melbourne: Oxford University Press, 1994), 119.
9. Gail Reekie, *Temptations: Sex, Selling, and the Department Store* (St Leonards, NSW: Allen & Unwin, 1993), 34.
10. 'Professional Shoppers', *World's News*, 21 December 1901, 2; 'The Professional Shopper', *Daily News*, 26 May 1903, 2, 'Professional Shoppers: New Occupation for. Women with Brains', *Ballarat Star*, 23 February 1904, 4; 'The Professional Shopper', *Tasmanian News*, 13 September 1907, 3.
11. 'Professional Shoppers', *Weekly Times*, 30 May 1914, 9; 'Smith's Appoints Expert Shopper', *Smith's Weekly*, 1 November 1924, 1.
12. Rappaport, Erika D. '"The Halls of Temptation": Gender, Politics, and the Construction of the Department Store in Late Victorian London', *Journal of British Studies* 35, no. 1 (Jan. 1996): 61. https://www.jstor.org/stable/175745
13. 'Can Women Shop?' *Age*, 13 October 1906.
14. 'Can Women Shop?'. For earlier critiques of 'shopping for pleasure', see Erika Rappaport, *Shopping for Pleasure: Women in the Making of London's West End* (Princeton University Press, 2000), 16–41.
15. 'Men and Women as Shoppers', *Albury Banner and Wodonga Express*, 30 May 1902, 9.
16. 'The Difference', *Geelong Advertiser*, 25 November 1905, 5.
17. 'Tea Table Topics', *Sunday Times*, 19 November 1905, 6.
18. 'Three Kinds of Shoppers', *Chronicle*, 30 July 1904, 48.

19. 'The Professional Shopper', *Colac Herald,* 2 April 1886, 2.
20. 'Shoppers and Shopping', *Star,* 18 September 1909, 13.
21. 'Women are Poor Shoppers', *Prahran Telegraph,* 11 July 1908, 6.
22. 'Lady Shoppers', *Barrier Miner,* 3 November 1904, 2. For middle-class women and shoplifting, see Elaine Abelson, *When Ladies Go A-Thieving: Middle-Class Shoplifters in the Victorian Department Store* (Oxford: Oxford University Press, 1989).
23. Elizabeth Block, 'Trials of the Girl Behind the Counter', *Daily Telegraph,* 2 April 1913, 15.
24. 'Some Tricks of Shoppers', *Darling Downs Gazette,* 5 June 1909, 6; 'Professional Shoppers', *Weekly Times,* 30 May 1914, 9.
25. 'Club For Shoppers', *Examiner,* 1 June 1907, 2.
26. 'Club For Shoppers'.
27. 'Searching for the Shoppers' Paradise', *Evening Journal,* 28 November 1908, 5.
28. 'A Woman's Paradise', *Table Talk,* 14 September 1916, 8.
29. 'Business Extension: Two City Firms to Spend Over £80,000', *Sunday Times,* 3 December 1911, 9; 'Business Expansion: Store Proprietors Spending Over £250,000. Great Demand for Room', *Sunday Times,* 10 December 1911, 9; Helen O'Neill, *David Jones 175 Years* (Sydney: NewSouth, 2015), 82, 84, 87.
30. 'The Shop Girl', *Sunday Times,* 25 February 1906, 2; 'The Girl behind the Counter', *Daily Telegraph,* 4 December 1909, 16.
31. 'The Girl behind the Counter', *Sydney Morning Herald,* 9 June 1911, 7; 'Bijou Theatre: The Girl behind the Counter', *Age,* 16 June 1913, 7; 'The Shop Girl', *Maitland Daily Mercury,* 7 November 1914, 4; 'The Shop Girl', *Richmond Guardian,* 16 October 1920, 3.
32. Lillian Quiller Couch, 'The Girl behind the Counter', *Journal,* 12 July 1913, 2.
33. Couch, 'The Girl behind the Counter'.
34. Couch, 'The Girl behind the Counter'.
35. 'The Second Visit', *Bathurst Times,* 1 April 1911, 3.
36. Ian Grosvenor, 'A Cheserby Sensation', *Express and Telegraph,* 17 February 1912, 5.
37. Reinette Lovewell, 'More Than Money', *Freeman's Journal,* 22 July 1915, 4.
38. 'The Little Girl Who Stayed', *Catholic Advocate,* 31 August 1912, 39.
39. 'The Tempter and Maria', *Sunday Times,* 15 March 1914, 24.
40. 'S.V. Reilly, 'The Lesson of the Day', *Freeman's Journal,* 29 February 1912, 4.
41. Friedrich Engels, *The Condition of the Working Class of England* (Oxford: Oxford University Press, 1993), 58.

42. Leach, 'Transformations in a Culture of Consumption', 320.
43. Melita Schaum, '"Just Looking:" Class, Desire, and the Consuming Vision in T. S. Eliot's "In the Department Store"', *Journal of Modern Literature* 23, no. 2 (1999–2000): 335–50.
44. H.G. Wells, *The History of Mr Polly*. London: Thomas Nelson and Sons, 1910.
45. Stuart Macintyre, 'The Making of the Australian Working Class: An Historiographical Survey', *Historical Studies* 18, no. 71 (1978): 233–53.
46. Reekie, *Temptations*, 32.
47. Susan Porter Benson, *Counter Cultures: Saleswomen, Managers, and Customers in American Department Stores, 1890–1940* (Urbana and Chicago: University of Illinois Press, 1986), 78; Ellen McArthur, 'Towards a Theory of Retail Evolution: An Australian History of Retailing in the Early Twentieth Century', PhD thesis (Sydney: University of Technology, 2005), 47.
48. 'Collins Street', *Punch*, 18 December 1902, 16.
49. 'George and George Limited', *Leader*, 1 January 1901, 98.
50. Philip Kotler, 'Atmospherics as a Marketing Tool', *Journal of Retailing* 49 (1974): 48–64.
51. Walter Benjamin, 'The Work of Art in an Age of Mechanical Reproduction', in *Illuminations*, ed. Hannah Arendt, trans. Harry Zohn, from the 1935 essay (New York: Schocken Books, 1969).
52. Elizabeth Outka, 'Crossing the Great Divides: Selfridges, Modernity, and the Commodified Authentic', *Modernism/modernity* 12, no. 2 (April 2005): 311–28.
53. Catherine Kovesi, 'The Aura of Luxury: Cultivating the Believing Faithful from the Age of Saints to the Age of Luxury Brands', *Luxury* 3, no. 1–2 (2016): 105–22.
54. Kovesi, 'The Aura of Luxury'.
55. Nicholas Alexander and Anne Marie Doherty, 'Theorising Brand Aura', *Journal of Service Management* 34, no. 1 (2023): 126–46.
56. 'Store Character and Personality: Winning Friends and Influencing People', *Retail Merchandiser*, April 1959, 11
57. 'Store Character and Personality', 11.
58. 'Store Character and Personality', 11.
59. 'Store Character and Personality', 11.
60. Pierre Martineau, 'The Personality of the Retail Store', *Harvard Business Review* 36, no. 1 (1958): 47–55, 48–9.
61. E.P. Thompson, *The Making of the English Working Class* (1963), 8–11; Erving Goffman, 'The Interaction Order', *American Sociological Review* 48, no.1 (1983): 4–6.

62. Delphine Dion and Stephane Borraz, 'Managing Status: How Luxury Brands Shape Class Subjectivities in the Service Encounter', *Journal of Marketing* 81 (September 2017): 68.
63. Dion and Borraz, 'Managing Status', 78.
64. Dion and Borraz, 'Managing Status', 69; Pierre Bourdieu, *Distinction: A Social Critique of the Judgement of Taste* (Cambridge: Harvard University Press, 1984), 102.
65. J. César Félix-Brasdefer, *The Language of Service Encounters* (Cambridge: Cambridge University Press, 2015), 8, 13.
66. Amy Hanser, *Service Encounters: Class, Gender and the Market for Social Distinction in Urban China* (Stanford: Stanford University Press, 2008), 3.
67. Leach, 'Transformations in A Culture of Consumption', 326.
68. 'The Constant Shopper', *Sydney Morning Herald*, 4 July 1906, 5.
69. Benson, *Counter Cultures*, 90–91.
70. 'Declining Credit and Retaining the Good Will of the Person Declined', *Credit World* 5, no. 2 (January 1915): 12.
71. 'City Stores Cultural Training Plan', *Argus*, 25 July 1944, 10; 'Educational Festival', *Sun News-Pictorial*, 31 October 1945, 14.
72. 'George and George', *Herald*, 18 December 1905, 3.
73. 'George and George'.
74. 'Bargain Counter Mania', *Braidwood and Araluen Express and People's Advocate*, 12 June 1903, 1; 'Woman Killed at Bargain Sale', *Daily News*, 18 September 1906, 3; 'Sequel to Bargain Sale', *Glen Innes Examiner and General Advertiser*, 16 October 1906, 3; 'The Shopping Face', *Daily Telegraph*, 3 March 1906, 15.
75. 'Hunting for Bargains', *Evening News*, 7 March 1905, 7.
76. 'Woman Killed at Bargain Sale', *Daily News,* 18 September 1906, 3; 'Fatal Bargain Rush', *Bundaberg Mail and Burnett Advertiser*, 6 June 1910, 2.
77. 'Women's Column: The Shoppers', *Watchman,* 28 July 1910, 2.
78. 'A Victim of the Sales', *Australian Star*, 9 August 1907, 2; 'Crush at Farmer's', *Maitland Daily Mercury*,19 July 1920, 5; 'Injured in Sales Rush', *Sydney Morning Herald*, 3 October 1940, 8; 'Crush At City Sale', *Daily Telegraph*, 29 June 1948, 7; 'Four Faint in Sale Crush', *Mercury*, 20 December 1949, 5; 'Window Goes in Bargain Crush', *Brisbane Telegraph,* 1 October 1951, 1.
79. 'Sale Crush: Five Lost', *Courier-Mail,* 21 January 1954, 6.
80. Leach, 'Transformations in a Culture of Consumption', 330.
81. 'Shops and Shoppers', *Examiner*, 6 April 1901, 13.
82. 'Shops and Shoppers'.
83. 'Cash and Credit', *Illawarra Mercury*, 12 June 1883, 4.
84. M.W., 'Credit', *Bathurst Times,* 8 March 1913, 4.
85. 'Railwaymen's Request', 17 July 1904, 3.

86. 'State Servants', *Gympie Times and Mary River Mining Gazette*, 29 August 1905, 3.
87. 'Victorian Parliament: Legislative Assembly, *Age*, 17 October 1902, 7; 'The Public Service Fortnightly Pay', *Age*, 21 August 1905, 4; 'Fortnightly Pay', *Clarence and Richmond Examiner*, 17 October 1905.
88. Reekie, *Temptations*, 32.
89. Josh Lauer, *Creditworthy: A History of Consumer Surveillance and Financial Identity in America*. New York: Columbia University Press, 2017.
90. 'Credit Bureaux – Their History', *Retail Merchandiser*, January 1959, 30–31.

References

Arendt, Hannah. *Illuminations*, ed., trans. Harry Zohn. New York: Schocken Books, 1969 [1935].

Abelson, Elaine S. *When Ladies Go A-Thieving: Middle-Class Shoplifters in the Victorian Department Store*. Oxford: Oxford University Press, 1989.

Barber, Stella. *Your Store Myer: The Story of Australia's Leading Department Store*. Woolloomooloo, NSW: Focus, 2006.

Benson, Susan Porter. *Counter Cultures: Saleswomen, Managers, and Customers in American Department Stores, 1890–1940*. Urbana and Chicago: University of Illinois Press, 1986.

Bourdieu, Pierre. *Distinction: A Social Critique of the Judgement of Taste*. Cambridge: Harvard University Press, 1984.

Crawford, Robert, Kim Humphery, and Judith Smart, eds. *Consumer Australia: Historical Perspectives*. Newcastle: Oxford Scholar, 2010.

Dion, Delphine and Stéphane Borraz. 'Managing Status: How Luxury Brands Shape Class Subjectivities in the Service Encounter', *Journal of Marketing* 81 (September 2017): 67–85. https://doi.org/10.1509/jm.15.0

Engels, Friedrich. *The Condition of the Working Class of England*. Oxford: Oxford University Press, 1993 [1845].

Félix-Brasdefer, J. César. *The Language of Service Encounters*. Cambridge: Cambridge University Press, 2019.

Goffman, Erving. 'The Interaction Order', *American Sociological Review* 48, no. 1 (1983): 1–17. https://doi.org/10.2307/2095141

Hanser, Amy. *Service Encounters: Class, Gender and the Market for Social Distinction in Urban China*. Stanford: Stanford University Press, 2008.

Hower, Ralph M. *History of Macy's of New York 1858 1919: Chapters in the Evolution of a Department Store*. Cambridge, Massachusetts: Harvard University Press, 1946.

Kingston, Beverley. *Basket, Bag and Trolley: A History of Shopping in Australia*. Melbourne: Oxford University Press, 1994.

Kotler Philip. 'Atmospherics as a Marketing Tool'. *Journal of Retailing* 49 (1974): 48–64.

Kovesi, Catherine. 'The Aura of Luxury: Cultivating the Believing Faithful from the Age of Saints to the Age of Luxury Brands', *Luxury* 3, no. 1–2 (2016): 105–22. https://doi.org/10.1080/20511817.2016.1232468

Lauer, Josh. *Creditworthy: A History of Consumer Surveillance and Financial Identity in America*. New York: Columbia University Press, 2017.

Leach, William R. 'Transformations in a Culture of Consumption: Women and Department Stores, 1890–1925,' *The Journal of American History* 71, no. 2 (1984): 319–42. https://doi.org/10.2307/1901758

McArthur, Ellen. 'Towards a Theory of Retail Evolution: An Australian History of Retailing in the Early Twentieth Century'. PhD thesis. Sydney: University of Technology, 2005, 47.

Macintyre, Stuart. 'The Making of the Australian Working Class: An Historiographical Survey', *Historical Studies* 18, no. 71 (1978): 233–53.

Marshall, Alan. *The Gay Provider: The Myer Story*. Melbourne: F.W. Cheshire, 1961.

Martineau, Pierre. 'The Personality of the Retail Store', *Harvard Business Review* 36, no. 1 (1958): 47–55.

Merrett, David T. 'Capital Markets and Capital Formation in Australia, 1890–1945', *Australian Economic History Review* 37(1997): 181–201. https://doi.org/10.1111/1467-8446.00014

Miller, Michael. *The Bon Marché: Bourgeois Culture and the Department Store 1869–1920*. New Jersey: Princeton UP, 1981.

O'Neill, Helen. *David Jones:175 Years*. Sydney: NewSouth Publishing, 2013.

Outka, Elizabeth. 'Crossing the Great Divides: Selfridges, Modernity, and the Commodified Authentic'. *Modernism/modernity* 12, no. 2 (April 2005): 311–28.

Reekie, Gail. *Temptations: Sex, Selling, and the Department Store*. St Leonards, NSW: Allen & Unwin, 1993.

Retail Merchandiser: Official Journal of the Masters Drapers and Traders' Association of Victoria. Melbourne, Vic.: Masters Drapers and Traders' Association of Victoria, 1949–1967.

Schaum, Melita. '"Just Looking": Class, Desire, and the Consuming Vision in T.S. Eliot's "In the Department Store"', *Journal of Modern Literature* 23, no. 2 (1999)–2000: 335–50. gale.com/apps/doc/A67408634/AONE?u=anon~d743daa0&sid=googleScholar&xid=1ddd5c08. Accessed 11 July 2025.

Stobart, Jon. 'Cathedrals of Consumption? Provincial Department Stores in England, c. 1880 1930', *Enterprise & Society* 18, no. 4 (December 2017): 810–45.

Thompson, E.P. *The Making of the English Working Class*. London: Victor Gollancz, 1963.

Trentmann, Frank. *Empire of Things: How We Became a World of Consumers, from the Fifteenth Century to the Twenty-First*. UK: Penguin, 2016.
Wells, H.G. *The History of Mr Polly*. London: Thomas Nelson and Sons, 1910.
Williams, Rosalind. *Dream Worlds: Mass Consumption in Late Nineteenth-Century France*. California: University of California Press, 1982.

CHAPTER 3

Innovation and Critique

Abstract From the 1890s, retailers began to seek safer, more scientific ways of providing and managing credit. Emanating from the United States, innovations in credit technology and management were implemented in Australia. Department stores adopted different credit forms depending on their own distinctive atmosphere or aura, helping to consolidate a hierarchy of credit. Australian workers became entangled in this emerging culture of credit in the broader context of society's ambiguous attitudes towards usury and credit in general. These included Christian teachings that allowed moneylending without excessive interest rates and the more critical position of socialists, who identified usury as a key component of capitalist exploitation and explored the issue in utopian novels.

Keywords Credit • Retail • Technology • Workers • Moneylending • Australian history

Given Australia's modern history as a collection of British colonies until federation in 1901, it is no surprise that British credit practices influenced early ideas about the ways in which credit should be managed in Australia. Retailers offered credit facilities to their regular customers, but these usually operated on a small scale, with stores keeping a record of a customer's debt, a system known as buying 'on tick' (short for 'ticket') or 'on the

J. Dickenson, *Credit and the Australian Department Store Since 1900*, https://doi.org/10.1007/978-3-032-16612-8_3

slate' (based on the old custom of recording debts with chalk on a piece of slate).[1] From the 1870s, British immigrant drapers such as Sydney's William Buckingham transformed retail credit in Australia by introducing the cash-order system, which will be examined in depth in the following chapter. Despite the influence of British retailers, it would be the United States that would have the biggest impact on the management of retail credit in Australia.

Managing Credit: United States

As department stores developed and more customers applied for charge or monthly (also known as 'entry') accounts, retailers sought safer, more scientific ways of extending and managing credit.[2] As in many things retail, the United States led the way.[3] When one Chicago department store was reported as struggling to manage the authorisation files of 'about 200,000 accounts', the maxim became 'speed, speed, and then again speed'.[4] The achievement of faster and more accurate ways of processing credit applications required, in part, more efficient filing and indexing equipment.[5] But it would take more than better filing systems to improve credit efficiency—and profitability—in department stores. Central to these systems would be two new technologies: the harnessing of electricity and the development of telecommunications.

Towards the end of the nineteenth century, US credit managers began to work out why their departments were struggling under such heavy workloads. The problem was that each store investigated new applicants itself, which meant they were often doubling up on information already collected by a rival store. Sharing information between retailers would fix this inefficiency and, in 1896, the credit managers took a step towards this when, like many other occupational groups moving to professionalise in this period, they came together to form their own professional organisation, the Retail Credit Men's Association.[6] The Association aimed to improve what it called 'The Interchange of Credit Experience'.[7] Combining in this way allowed credit managers to adopt uniform management methods and to pool their resources to improve the gathering and dissemination of credit information. The Association's journal later explained the value of sharing this information:

> Suppose Mr. Alexander, of Geo. Muse, opened an account with Jim Jones. Three days later Jones comes in my store. If Mr. Alexander keeps this

> information in his file and does not let me see it, the work of investigating would be to do over, whereas, if he gave it to the reporting bureau, we will call the bureau and will know what he does.[8]

The Association went on to establish local credit bureaus across the country that provided 'all alive and useful credit information', helping credit managers to maintain tighter control of their debtors.[9]

In 1912, the Association launched the *Credit World*, a bi-monthly publication, featuring the latest news and developments from the credit industry.[10] *Credit World* outlined how the Association's Credit Department managed credit records. Previously, the department had recorded credit details in a credit-rating book (as did most privately owned collection agencies), but this information went out of date too quickly to be of use, so the Credit Department had shifted to using 'little cards' to keep a record of all applicants.[11] These cards documented the information the store forwarded to the Credit Department, such as the applicant's name and their references.[12] The Credit Department then checked the references using private telephone lines (to avoid eavesdropping switchboard operators), and stores paid for this service based on how many telephone calls were made. A credit report was then sent to the store. If required, debt collection was undertaken by mail and examples of collection letters were printed in *Credit World*.[13] The Association assured it members that the service it offered was cheaper than privately owned collection agencies, and gave the example of its work for the high-end department store, Stix, Baer and Fuller of St. Louis, Missouri.[14]

Over the next two decades, *Credit World* recorded the technological developments designed to improve the speed and accuracy of credit approval. Many of these innovations were promoted in advertisements, the Ellis Book Keeping Machine—'Accuracy Makes Profits, Errors Make Losses'—for example, and its rival, the Elliott-Fisher Bank Bookkeeping Machine, which gave credit managers 'Facts at Finger Tips'.[15] Other innovations included 'visible records', which replaced 'the old-fashioned card-in-the-box records'. Rand Visible Records made record-finding 'seven times faster' and the Acme Card System provided 'Greater Speed and Accuracy'.[16] The Rotosfled Stencil Duplicator printed 'a thousand excellent form letters for 20c' (for easier debt collection) and was 'easy to operate' with 'no type to set, no delay, no muss'[17]; the Protectograph, which printed cash amounts on cheques in words, ensured 'forgery-proof checks'.[18] Technologies used to improve communication between the sales floor and the credit office included pneumatic tubes (patented in 1854 and still in use today) and the telautograph. Invented in 1888, the latter was an electrical device that provided a rapid handwritten exchange of information, in essence, the first facsimile machine.[19]

The most significant of these innovations was, arguably, the 'electrical credit system', which was introduced circa 1914. Known colloquially as the 'OK system' of credit authorisation, this would be the dominant form of department store credit management for the next three decades, including in Australia.[20] The system used Credit Authorisation Telephones, known by staff as the OK Phones.[21] An advertisement promoting the National Electric Credit System in the United States explained why the system was necessary and how it worked. Once again, speed was its key selling point:

> Charge systems have undergone great changes in the past few years. Speed and accuracy are now the two great department store essentials. The National Electric Credit System is the speediest method yet invented. The credit office is in instant communication with all departments. The salesperson phones the inquiry. The O.K. comes back like a flash—electrically stamped on the sales-slip. The office is in direct, complete and immediate control of all authorizations. Everybody's time is saved. Minutes are clipped to seconds. Customers are pleased. Sales are rapid. Aisles are clear.[22]

As processing credit applications became easier and measuring credit risk improved, retail credit expanded rapidly.[23] More women began to sign up to credit accounts, and some even trained as credit managers. This forced the Retail Credit Men's Association to consider changing its name: the Association now had so many 'Lady Credit Men' that some sections were seriously considering the change 'so as to eliminate the masculine sex from our present title'.[24] In 1927, the Association became the National Retail Credit Association.

Managing Credit: Australia

Credit expanded rapidly in Australia, too, and Australian department stores would eventually adopt many of these scientific measures to manage their credit applications. Myer was an early adopter, but it took the store almost a decade after the OK system's launch in the United States to bring it to Australia, no doubt because of the First World War. The system was installed at Myer in 1922.[25] The Australian credit industry also lagged behind the United States in its move to professionalise. Its industry body, the Australian Institute for Credit Management (AICM), was established only in 1937 and not incorporated until 1967.[26]

Australian department stores were quicker to move on another US innovation. Charge account customers had previously been issued with a cardboard card to present when using their accounts in store. This changed with the arrival of the metal charge plate in Australia. The Charga-Plate—trademarked by the Farrington Manufacturing Company of *Massachusetts, United States,* in 1928—was a metal, dog-tag-style plate with the customer's name and city of residence imprinted on it and a paper backing that the customer signed. The Charga-Plate was mostly issued between the 1930s and the late 1950s, when the plastic charge card began to replace it, including in Australia.[27] Long-time customers of department stores such as David Jones and Myer (Figs. 3.1 and 3.2), however, would continue to use their metal Charga-Plates until well into the 1970s.[28]

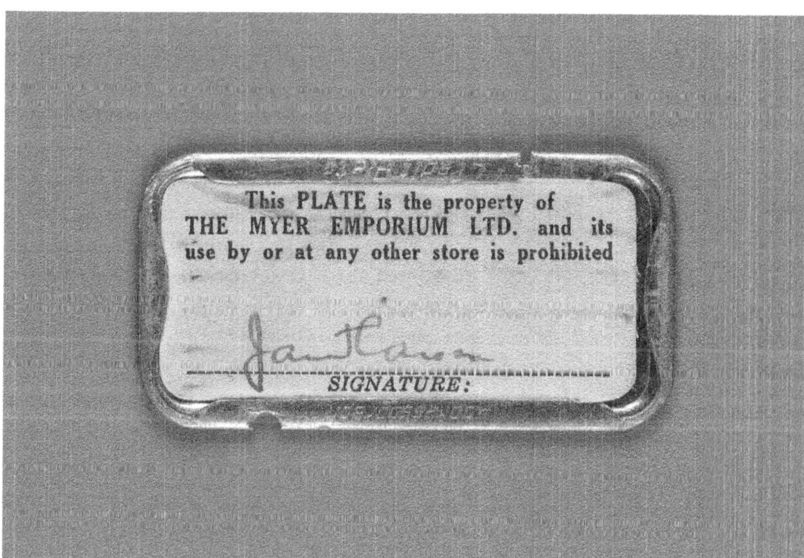

Fig. 3.1 Myer Emporium charge plate, 1960s. MS13468, Box 1715, COMY13383, SLV

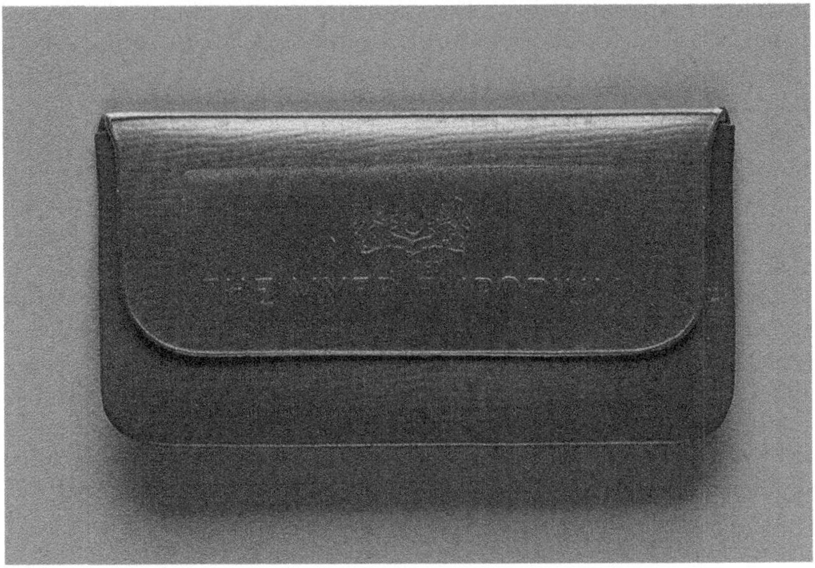

Fig. 3.2 Myer Emporium charge plate wallet, 1960s. MS13468, Box 1715, COMY13383, SLV

Those department stores pitched at less affluent shoppers were slower to adopt new credit technologies, continuing to preference cash sales over credit. One such store was The Mutual Store Ltd., which was Melbourne's first 'department store', incorporated in 1872.[29] Located at the corner of Flinders and Degraves streets, the store attracted comparisons to Paris's Le Bon Marché department store because of its profit-sharing model, through which profits were shared with staff via a yearly dividend.[30] This was intended to improve productivity and avoid the 'labour troubles' that were steadily increasing between employers and newly organising employees in the second half of the nineteenth century.[31] Over the next 50 years, this profit-sharing model would be adopted and extended by other Australian department stores. Myer, for example, offered a co-operative model—the Staff Partnership Scheme—in which employees were able to purchase shares in the company either by cash or over time through an instalment purchase plan at 10% interest.[32] Giving employees a stake in the financial success of the company would, it was hoped, make them more productive than those who just worked to draw wages.[33]

The Mutual Store's proximity to Flinders Street Station suggests a catch-all target audience. Pitched at the budget end of the market, the company provided a range of services to its customers, including access to short-term credit in the form of monthly accounts.[34] An examination of the minutes of the board's meetings between 1900 and 1918 shows that, although there was a gradual (if uneven) growth in credit approvals for the store's monthly account, the Mutual Store (like other Australian department stores) was slow to embrace the credit innovations emanating from the United States.

The minutes also reveal shifts in the ways in which a large store managed these accounts across the first two decades of the twentieth century.[35] In 1900, 107 applications were approved with around 18% of these being applications from women. The minutes recorded the names of those approved for a monthly account and, in most cases, the individual amounts that were owed, which ranged from £5 to £25.[36] As the number of monthly accounts grew, it was no longer possible to record individual names in the minutes and, from July 1906, noted instead the number of credit accounts that had been approved each month.[37] Between November 1911 and July 1918, an average of 24 new accounts were approved each month with the lowest number of approvals (5) in September 1915 and the highest number (56) in July 1918, which no doubt reflected shifting levels of confidence at different stages of the First World War.[38]

Despite this growth in monthly charge accounts, the promise of short-term credit was slow to appear in department store advertising. The Mutual Store, for example, did not promote its credit offering. In fact, the store rarely ran display advertising at all, relying on advertorial-type newspaper articles and its regular catalogue to promote its products and services long after display advertising became popular.[39] Those department stores that did use display advertising—the Myer Emporium, for example—only began to promote their credit facilities towards the end of the 1920s. Even then, this was for deferred payment plans, that is, long-term plans for major purchases such as furniture, sewing machines, and radios to be repaid weekly or monthly. Also known as hire purchase or instalment plans, these accounted for around 15% of department store credit business at the time.[40] A Myer advertisement for furniture, for example, marketed the plan as 'Easy Credit Terms', which were available to approved customers.[41] An earlier exception to this was the Sydney department store Anthony Hordern, which introduced the interest-free Deposit-Purchase System (known as the DPS) in 1928.[42] 'Not to be confused with cash orders and instalment plans', the DPS required a 'deposit of not less than 20% then instalments [paid] each month' with no interest charged.[43] By 1930, the Sydney department store Mark Foy had introduced a similar scheme, calling it 'lay-buy'.[44]

Some stores—Sydney's Grace Bros, for example—encouraged the use of cash rather than credit, even for large items such as furniture: 'Furniture on the cash system has proved a great success at Grace Bros. Mr. Grace remarks that the time-payment system may suit the unready, but that the man with the cash knows he can command best value'.[45] On the other hand, David Jones pitched its monthly account as 'the modern and most efficient way of shopping' that was more convenient than cash. By simplifying shopping, the account saved the customer time and made good business sense.[46] There was also an urgency to the store's messaging on credit. 'No Account? Don't Be Without One Any Longer!', one advertisement shouted, foreshadowing the appeal to (and encouragement of) a customer's hankering for instant gratification—or impulse buying—that, as we will see, gained traction after the Second World War.[47]

The earliest advertisement for Myer's entry account (its version of the charge or monthly account) appeared only in 1933.[48] Given the significance of this facility, it is surprising that it was not promoted earlier, but it might have helped maintain the image of exclusivity around the approval of a charge account. The account customer needed to feel their relationship with the store was special, that they alone deserved special rewards, and Myer's advertising emphasised the special consideration that the entry account customer received, for example, extended payment schedules to help them take early advantage of sales and ensure they had the pick of the bargains.[49] According to one advertisement, opening a Myer charge account would immediately raise a customer's social standing. '"I have a charge account at Myer's!" At once your rating in any community is placed at a high level', it reassured prospective members. Appealing to the Australian middle class's self-conception of its moral superiority to the working class, the advertisement assured them that the convenience of a Myer charge account was only available to 'responsible persons'.[50] Foreshadowing later developments, this sense of exclusivity was the foundation of the store loyalty programmes that would flourish in the last decade of the twentieth century. For its part, the Mutual Store continued to lag behind the more upmarket stores in its promotion of its credit facilities. As late as 1934, the board's minutes referred with evident surprise to 'the efforts being made by Myer's to increase sales, they had recently been devoting a great deal of attention to the use of credit accounts and were missing no possible opportunity of circularising prospects in this connection'. The implication was, perhaps, that the Mutual Store should start to do the same.[51]

The Usury Curse

So how did Australian workers become entangled in this new credit culture? As we will see in the next chapter, working-class women had long been dependent on credit to get the family through to payday. This did not mean they necessarily approved of credit or felt comfortable about seeking it out. Finding themselves in straitened circumstances, these women had little choice but to resort to its use.

Usury, or the charging of excessive interest on loans, was frowned upon by all classes in Australia, influenced by the Church's teaching on the topic, which condemned usurers—those lending the money—rather than those forced to use credit. As we will see, however, a deeper analysis underpinned criticism of usury by a newly influential sector of society—that is, the nascent labour movement, representing the working class.

For centuries, the key debate engaging thinkers on the topic of usury had been (and still is) whether all moneylending was wrong or just moneylending that charged excessive interest. According to Aristotle, all usury was unproductive, unnatural, and unjust.[52] Money existed for the purpose of exchange, but interest increased the amount of money itself: 'offspring resembles parent, and interest is money born of money; consequently this form of the getting of wealth is of all forms the most contrary to nature'.[53] The major religions also condemned usury. Judaism forbade lending for interest to fellow Jews and Islam used sections of the Quran to prohibit the charging of *riba* (interest).[54] However, adherents of both faiths had, over time, found ways to circumvent these prohibitions.[55]

Christianity was no different. From its earliest years, the Church regarded usury as a sin, despite there being no blanket prohibition in the scriptures on the earning of interest on investments or from the paying of interest on loans. Church leaders interpreted the Old Testament references to usury as implying that loans could be made to the poor or destitute, but that a moneylender should not demand interest from impoverished relatives or from members of the same social or religious group.[56] The New Testament did not address the issue of usury directly, but the Church interpreted two parables (Luke 19:23 and Matthew 25:27) as condemning usury because they implied that a person should not accumulate wealth and possessions at the expense of others. Moreover, Jesus was said to have encouraged his disciples to help those in need without charging interest: 'lend, hoping for nothing again; and your reward shall be great'.[57]

As capitalism gained momentum and the demand for business lending increased, a more flexible view of usury became necessary. In the sixteenth and seventeenth centuries respectively, the German theologian Martin Luther and the English philosopher Francis Bacon argued that charging interest should be allowed, but that it was immoral to charge excessive interest: Bacon, for example, wanted interest to be limited to a maximum of 5%.[58] By the beginning of the twentieth century, usury had been linked for a millennium to the antisemitic stereotyping of the Jewish community as scheming moneylenders, and we will see more of this ugly aspect of Australian attitudes to moneylending in the following chapter.

'He goes a sorrowing who goes a borrowing', observed *Tocsin*, Melbourne's socialist paper, in 1905.[59] For the labour movement, usury was a key feature of the exploitative capitalist system, as pernicious and undeserved as the charging of rent or the taking of excessive profits.[60] In Volume Three of *Capital*, Karl Marx addressed the role usury played in fuelling the exploitation of workers: it led to unstable financial interdependences and encouraged speculation and over production, which then led to low wages for industrial workers.[61] The *Worker* newspaper spelled out the link between usury and the exploitation of workers: 'Usury … guised as Interest sucks the life blood of nations'; 'People are poor because people are rich. Wages are low because Rent and Usury grind, of all, the faces of the poor'. [62]

The labour press took aim at usury using historical commentators, quoting Bacon:

> Usury bringeth the treasures of a realm or state into a few hands; for the usurer being at certainties, and all others at uncertainties, at the end of the game most of the money will be in his box; and over a state flourisheth most when wealth is more equally spread.[63]

and John Ruskin, the nineteenth-century English art critic: 'Large fortunes are all founded either on occupation of land, or usury, or taxation of labour'.[64] The English socialist Tom Mann linked the need to control usury to the moral standpoint and solidarity of the labour movement:

> Socialists, by endorsing a true morality that forbids robbery by usury (interest), rent, and profits (other than the right reward of labour, which sometimes is included in the latter term), are bringing about a system of righteousness, not by professions of faith, but by righteous relationships worthy of true Brotherhood.[65]

Mann's commentary reflected the utopian nature of labour's critique of usury. The purpose of trade unions was to make the world better, the *Worker* declared, and lowering usury would help achieve this.[66] George Black, the Labor politician and editor of *The Australian Worker*, dreamed of a 'limited Utopia' where: 'Usury will be annihilated, for no one will be denied the use of that which exists only for the well-being of all, and no one will be so foolish as to hoard that whose possession does not advantage him'.[67]

Analysis such as this featured prominently in the utopian novels of the last quarter of the nineteenth century. Edward Bellamy's utopian novel *Looking Backward, 2000 to 1887* (published in 1888), for example, told the story of a wealthy young protagonist Julian West, who reflects on his life in late-nineteenth-century Boston, where he lives in luxury at the expense of the working class. He describes the role that usury played in the inequities of his society:

> interest on investments was a species of tax in perpetuity upon the product of those engaged in industry which a person possessing or inheriting money was able to levy. It must not be supposed that an arrangement which seems so unnatural and preposterous according to modern notions was never criticized by your ancestors. It had been the effort of lawgivers and prophets from the earliest ages to abolish interest, or at least to limit it to the smallest possible rate. All these efforts had, however, failed, as they necessarily must so long as the ancient social organizations prevailed. At the time of which I write, the latter part of the nineteenth century, governments had generally given up trying to regulate the subject at all.

After falling into a deep sleep, West wakes up in the year 2000 to a completely transformed society. The capitalism of his own time has gone, replaced by a collective societal structure where the government has assumed control of production and labour for the benefit of all. Works such as this and Bradford Peck's *The World a Department Store: A Story of Life Under a Cooperative System (A Twentieth Century Utopia)*[68] included arguments for a co-operative utopia in which lending for interest would be rendered obsolete. In reality, the co-operative movement emphasised the granting of loans where necessary but without excessive profit.[69]

The political wing of the labour movement—the recently formed Australian Labor Party (ALP)—embraced this utopian ideal, positioning itself in opposition to usury. It was the party for 'all honest workers, whether clad in Bishop's lawn or navvy's moleskin', it argued. 'The only persons the Party did not represent', however, 'were the professional idle classes—landlords, usury lords, sweater lords, and all of like ilk—who toil not, neither mentally nor physically, but prey on the toil of others'.[70] 'Law Reform and the Rigid Regulation of Usury' were 'two measures worthy of a place on the Labor Party's platform'.[71] Some in the labour movement hoped that Australia's first federal (Protectionist) government would move on the abolition of usury and demanded its new representatives act to limit the amount of interest that moneylenders could charge. The first federal governments (including the first Labor government of 1904) were, however, 'seemingly content to let it be'.[72]

There were two drivers of this lack of urgency. First, responsibility for credit was divided between the federal government and the states. The federal government was responsible for legislating the banks, including their loan activities, such as mortgage loans (*Credit Foncier*, in the jargon of the day). The newly formed states were responsible for legislating consumer credit, for constraining usury and 'fringe-lending', that is, short-term high interest instalment loans.[73] Second was Labor's continuing ambivalence towards regulating credit caused by the gap between socialist idealism and liberal pragmatism. For the socialists, usury was unquestionably evil and deserving of eradication. For the labourites, moneylending might be exploitative of the poor, but access to credit should not be the preserve of the middle and upper classes. Just as working people deserved to have nice things,[74] they also deserved to be able to access credit where necessary. As we will see in the following chapter, this argument would be made forcefully in the Arbitration Court in the late 1920s as the movement argued its case for a rise in the basic wage.

The year before Australian federation, the UK parliament passed the Money-Lenders Act, 1900 (Imperial), which was applied in each colony and remained on the statute books in the newly federated states.[75] The Act mandated the registration of moneylenders but did not place a cap on interest rates and was judged to not go far enough. Its shortcomings drew attention from the Australian press: 'The Moneylenders Act has clipped the wings of the late Isaac Gordon's [an infamous and recently-deceased

English moneylender] imitators, but much remains to be done to obviate the ingenuity of the fraternity in evading the law'.[76] Based on a Scottish report, the article also included condemnation of working-class moneylenders. These flourished 'amongst the poorest sections of the working classes' and their profits were 'such as might make Shylock green with envy'.[77] Their profits were excessive (at least 433% it was claimed!), because, unlike more 'respectable' moneylenders, working-class moneylenders refused to charge a 'modest' rate of interest. Moreover, the illicit moneylender was usually a workman himself and, because he was 'steadier' than his colleagues, was likely to be promoted to foreman or assistant foreman, which then gave him 'crushing powers of extortion' over his fellow workers.[78] Missing from this report was any reflection on why the poor might be especially vulnerable to the predatory credit practices it described, or, for that matter, what kind of system allowed men capable of illicit behaviour to flourish and be promoted.

The first of the states to act on usury was New South Wales (NSW), which had resolved to establish its own rules. The colony had a long history of rejecting the application of British usury laws. Rather than adopt a 1834 British law, NSW proposed its own Act to set a limit of 8% on interest charged on loans 'which may be recovered in cases where it hath not been previously agreed on between the parties'.[79] In the 1870s, 'drastic' legislation was first proposed to fix a maximum rate of interest that was chargeable on loans and to protect minors from 'what might be alluring devices of money-lenders'.[80] Introduced in 1900 and again in 1902, the Money-lenders and Infants Loans Act No. 43 set an 8% limit on interest. [81] The *Worker* was dissatisfied.[82] Although the NSW Parliament had 'at last devoted some attention to the usury evil' and was willing to deal with 'the bloodsuckers', the bill did not go far enough for the *Worker*: 'For one thing, it leaves the pawnshop people, whose security is always certain and in hand, absolutely untouched. Some measure of protection is provided for the "better class" borrower, but the poor, as usual, are forgotten'.[83] The Bill lapsed on prorogation and was later reintroduced: the Money-lenders and Infants Loans Act No. 24 passed in November 1905 and remained in place until 1941.[84]

The other states also moved to legislate on usury in this period. In 1895, the Victorian government commissioned a report on 'usurious lenders' and this was followed by repeated attempts to pass a Usury Prevention Bill. Labor members reintroduced the Usury Prevention Bill in 1905. It proposed a maximum interest charge of 10% and was passed in

1906.[85] South Australia legislated the Money-lenders Act No. 820 in 1903; Western Australia followed with the Money-Lenders Act No. 65 in 1912.[86] In Queensland, the Money-Lenders Act of 1916 repealed the Usury Act of 1834, which had been adopted when Queensland was still part of NSW. The new act nodded towards the structural underpinning of the 'evils' of usury, admitting that 'dire necessities' had forced 'ignorant and incapable' clients into the hands of the moneylender.[87]

Overall, though, the discourse around the regulation of moneylending ignored the reasons the poor might seek out credit and concentrated on blaming usurers and their victims alike. Rather, the emphasis on regulation in this period reflected growing anxieties regarding the increasing forms of credit available and the growing numbers of working people who were able to access them, through increased spending power.[88] Moves by retailers were all designed to make spending easier. Instalment accounts (also known as time payments or hire purchase) and charge accounts expanded, and a new system of purchasing also gained popularity.[89] The Lay-By (or Lay-Buy) system (known as 'lay-away' in the United States and sometimes in Australia) was an interest-free cash facility by which the customer put down a deposit and paid off the balance in regular instalments.[90] Unlike time payments or charge cards, the customer had to wait to take the goods home until payment was complete.[91] Stores promoted the lay-by as a service to customers because it allowed them 'to get what you want instead of having to be satisfied with something else, which invariably happens when left till the rush is on'.[92] Cash-strapped customers could also take advantage of sale prices: 'At and under cost cash sale: of all goods in our China and Glassware departments. … Lay by and save money'.[93] According to Myer, it was also an option for those responsible shoppers who lacked ready cash: 'We call It "LAY-BY" today, but really it is plain honest-to-goodness, old-fashioned "THRIFT." You see something you need or desire, you haven't the ready money so pay a small deposit, Myer's keep it for you, and you immediately begin to SAVE UP for it'.[94]

The groundwork for new forms of retail credit had been laid in the 1920s and was primed for expansion after the Second World War. However, the US stock market crashed in October 1929 and the resulting economic collapse had devastating effects in Australia between 1930 and 1933, effects that reverberated through to the outbreak of war in 1939.[95] Hundreds of thousands of Australians were thrown out of work, growth stalled, as did discretionary spending. Janet McCalman has shown how, though less affected by the Great Depression than the working class, the middle class were increasingly 'anxious', valuing respectability above all else and defining themselves against the class 'below' them: 'Survival in the real world depended on their personal respectability, their mental competence and on the intangibles of caste'.[96] The 'moral middle class', as Judith Brett has called them, judged harshly those less well-off individuals who borrowed 'beyond their means', viewing it as evidence of a lack of thrift and personal character and restraint.[97]

Technological innovation facilitated the expansion of retail credit in the interwar years, despite society's misgivings about credit, in general, and working-class credit, in particular. Those unsettled by the expansion of credit to Australians on low incomes were particularly concerned with one form of credit—the popular cash-order system—which operated separately from store-run charge accounts and instalment plans. As we will see in the following chapter, the cash-order system helped ease workers into a burgeoning culture of credit.

Notes

1. Jackie Dickenson, 'The Poor Man's Overdraft: A Longer History of Australian Retail Credit.' *History Australia* 21, no. 4 (May 2024): 550.
2. By 1915, at least 60% of retail business in the United States was done on a credit basis, F.M. Couch, 'Credit and the Credit Man', *Credit World: Official Organ of the Retail Credit Men's Association* 6, no. 1 (June 1915): 36.
3. Frederick W. Walter, ed. *The Retail Charge Account* (New York: Ronald Press Company, 1922).
4. John T. Bartlett and Charles M. Reed, *Retail Credit Practice* (New York and London: Harper & Brothers, 1928), 122.
5. Couch, 'Credit and the Credit Man'; Bartlett and Reed, *Retail Credit Practice*, 122.
6. 'Making the Credit Bureau Efficient', *Credit World* 8, no. 9 (May 1920): 9.
7. *Credit World*, 'Rules for Bringing About The Interchange of Credit Experience Between Members of the National Association of Credit Men', 1915; Josh Lauer, *Creditworthy: A History of Consumer Surveillance and Financial Identity in America* (New York: Columbia University Press, 2017).
8. 'Using the Mercantile Agencies for Information', *Credit World* 8, no. 9 (May 1920): 16.

9. Douglas G. Baird, 'The Credit Men' in *The Unwritten Law of Corporate Reorganizations* (Cambridge University Press, 2022), 48; 'Making the Credit Bureau Efficient', *Credit World* 8, no. 9 (May 1920): 9.
10. Sam Kawin, 'Educating the Charge Customer', *Credit World* 6, no.1 (1915): 62.
11. 'Discussion on Credit Department Methods', *Credit World* 4, no. 6 (1914): 18–21. See Advertisement, 'The Credit Rating Book. The Retailer's Reporting Agency: Creates Business, Protects Credit. Insures Against Loss', *Credit World* (Los Angeles No.) 6, no. 1 (1915): 2.
12. 'Discussion on Credit Department Methods'.
13. 'Discussion on Credit Department Methods'.
14. 'Discussion on Credit Department Methods'.
15. 'Accuracy Creates Profits', *Credit World* 8, no. 8 (April 1920): 2; 'Every Record Complete', *Credit World*, no. 8 (April 1920): 7; 'Facts At Finger Tips', *Credit World*, 8, no. 9 (May 1920): 5.
16. 'Make Business Control Easier—and Cheaper', *Credit World* 8, no. 8 (April 1920): 37. 'Acme Visible Records', *Credit World*, no. 8 (April 1920): 9.
17. 'Collection Letters', *Credit World*, 8, no. 8 (April 1920): 25.
18. 'A Letter from President Lewis', *Credit World*, 8, no. 8 (April 1920): 21; Museums Victoria, Item ST 34275, Cheque Writer - GW Todd & Co, 'Protectograph', Rochester, New York, USA, circa 1916, https://collections.museumsvictoria.com.au.
19. John T. Bartlett and Charles M. Reed, *Retail Credit Practice* (New York and London: Harper & Brothers, 1928), 120.
20. 'How to Use the "O.K."', *Sales System Guidebook*, 53.
21. 'Shall It Be?', *Credit World* 5, no. 2 (January 1915): 9.
22. 'National Electric Credit System', *Credit World* 8, no. 9 (May 1920): 7; University of Melbourne Archives (hereafter UMA) Myer Emporium (hereafter ME) 1979-0180, Unit 141, *Sales System Guide*, 1935, 55.
23. Philip Klein, *The Cyclical Timing of Consumer Credit, 1920–67* (New York, 1971); Tobias Rötheli, 'Innovations in US Banking Practices and the Credit Boom of the 1920s', *Business History Review* 87 (Summer 2013): 309–27. https://doi.org/10.1017/S000768051300041X.
24. 'Mrs T.H. Daly', *Credit World* 8, no. 9 (May 1920): 10.
25. State Library of Victoria, Records of Coles-Myer Ltd. and its predecessors, ca. 1840–ca.1990 (hereafter CM), MS 13468, Box 181, 'The New O.K.', *Myer Store News*, January 1949, 8–9; Walter, *The Retail Charge Account*, 58–60; Sales System Guide 1935; ME, Unit 141, 'The Myer Emporium Souvenir Booklet'.
26. https://www.arca.asn.au, accessed 8 April 2025.

27. https://americanhistory.si.edu/collections/object/nmah_1251614; 'The Mechanics of Credit', *Retail Trader*, October 1959, 44.
28. https://scuablog.lib.vt.edu/2023/07/21/charge-it-with-charga-plate/.
29. https://www.emelbourne.net.au/biogs/EM01036b.htm, accessed 11 July 2025.
30. Tartuffe, Jr, 'The Paris Bon Marche', *Queensland Sentinel, Drysdale, Port Arlington and Sorrento Advertiser*, 21 June 1890, 3; UMA, Mutual Stores Ltd (hereafter MSL) 1973.0078, Unit 70, Minutes 1900–1918, Minutes of Special Board Meeting, 20 August 1918, 370.
31. Nikola Balnave and Greg Patmore, 'A Short History of Co-operatives in Australia', *History* (March 2004): 4–5.
32. 'The American Way: Successful Profit-Sharing', *Register*, 22 January 1921, 7; Balnave and Patmore, 'A Short History of Co-operatives', 4–5.
33. 'Profit Sharing For Employes', *Herald*, 25 October 1927, 27.
34. https://www.auspostalhistory.com/articles/1894.php
35. https://www.emelbourne.net.au/biogs/EM01036b.htm; Tartuffe, Jr, 'The Paris Bon Marche', *Queensland Sentinel*, 21 June 1890, 3.
36. MSL, Unit 70, Minutes 1900–1918, 29 November 1900, 43. The relative value of £5 in 1900 was A$836.20 in 2024, https://www.measuringworth.com/calculators/australiacompare/relativevalue.php. https://www.thomblake.com.au/secondary/hisdata/calculate.php
37. MSL, Unit 70, Minutes 1900–1918, 26 July 1906, 72.
38. MSL, Unit 70, Minutes 1900–1918, 9 November 1911, 26; 25 July 1918, 366.
39. 'Mutual Store', *Punch*, 15 December 1904, 27; 'The Mutual Store', *Punch*, 9 March 1911, 30.
40. 'Myer Display Ad', *Herald*, 3 December 1929, 11.
41. 'Advertising', *Herald*, 4 October 1938, 11.
42. 'Anthony Hordern's Meeting', *Sydney Morning Herald*, 17 May 1928, 1
43. 'Anthony Horderns' [sic] Catalogue', Easter 1934, Sydney, 1.
44. 'Foy's Lay-Buy Will Help You Here', *Sydney Morning Herald*, 16 October 1930, 2.
45. 'Grace Bros', *Wingham Chronicle*, 23 December 1899, 13.
46. 'Good Business', *Sun*, 22 April 1936, 3.
47. 'David Jones News', *Sydney Morning Herald*, 16 April 1936, 25.
48. *Herald*, 26 August 1933, 22.
49. 'Your Credit is Good at Myer's', *Herald*, 27 May 1937, 13.
50. 'It's Wise to Open a Charge Account', *Herald*, 30 September 1933,15.
51. MSL, Box 68, Minutes 1918–1941, 27 May 1934, 54.
52. Aristotle, *Politics*, trans. Benjamin Jowett (Dover Publications, 2000), 1258b.

53. David Hawkes, *The Culture of Usury in Renaissance England* (New York: Palgrave Macmillan, 2010), Chapter 2, 47.
54. Daniel Klein, *The Islamic and Jewish Laws of Usury: A Bridge to Commercial Growth and Peace in the Middle East*, Denver *Journal of International Law & Policy* 23, no. 3 (January 1995): 536; Hasan Gürak and Neelamber Hatti, *The Law of Riba in Islamic Banking: Conventional and Unconventional Approaches to Interest-Free Financing* (London and New York: Routledge, 2024), 1–2.
55. The Hon Justice Peter Applegarth AM, 'Credit and Unconscionability', WA Lee Equity Lecture 2020 Supreme Court of Queensland, 19 November 2020, accessed online 31 March 2025.
56. Deuteronomy 23:20.
57. Luke 6:35. For shifts in the Church's attitudes to usury in the medieval period, see John T. Noonan, *The Scholastic Analysis of Usury* (Cambridge, Mass.: Harvard University Press, 1957) and Jacques Le Goff, *Your Money or Your Life: Economy and Religion in the Middle Ages*, trans. Patricia Ranum (New York: Zone Books, 1988).
58. https://tifwe.org/usury-in-the-gospels/
59. 'The Way of the Moneylender', *Tocsin*, 28 December 1905, 5.
60. Ian Manning and Alice de Jonge, 'Regulating the Cost of Credit', Research Paper No. 6 (Melbourne: Consumer Affairs Victoria, 2006), 8.
61. Karl Marx, *Capital III*, Chapters 25 and 27; Maurizio Lazaretto, *The Making of the Indebted Man: An Essay on the Neoliberal Condition*. Los Angeles: Semiotexte, 2012, 61–65.
62. 'Compulsory Arbitration', *Worker*, 7 April 1900, 4; 'Work Better Than Prayer', *Worker*, 14 April 1900, 7.
63. Francis Bacon, 'On Usury' (1601) *The Essays* (London: Penguin, 1986) quoted in 'Swindling Shylocks', *Worker*, 17 December 1904, 8; David Boyle, ed. The *Moneychangers: Currency Reform from Aristotle to E-Cash* (London: Earthscan Publications, 2002), 90.
64. John Ruskin, 'Usury', quoted in the *Worker*, 4 April 1903, 3; John Ruskin, *On the Old Road Vol. II*, 'Home and Its Economies 145' (New York-Chicago: National Library Association, 1834–85), 311, https://www.gutenberg.org/files/21263/21263-h/21263-h.htm, accessed 24 June 2025.
65. 'Tom Mann on Churchianity', *Tocsin*, 19 October 1905, 9.
66. 'Trade Unions', *Worker*, 7 June 1902, 2.
67. George Black, 'What Might Be', *Worker*, 26 April 1902, 2.
68. Bradford Peck. *The World a Department Store: A Story of Life Under a Cooperative System. A Twentieth Century Utopia* (Bradford Peck, Maine, 1900).

69. For co-operatives in Australia, see Nikola Balnave, Greg Patmore and Olivera Marjanovic, *A History of Australian Co-operatives 1827–2023* (Abingdon, Oxon: Routledge, 2024).
70. 'The Song of the Republic', *Tocsin*, 25 July 1901, 8.
71. 'Truths and Trifles', *Worker*, 29 July 1905, 1.
72. 'Federal Banking and Insurance', *Worke*r, 25 May 1901, 3; 'Compulsory Arbitration', *Worker*, 7 April 1900, 4.
73. Ian Manning and Alice de Jonge, 'Regulating the Cost of Credit', Research Paper No. 6
    (Melbourne: Consumer Affairs Victoria, 2006), 9.
74. Jackie Dickenson, 'Luxury and the Australian Labour Press, 1890–1918', *Labour History* 124 (May 2023): 19, 24.
75. Sean O'Connell, 'The Moneylender Unmasked', in *Credit and Community: Working-Class Debt in the UK since 1880* (Oxford: Oxford Academic, 2009).
76. 'Factory Pests: Working-Class Moneylenders', *Australian Star*, 22 August 1905, 3.
77. 'Factory Pests'.
78. 'Factory Pests'.
79. Warren Swain and Karen Fairweather, 'To Your Marrowbones All: Loan Transactions and the Law in 19th Century New South Wales', *Law & History* 10, no. 1 (Jan 2024): 82–109.
80. 'Heirs and Money Lenders', *Brisbane Courier*, 31 May 1873, 7; 'Loans to Minors', *Age*, 26 May 1894, 8; 'Dealing with Money-lenders', *Richmond River Herald*, 2 November 1900, 2.
81. 'Swindling Shylocks', *Worker*, 17 December 1904, 8; 'Minors and Moneylenders Bill', *Daily Telegraph*, 26 October 1905, 3.
82. ' A Usury Law Wanted', *Tocsin*, 24 July 1902, 2
83. 'Mainly Political', *Worker*, 16 November 1905, 1.
84. 'Money Lenders Bill', *Sydney Morning Herald*, 20 October 1905, 6.
85. 'Usury Prevention Bill', *Tocsin*, 16 August 1906, 9, 'Money-Lenders Bill', *Age*, 13 October 1938, 14
86. This was repealed by Act No. 1617 in November 1924, which was amended 1913 and 1937.
87. Queensland, 'The Money Lenders Act 1916 to 1859', 31 March 1961; Queensland Money-Lenders Act 1917. Money Lenders Acts, 1916 to 1962, 251.
88. 'Living on Credit: Easy Payments', *Daily Mercury*, 17 June 1927, 7.
89. 'Be Convinced That It Pays To Shop The Lay-By Way', *Illawarra Mercury*, 26 November 1920, 8.
90. https://www.austlii.edu.au/cgi-bin/viewdoc/au/legis/cth/consol_act/caca2010265/sch2.html, accessed 5 May 2025.

91. 'The Mechanics of Credit', *Retail Trader*, October 1959, 43; 'Lay-By Means'.
92. 'Lay-By Means'.
93. 'Snow's Dressing Gowns', *Raymond Terrace Examiner and Lower Hunter and Port Stephens Advertiser*, 22 October 1926, 3; 'Lay-By Means', *Williamstown Advertiser*, 20 December 1924, 3.
94. 'Your Credit is Good at Myer's', *Herald*, 27 May 1937, 13.
95. https://unreserved.rba.gov.au/nodes/view/46377.
96. Janet McCalman, 'Private Life in the Garden Suburbs between the Wars Or "What Will People Say?"', in *The Cream Brick Frontier: Histories of Australian Suburbia*, ed. Graeme Davison, Tony Dingle and Seamus O'Hanlon (Melbourne: Monash Publications in History, 1995), 53.
97. Judith Brett, *The Moral Middle Class* (Melbourne: Melbourne University Press, 2001), 135–37.

References

Applegarth, Peter. 'Credit and Unconscionability – The Rise and Fall of Statues. WA Lee Equity Lecture 2020'. 19 November 2020, accessed online 31 March 2025.

Aristotle. *Politics*, trans. Benjamin Jowett. New York: Dover Publications, 2000.

Bacon, Francis. *The Essays*. London: Penguin, 1986.

Baird, Douglas G. *The Unwritten Law of Corporate Reorganizations*. Cambridge: Cambridge University Press, 2022.

Balnave, Nikola, Greg Patmore, and Olivera Marjanovic. *A History of Australian Co-operatives 1827–2023*. Abingdon, Oxon: Routledge, 2024.

Bartlett, John T. and Charles M. Reed. *Retail Credit Practice*. New York and London: Harper & Brothers, 1928.

Boyle, David, ed. The *Moneychangers: Currency Reform from Aristotle to E-cash*. London: Earthscan Publications, 2002.

Brett, Judith. *The Moral Middle Class*. Melbourne: Melbourne University Press, 2001.

Credit World, The. The Official Organ of Retail Credit Men's Association. St. Louis, Mo.: The Association, 1914–1990.

Davison, Graeme, Tony Dingle and Seamus O'Hanlon, eds. *The Cream Brick Frontier: Histories of Australian Suburbia*. Melbourne: Monash Publications in History, 1995.

Dickenson, Jackie. 'Luxury and the Australian Labour Press, 1890–1918'. *Labour History* 124 (May 2023): 1–29. https://doi.org/10.3828/labourhistory.2023.2

Dickenson, Jackie. '"The Poor Man's Overdraft": A Longer History of Australian Retail Credit.' *History Australia* 21, no. 4 (May 2024): 546–65. https://doi.org/10.1080/14490854.2024.2343388

Gürak, Hasan and Neelamber Hatti, eds. *The Law of Riba in Islamic Banking: Conventional and Unconventional Approaches to Interest-Free Financing*. London and New York: Routledge, 2024.

Hawkes, David. *The Culture of Usury in Renaissance England*. New York: Palgrave Macmillan, 2010.

Klein, Daniel. 'The Islamic and Jewish Laws of Usury: A Bridge to Commercial Growth and Peace in the Middle East.' *Denver Journal of International Law & Policy* 23, no. 3 (January 1995): 535–54. https://digitalcommons.du.edu/cgi/viewcontent.cgi?article=1719&context=djilp

Klein, Philip. *The Cyclical Timing of Consumer Credit, 1920–67*. New York, 1971.

Lauer, Josh. *Creditworthy: A History of Consumer Surveillance and Financial Identity in America*. New York: Columbia University Press, 2017.

Manning, Ian and Alice de Jonge. 'Regulating the Cost of Credit', Research Paper No. 6. Melbourne: Consumer Affairs Victoria, 2006.

Marx, Karl. *Capital III*. 1894, https://www.marxists.org/archive/marx/works/1894-c3/

O'Connell, Sean. *Credit and Community: Working-Class Debt in the UK since 1880*. Oxford: Oxford Academic, 2009.

Peck, Bradford. *The World A Department Store: A Story of Life Under a Cooperative System (A Twentieth Century Utopia*. Maine: Bradford Peck, 1900.

Records of Coles-Myer Ltd. and its predecessors, ca. 1840–ca.1990, MS 13168, State Library of Victoria.

Records of Myer Emporium Ltd. 1979.0180, 1908–1972. University of Melbourne Archives.

Retail Trader. Sydney: Retail Traders' Association of NSW, 1921–2006.

Ruskin, John. *On the Old Road Vol. II*. New York-Chicago: National Library Association, 1834–85. https://www.gutenberg.org/files/21263/21263-h/21263-h.htm, accessed online 24 June 2025.

Swain, Warren and Karen Fairweather. 'To Your Marrowbones All: Loan Transactions and the Law in 19th Century New South Wales', *Law & History* 10, no. 1 (J 2024): 82–109. doi:10.2139/ssrn.4061256

Walter, Frederick W. ed. *The Retail Charge Account*. New York: Ronald Press Company, 1922.

CHAPTER 4

A Bridge to the Future

Abstract Since at least the 1870s, middle-class Australians had used retail credit to supplement their incomes, take advantage of special offers, deal with unexpected expenses, and indulge impulsive desires. Those with more limited and less regular incomes—working-class families unable to secure credit from banks or department stores—also became enmeshed in credit culture, but through a different route. First introduced in the mid-nineteenth century, the cash-order system provided a bridge between older forms of working-class credit such as 'the tick' and 'the slate' and the store-run revolving credit accounts that gained popularity after the Second World War. The cash-order system played a crucial role in preparing working-class consumers for the post-war boom in credit culture.

Keywords Credit • Retail • Class • Workers • Women • Australian history

In 1941, a witness to the Commonwealth board of inquiry into the cash-order system explained its value. The cash order was 'the poor man's overdraft' and constituted 'a form of compulsory saving' for those living on or near the basic wage.[1] Consumers applied for a (for example) £5 cash order from a dedicated cash-order company, paying 5 shillings commission. They used this order to make a purchase at an approved retailer, and then

J. Dickenson, *Credit and the Australian Department Store Since 1900*, https://doi.org/10.1007/978-3-032-16612-8_4

repaid the issuer at the rate of 5s weekly for 20 weeks. The consumer paid £5 5s for £5 worth of goods at cash prices, had five months credit at the cost of 3 pence a week, and avoided time-payment prices.[2] The system enabled working-class families who lacked ready cash to buy items using a proxy for cash and thereby earn themselves a cash discount.[3] Though the cash-order system was popular with cash-strapped Australian shoppers before the Second World War, many large retailers decried the scheme, arguing that it gave shoppers on limited incomes a false sense of prosperity, encouraging extravagance and economic waste.[4] Underlying this critique was the reality that the system meant fewer shoppers signed up for the retailers' in-house credit schemes, which undercut their profits. The 1941 inquiry was just one of a number of formal investigations set up under pressure from retailer associations to assess the cash order's impact and determine its future.

The Cash-Order System

Those unsettled by the expansion of credit were particularly concerned with the popular cash-order system, which operated separately from the store-run provision of time-payments and hire purchase outlined in the US retailers' guide.[5] When cash orders were first brought to Australia is unclear, but it was likely to have been by a draper, as the system would be used predominantly for clothes.[6] Two drapers claimed to have introduced the system. Edward Arnold, a drapery located in Oxford Street, Sydney, claimed to have begun to use cash orders in the 1850s, but William Buckingham, an English-born draper, later explained that he had brought the cash order to Australia in 1878.[7] 'Anxious to meet the needs of the people', Buckingham had found that the cash order was 'of great assistance to housewives' and he had built his extensive business, which became a large department store, on the system.[8] His system had evolved from the discount coupon system of trading observed in Britain: customers received coupons when they paid cash which they could then redeem at the retailer whose advertisement featured on the coupon. Similar schemes became popular in Australia in the 1890s.[9]

Conceived as a substitution for existing credit schemes, rather than as an addition to them, the cash order was said to be 'simpler and more effective than Time-Payment and Money-lending'.[10] Supporters argued that the system was unique, as it brought together 'the advantages of cash-buying (by paying lower prices than charged on standard credit) with those of credit-buying (the relief to the cash-strapped of paying through instalments)'.[11] Besides New South Wales, the system had been operating for some time in New Zealand where it was used 'to very large extent' and in England, where it was known as 'check trading'.[12] Independent companies sold 'checks' to the consumer on credit. The check (or cash order) could then be redeemed at certain associated stores, and the stores were reimbursed by the issuing company. Check or cash-order companies made their profits from the interest received on money held from customers' purchase of orders before that money was paid out to the trader: the longer it took the customer to use the cash order the more money the check or cash-order company made.[13] They also redeemed orders at 10–15% below their face value—in other words, the companies charged the retailers commission for supplying them with extra trade.[14] The cash order enabled working-class families 'in receipt of small regular incomes' to purchase necessary non-consumable goods 'with the minimum of burden and inconvenience', using a proxy for cash and thereby earning themselves a cash discount.[15] Despite (or perhaps because of) its usefulness to working families, the cash order would prove much less popular with other sections of consumer society.

The moral panic around the cash order grew in Australia from about 1908—perhaps influenced by the experiences of the 1890s land boom and crash—when the scheme expanded out from New South Wales and into Victoria.[16] Over the next 40 years, Australian state and federal governments held investigations into cash orders at regular intervals, sometimes as part of a broader inquiry into Australian monetary systems, sometimes concerned only with the cash-order system. These investigations were usually the result of pressure from retailer associations such as the Drapers' Association of Victoria (DAV), whose members offered their own in-house credit facilities and believed the cash-order system threatened their profits.[17]

Opposition to the cash-order system in Victoria began almost immediately. In 1910, the DAV spoke up against it: 'In Sydney the system is gripping drapery houses like an octopus', one draper told the *Argus*. 'The system so far in Melbourne is not extensively followed', another observed, 'but if not checked it may become a great evil'.[18] The key reason for opposition was revealed in the title of the report: 'Money for the Middleman'. The system, which was 'as bad if not worse than coupons', affected the profits of drapers by undercutting their prices.[19] The cash-order firms had lower overheads than drapers and so could offer larger discounts. 'Who is to know whether the house which gives the 15% discount does not add 15% to the price of the goods', another draper argued. 'No draper that I know of makes the large net profit of 15%. How can he possibly if he trades honestly allow a 15% discount'.[20] Representatives from the cash-order companies immediately defended the system, arguing that it was an improvement on other credit systems and 'a boon to the thrifty as well as the struggler'.[21] The system legitimised small credit without making the user pay excessively and the legitimate shopkeeper obtained extra trade without having to employ travellers who cost far more than 15%.[22]

Despite this defence, retailer associations continued to lobby the government to act on their concerns and, in July 1912, a bill to abolish the cash-order system was introduced into the Victorian Parliament.[23] Debate around the system's merits and abuses continued well into 1913. On the one hand, warnings against the middleman getting between the retailer and the customer were again advanced.[24] On the other hand, a Melbourne *Age* reader recommended research into the operation of the scheme in England: the need for the cash order was not so great in Australia, he noted, but there were 'undoubtedly many whose needs come all at once, whose positions do not warrant retailers in advancing credit, but who could under the cash-order system, have their payments spread over a period of months'.[25]

Retailer associations that opposed the scheme came up with four key criticisms to argue for the abolition of the cash-order system and to obfuscate the real source of their opposition: that the schemes threatened the profits they earned by offering in-house credit. First, they argued that the system encouraged bad debts.[26] Underpinned by class anxiety, this claim emerged from a paternalistic middle-class impulse to regulate the economic life of working-class families. This impulse arose in part from the middle class's need to assert its ostensible 'virtues'—for example, the capacity to save, not living beyond your means, and paying your way in the world—in contrast to the 'vices'—for example, poor financial planning and wastefulness—of an increasingly assertive working class.[27] This moral position fed into anxieties about the working class's use of credit, in general, and the cash-order system, in particular. In 1918, for example, it was suggested that cash-order agencies were encouraging returned soldiers or their dependants (presumably their wives, see below), who had received grants for furniture and tools of trade, to run into debt, 'knowing that the articles could be distrained upon at the end of 12 months'.[28]

Second, critics claimed that the cash-order system increased prices for customers. In 1921, a deputation from the Victorian United Retailers' Council (VURC) to the Victorian State Attorney-General argued that participating retailers passed on the costs of the system to customers in order to maintain their profit levels: customers paid higher prices, it was claimed, and so the cost of living rose.[29] Third, critics argued that the system was unfair, that traders who were not on the lists of retailers where cash orders could be used were at a disadvantage compared with those on the lists.[30]

Finally, they maintained that the system encouraged extravagance, especially amongst women and especially amongst working-class women who used cash orders to supplement their cash supply at times of shortage.[31] Given the gender stereotypes that operated in Australia in this period, it comes as no surprise that women consumers were accused of extravagance. Women were at the frontline of emerging mass consumer society: conventionally, they shopped for the family and many also managed the household budget.[32] In addition, masculinity had long been associated with 'manly independence', so that indebtedness, with the implication of a failure to support yourself and your family, was viewed or framed as implicitly 'feminine'.[33] At the 1921 Victorian investigation, critics offered the example of a woman buying a fur coat with a cash order to support their claim that cash orders were used 'exclusively to facilitate the purchase of luxuries by women': this story would persist in Victoria, becoming a type of urban myth to be used whenever cash orders were again under investigation.[34]

Cash-order companies and supporters of the system defended it against these criticisms. On the charge of encouraging bad debts, Henry Brook, the proprietor of the Brook Cash Order Company, defended his record in April 1918 at a hearing of the Melbourne session of the Interstate Commission, which had been set up in 1912 to investigate interstate trade and commerce.[35] Brook had recovered just £10 by legal proceedings during the 10 years he had been in the business, he recalled, and his bad debts amounted to just 1%.[36] Drawing attention to the role of department stores in normalising retail credit, Brook also noted: 'The better holders of cash orders were known to a firm like Myer's, the cheaper they could get their goods. Myer's turnover with [Brook] would amount to between £18,000 and £10,000 a year'. The average amount of a cash order was £4 and Brook's net profits, leaving out bad debts, was about 7½%. With between 2000 and 3000 customers on his books and about £75,000 worth of business done annually in Victoria under the cash-order system, the public clearly found it useful.[37] William Buckingham agreed. When the issue of bad debts was raised with him, Buckingham admitted that the system had been abused at times 'by the few' but argued that this had been 'more than balanced by the many thousands' who had found it a boon.[38]

A representative of Read's department store in Prahran in Melbourne dismissed the charge that the system encouraged women to purchase luxuries, arguing that there was almost a total absence of spending on luxuries; most cash orders were spent on Manchester and clothing.[39] Working-class women supported this account. Annie Hayne told the Interstate Commission in 1918 that the system was of great benefit to the working classes: she had used the cash-order system to obtain clothes for one of her girls who was about to apply for a position in the city and who otherwise could not have been 'well clothed cheaply and at once'.[40] Sophie Downey used cash orders for household goods when 'money was scarce and credit unobtainable'. Mary Dalton explained how she had saved money by using the cash-order system: with a time-payments firm, she would have paid 'three or four times more interest'. 'The taking [abolition] of the cash order system would cause hardship', Dalton concluded.[41] By giving an account of their experiences with cash orders, these working-class women underlined the necessity of the system for obtaining household goods.

A 1926 Queensland inquiry into profiteering in the clothing trade found that the system did not encourage extravagance, pointing out that this would not be in the interest of the 'Cash Order Office' which bore the risk of defaults on payments. Moreover, the system was only available for non-consumable goods, enabling those 'in receipt of small regular incomes ... to make necessary purchases with the minimum of burden and inconvenience'.[42] Nevertheless, anxieties about women wasting money on luxuries rather than buying necessities remained and criticism of the system continued to flare up, especially in the tough economic circumstances that lay ahead.[43]

The Interwar Years

Criticisms of credit ebbed and flowed, tied specifically to the prevailing economic conditions. Credit attracted more criticism during economic downturns, ironically exactly the circumstances in which workers might need access to it.[44] At the end of the 1920s, as the Australian economy began to contract, cash orders were reported to be 'growing into nearly every business', including dentists and opticians.[45] Supporters argued this was a good thing because it encouraged production; US advocates argued that the cash-order system permitted 'a steadier factory output'.[46]

Governments across Australia launched inquiries into the retail trade, including into its credit systems. Retailers remained split over the business value and moral worth of cash orders, and familiar tropes were resurrected. At the 1926 Queensland inquiry, the draper A.C. Byerley explained that if he introduced cash orders into his business, prices would have to be increased 22½% unless he did as other firms had done, and 'made the cash traders help carry the burden of this extravagant form of service'. Byerley declared that 'the day has come when every house must be put in order. ... Let us put a stop to the extravagant orgy'.[47]

Opponents pointed out that 'for its users it was a very expensive system, and the effect on the national economy of its undoubted contribution to extravagance had yet to be proved harmless'. [48] At a Victorian Ad-Men's luncheon in September 1927, members debated the proposition 'Should the Cash Order System Be Abolished?'; the affirmative case won.[49] Meanwhile, there were more calls for legislation to curb moneylenders, including cash-order companies.[50] Newspapers carried reports of the social problems cash orders allegedly caused, particularly their impact on 'vulnerable' women: one young mother was said to have been 'easy prey for plausible, persuasive and persistent cash-order canvassers'.[51] During debate in the Victorian Legislative Council on the Wages Attachment Bill, which aimed to set a level at which debt-collectors could 'garnish' a working man's wage, J.H. Disney, an Honorary Minister in the Victorian Labor government, argued that the need for such a bill had 'become much greater during the last few years, more particularly since the cash order system has come into vogue'.[52] Action needed to be taken to stop women purchasing cash orders behind their husbands' backs, accruing debt for which the husband was then responsible.

Disney repeated the urban myth of a woman using cash orders to buy a fur coat to illustrate his argument for better regulation of the cash-order system.

> I believe that very much domestic unhappiness is brought about by women obtaining goods at prices greater than they can afford to pay. In many cases the husband has such a load put upon him, and gets so tired of it, that he leaves his wife and family, who are thrown as a burden on the State.[53]

Anxieties about the irresponsible use of the cash-order system by women on limited incomes were fuelled by the activities of cash-order canvassers, roaming the suburbs, calling at homes when men were away at work, and it was assumed that women were vulnerable to their wiles. Later, moves would be made to ban canvassing in NSW.

Another problem emerged for critics: were cash orders a form of moneylending or a legitimate business tool?[54] The link to moneylending unsurprisingly led to the use of antisemitic stereotypes in arguments against cash orders and credit in general. Disney, for example, claimed not to oppose the cash-order system as long as it was conducted 'in a proper manner' by 'respectable people', but this did not include Jews, who Disney linked to moneylending in an unpleasant and contrived 'anecdote' on the Hansard record:

> Listen to the cash-order and time-payment people singing out! Only to-day, going down Brunswick-street, Fitzroy, I saw a glaring sign on a window, which read 'Jacob Graball, money lender, cash orders a specialty'. Just imagine going to such a man for a cash order![55]

Again, the cash-order system was vigorously defended, especially by working women. The Labor Women's Organising Committee Conference resolved that, as present-day society made no provision for sickness and unemployment, and the basic wage was insufficient to provide the necessary seasonal comforts for the people, the proposed abolition of the cash-order system would 'entail serious hardship amongst a large section of the people'.[56] 'A Mother' from the Melbourne inner suburb of Richmond wrote to the *Herald* to defend the system:

> I think that cash orders are useful to the working class. I for one could not keep my little ones in warm clothing for the winter but for the cash orders and I have only to pay a shilling in the £. If my husband is not working, I have never been worried until he has been working again.[57]

The class-based nature of earlier credit discourse began to moderate in this period. After noting the class and gender-based nature of much of the criticism, one commentator observed that the cash-order system was 'merely' one method of extending to the working class the ordinary credit facilities which had been increasingly enjoyed by other classes for many years. Credit might have been extended too easily but this was as much true for 'the respectable overdraft' and 'the aristocratic mortgage', as it was for 'the plebeian cash order'. The cash-order system should not be made 'the whipping boy' for the whole of the credit system: it was not without significance that in 1926, after careful investigation, the Board of Trade inquiry in Queensland had reported in favour of the system.[58] A deputation was charged with meeting the Victorian Attorney-General 'to urge that an exhaustive investigation be made into the cash-order system, time payments, money lenders, and pawn-brokers'.[59] The Member for Prahran in the Victorian parliament sought a Royal Commission into the issue. The Labor Premier rejected a Royal Commission but did instigate an enquiry.[60]

As Australia's economy recovered in the mid-1930s, the cash-order system remained a topic of debate and concern. Retailers continued to demonstrate ambivalence, regularly speaking for and against the system. The Sydney store Edward Arnold's defended cash orders, arguing that the system benefitted the consumer and the retailer. Cash-order purchase had been the means of thousands of poorer families being able to keep themselves well clothed and their homes well furnished. It enabled householders to spread the payment of goods over a convenient period and was now a regular method of merchandising that had been adopted by the greater part of the whole retail community. The firm's recognition of the necessity of assisting people on small incomes to purchase things that they require had been one of the strongest factors in building Edward Arnold's business.[61] In contrast, on a visit to Australia in 1936, the British clothing magnate Montague Burton declared the system to be an undesirable form of trading, alleging that on the issue on a £1 cash order, a trading firm would receive 18 shillings which meant that 15% of the amount was involved in the collection of money from the consumer. A firm dealing with a cash-order organisation might show a loss on a years' trading. Cash-order companies refused to comment on Burton's allegations.[62] The 1937 Royal Commission into the banking system examined the links between credit and production and again exposed divergent views between retailers about the value of the cash-order system.[63] The same year, Queensland traders agreed not to deal with cash orders.[64] Workers were accused of assuming a higher standard of living than the Industrial Commission laid down, which helped the cash-order system flourish and increased the 'profits of the low-wage financial dictators, viz., the Cash Order company shareholders'.[65]

In May 1939, another inquiry began, this time in New South Wales. The Labor MLA George Booth raised the issue of cash orders in parliament, calling for canvassing to be banned because of the risk to husbands' pay packets of women at home being bamboozled by the canvasser to buy goods she could not afford.[66] The Bill went to Cabinet to discuss.[67] Discussion was still underway in December, with calls for cash orders to be covered by the Money-lending Act. This had implications for other forms of consumer credit. If cash orders were found not to be a form of money-lending but a legitimate facility offered by businesses, then other forms of consumer credit might be subject to additional restrictions. Further discussion seems to have been overtaken by events: the escalating war followed by the Federal Government's desire to control unnecessary spending in wartime.

The increasing popularity of time payments, including cash orders and lay-bys, came under scrutiny in 1941, when, in an attempt to restrain spending in wartime,[68] the Federal Government set up a Board of Inquiry under the National Security (Inquiries) Regularities to investigate the cash-order system (as well as hire purchase). This was clearly a sensitive topic: board members commented that witnesses from reputable companies seemed reluctant to give information. One witness in Sydney said retailers were frightened to appear because cash-order companies would end relations with them; 'he was speaking for hundreds of retailers who were frightened to come'.[69] Representatives from nine cash-order companies did give evidence to the inquiry when it visited Sydney.

Again, the focus was on working-class women misusing the system. Ormond Bisset from the Mutual Acceptance Co. Ltd. suggested that there should be some law to prevent wives taking out cash orders without their husband's written consent.[70] Timms had recently raised the issue of 'Married Women's Liability', arguing that purchases must match 'husband's station in life'.[71]

> Any trader who supplies luxuries to married women on credit, particularly where such goods are out of all proportion to her husband's apparent income would do well to pay special attention to this point. The Court does not look with favour upon such transactions and will protect the harassed husband from his wife's foolishness when goods have been extravagantly supplied without this knowledge and consent.[72]

This anxiety about women's use of cash orders was part of the moral panic around wasteful luxury and extravagance, especially in wartime, but it became clear that cash orders were being used for necessities, particularly clothing. The greatest demand for cash orders, one witness said, was in the winter and early summer when they were obtained to purchase outfits for the coming season. An analysis of the cash orders issued in one period of 12 months showed that only 800 were used to obtain goods from jewellers and opticians, but 177,000 were presented in drapers and general outfitters, 22,500 at drapers' shops, 64,500 at men's and boy's outfitters, and 42,000 at boot shops.[73] Arguments about class inequalities were used to support the system: about 95% of the users of cash orders were people on or near the basic-wage level.[74] One retailer argued that cash-order trading was essential for the lower wage group, but that it should be under proper control.

Cash-order companies were making up to 90% profit a year and guaranteed 50%. Some retailers increased the cost of goods when they saw cash orders in customers' hands. Another retailer said he thought prices would fall if cash orders were eliminated.[75] A team from the University of Sydney presented the results of research into cash orders and the hire purchase system. The team had interviewed 544 homes in 14 municipalities and found that 95% of cash orders were used for the purchase of clothing and household necessities, and that 75% of hire purchase agreements covered furniture. In 73.7% of the households visited, householders felt they could not get along without cash orders.[76] The inquiry moved on to Melbourne. Ben Chifley, a member of the board of inquiry and future Prime Minister, interviewed Jean Daly, who was representing Trades Hall Melbourne. Chifley raised the Labor women's resolution against the proposed legislation to abolish cash orders in 1927 and proposed that cash orders were a necessary form of credit for working-class women.[77] 'You consider cash orders are the best form of credit for the people who use them?', Chifley asked Daly. 'Not the best', she replied, 'but the only form'.[78]

Cash Orders and the Department Store

The department stores were ambivalent towards the cash-order system from the start. The reason behind this ambivalence was revealed by director of Dimmey's Model Store in Richmond, Melbourne in his evidence to the 1918 inquiry: cash orders competed with Dimmey's own credit systems, he explained, and removed opportunities for the firm to accumulate interest.[79] In 1927, the Myer Emporium secretary, Beresford Barry, told the Royal Commission that Myer had done business with almost all the cash-order companies, but the firm now dealt with just one company and had reduced the commission they charged to 10% (from 15%). Overall, Myer did not regard the cash-order system as desirable, as 'the fear existed that it might get beyond reasonable limits and prices would have to be raised to the public'.[80]

In other words, the cash-order system threatened to undercut the department stores' interest charges and, therefore, their profits. The city's leading department store remained ambivalent about cash orders: Myer's managing director Lee Neil explained that cash orders represented less than 5% of his firm's total turnover. Although not in favour of the system as a general practice, Lee Neil believed it provided 'a definite service' and his firm exercised a very strict control over the volume of cash-order business transacted. There was never any discrimination between charges made to customers who paid by cash and those using cash orders: the employee who served the customer was usually unaware until after the sale had been made that the goods were to be paid for in this manner. Reports concerning arrests and seizures made in connection with non-payment for cash orders had been exaggerated, in Lee Neil's view. Figures from the Economic Cash Buying Co. Pty. Ltd, the cash-order firm used and partly owned by Myer, showed that over the past 18 months the percentage of summonses issued in connection with purchases from the store had been less than 1%. If clients were found to be in straitened circumstances through sickness or unemployment, Myer withdrew the summons.[81] In contrast, the manager of a large store that did not accept cash orders explained his objections to the scheme. It gave people on limited incomes a 'sense of false prosperity', he argued, and in bad economic times, when unemployment increased, the first people to be hard pressed were those with cash-order commitments: 'Those who are buying articles on time payment fear at most that the articles will be seized, but purchasers of cash orders have no such asset to cover their liabilities'.[82]

By 1941, many of Melbourne's cash-order companies had consolidated into the Victorian Shopping Service (VSS), 'a clearing house for nearly all cash orders'.[83] At the same time, department stores had developed their own means of handling the cash-order quandary. Dimmey's Model Store had now opened their own cash-order company (Fig. 4.1) and Myer offered its customers the convenience of the cash order, but only through its subsidiary company, the Economic Cash Buying Company. The

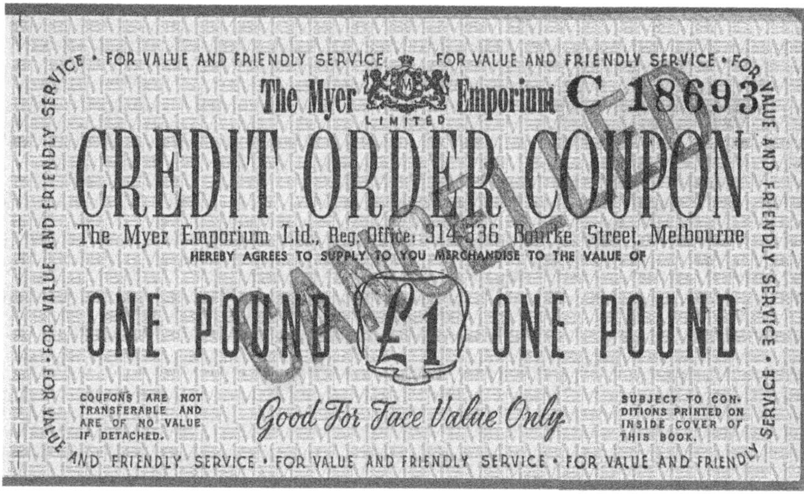

Fig. 4.1 Myer Emporium Credit Order Coupon. MS13468, Box F3352, COMY15380, SLV

Economic Cash Buying Company was positioned as an alternative to the Thrift Budget Accounts administered by rival department stores such as Snows.[84] The staff journal helped train staff to inform customers of the existence and benefits of the cash order or the 'Credit Order Coupon', as the infamous cash order was rebranded by Myer.[85] An article showed how 'Economic Cash Buying' could come 'to the rescue' of a customer who, though short of ready cash, wanted a frock to wear on the coming weekend: 'No Money Doesn't Necessarily Mean No Sale'. Staff should suggest to the customer that they popped around the corner to 'Myer's credit company', the Economic Cash Buying Company. There, 'comfortably seated' in a 'spacious hall', the customer could 'borrow coupons as money'.[86] Credit Order Coupons (Fig. 4.1) came in books of up to £12 and could be used anywhere in the Store: 'We treat them just as cash and ring through the register'.[87] Staff should assure the customer that the Economic Cash Buying Company was 'much better' than Thrift Accounts elsewhere: interest charged was 'less than 9d. in the £, 3d less than is charged for most Thrift Accounts'.[88]

The Economic Cash Buying Company provided credit facilities for Myer customers and financed car hire purchases from motor car dealerships.[89] Myer had part-owned Economic since the late 1920s and bought the company out after the death of its founder and managing director, Otto Neuendorf, in 1951.[90] Speaking that year at Myer's annual meeting, the chairman Norman Myer said of Economic: 'we always feel that in addition to being a profitable undertaking, it serves a very useful purpose in the community by providing short-term credit to people who desire this particular form of accommodation'.[91] In 1954, Myer formed Economic Holdings 'to acquire the capital of the Economic Cash Buying Company', then floated the new company, issuing 500,000 shares to the public.[92] The float appears to have been in anticipation of increased growth in consumer credit: noting that Economic had doubled its turnover in the last four years, Myer observed that 'demand for consumer credit was increasing'.[93] Arnot ('Harry') Tolley, the joint managing director of the Myer Emporium Ltd., explained to the 1941 inquiry that Myer paid this company 7½% discount. The policy of the Myer Emporium was to keep prices down to the lowest level for its customers. The position of people who purchased cash orders was different from Myer's regular customers because they were unable to access regular credit and The Economic Cash Buying Co. gave these people a definite service.[94]

The volume of cash-order trade fell off during the war, limited by the high level of employment and rising wages.[95] These conditions would consolidate in the coming decades, helping to change Australians' relationship to retail credit, seemingly irrevocably: a 1965 report observed that it was now 'customary for the public to live today off tomorrow's income … Stores which offer better credit plans are gaining the customers' loyalty because they have declared themselves interested in securing it'.[96] Retailers adjusted their facilities accordingly. Myer reassessed its use of cash orders. In 1953, the retailer introduced the Permanent Budget Account (PBA), which offered the cash-strapped shopper similar facilities to the cash order. In 1959, Myer sold off the Economic Holdings Company and embarked on a new era of consumer credit. That said, Myer subsidiary companies such as the Canberra stores J.B. Young (Figs. 4.2 and 4.3) and Meager continued to offer their versions of the cash order well into the 1970s.

The history of the cash order in Australia reveals a longer history of retail credit than is usually assumed. Australians' appetite for credit did not begin in the 1950s in the heady days of the early post-war boom. Middle-class Australians had long made use of available credit forms such as monthly accounts to supplement their incomes, take advantage of special offers, deal with unexpected expenses, or indulge impulsive desires. For

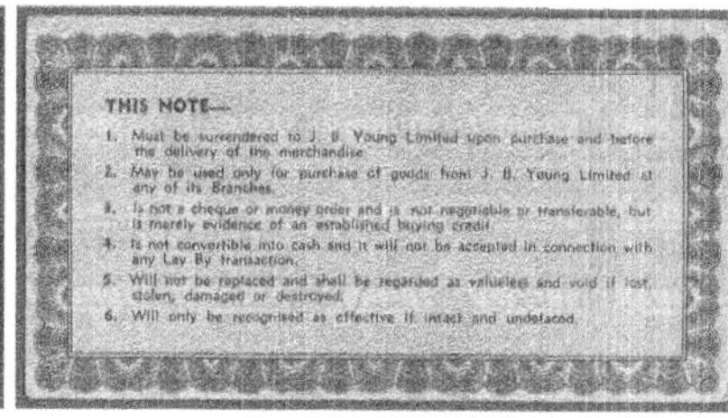

Figs. 4.2 and 4.3 J.B. Young's department store cash order from before the introduction of decimal currency to Australia in 1966. MS13468, Box 3353, COMY21851, SLV

working-class Australians, the cash order provided a bridge between older forms of working-class consumer credit such as the tick and the slate, and modern forms such as the department store budget accounts that became widely available after the Second World War.

The history of the cash order also complicates the usual presentation of the extension of consumer credit in the twentieth century as inexorable. The availability of this particular form of consumer credit was by no means assured as it was repeatedly contested by retailer associations who lobbied governments to interfere in the forms of credit available and the types of people who could access them, in particular, to prevent working-class women from accessing them. Governments responded to this lobbying by holding frequent, but often half-hearted, inquiries at which working-class women testified to the necessity of this form of credit. In this way, the long history of retail credit in Australia is shown to have been both classed and gendered.

The retailer associations won the battle against the cash order: by the late 1950s, most of the cash order companies had closed up shop.[97] However, cash orders survived: a few department stores retained them well into the late 1970s, when they were supplanted by the introduction of the Bankcard. That said, most department stores evolved cash orders into 'modern' revolving credit accounts in the 1950s. These were operated by the stores themselves, ensuring that the stores retained the associated profits. The next chapter turns to the introduction of these new accounts and the technological advances that accompanied them, developments that represented a significant step in the 'democratisation' of retail credit.

Notes

1. An earlier version of this chapter was published as Jackie Dickenson, 'The Poor Man's Overdraft: A Longer History of Australian Retail Credit', *History Australia* 21, no. 4 (May 2024): 546–65; 'Cash Orders Defended. "The Poor Man's Overdraft"', *Sydney Morning Herald*, 30 April 1941, 6.
2. 'Clothes Without Cash', *Age*, 18 January 1911, 11; 'Luxuries Not Bought', *Age*, 26 October 1921, 14; Catherine Alexander, 'The Simple Bare Necessities: Scales and Paradoxes of Thrift on a London Public Housing Estate', *Comparative Studies in Society and History* 64, no.4 (October 2022): 958; 'Trading Coupons Abolition Bill', *Argus*, 1 November 1899, 5. See also 'Cash Order Abolition Bill', Victoria Legislative Assembly, 13 October 1913, 1110–123.
3. Paul Johnson, *Saving and Spending: The Working-Class Economy in Britain, 1870–1939* (Oxford: Oxford University Press, 1985), 151–53.
4. 'Cash Order Systems: Conflicting Views', *Argus*, 3 May 1918, 4.
5. See J.C. Timms, *Time-Payment Trading and Accounts: Hire-Purchase, Instalment Sales, Cash Orders, Lay-Bys* (Melbourne: Sir Isaac Pitman & Sons, 1941), 12–13, 144–76.
6. The 'order' had long been used for a range of financial transactions in Australia, including privately issued 'cheques' and as the payment of wages to be used at a specific shopkeeper, S.J. Butlin, *Foundations of the Australian Monetary System 1788–1951* (Melbourne: Melbourne University Press, 1953), 124, 168, 254, 268–9, 288–90, 342, 371–8, 382, 552.
7. 'Edward Arnold's Cash Order System', *Labor Daily*, 23 August 1935, 13; Beverley Kingston, 'Buckingham, Ashley James (1898–1962)', Australian Dictionary of Biography, National Centre of Biography, Australian National University, https://adb.anu.edu.au/biography/buckingham-ashley-james-9613/text16949, accessed online 13 January 2023.
8. 'Edward Arnold's Cash Order System'.
9. 'Only Had An Idea', *Daily Telegraph*, 16 March 1928, 6; 'The Discount-for-Cash Coupon', *Newsletter*, 24 May 1902.
10. *The Cash Order System*, 16 pages, s. n. [S.I. :1926?], National Library of Australia (NLA) RIL 2101, 1
11. 'Clothes Without Cash', *Age*, 18 January 1911, 11; 'Luxuries Not Bought', *Age*, 26 October 1921, 14; Johnson, *Saving and Spending*, 151; Alexander, 'The Simple Bare Necessities', 941; 'Trading Coupons Abolition Bill', *Argus*, 1 November 1899, 5.
12. *The Cash Order System*, 5; 'Only Had an Idea'.
13. Johnson, *Saving and Spending*, 151.
14. Johnson, *Saving and Spending*, 151.
15. *The Cash Order System*, 1; Johnson, *Saving and Spending*, 151–53.

16. 'Clothes Without Cash', *Age*, 18 January 1911, 11; 'Cash Order Plan', *Herald*, 30 April 1918, 8. For the 1890s depression, see Lionel Frost, 'The Economy', in ed. Alison Batchford and Stuart Macintyre, *The Cambridge History of Australia* (Cambridge: Cambridge University Press, 2013), 338–40.
17. *The Cash Order System*, 5; 'Cash Order System', *Herald*, 4 September 1913, 8; 'Cash Orders', *Herald*, 6 September 1913, 12; 'Abolishing Cash Orders', *Argus*, 7 October 1921; 'The Cash Order System', *Age*, 3 May 1918, 8; Harold Burston, 'Merits and Abuses of Cash-Orders', *Herald*, 21 September 1927, 12.
18. 'Money for the Middleman', *Argus*, 21 June 1910, 6.
19. 'Money for the Middleman'
20. 'Money for the Middleman'.
21. 'The Cash Order System', *Argus*, 22 June 1910, 9; Victorian Hansard 1913, vols. 133, 134, 135, 'Cash Order System Abolition Bill', 15 October 1913, 1904–1905.
22. 'The Cash Order System', *Age*, 22 June 1910, 9.
23. 'Cash Orders', *Australasian*, 3 August 1912, 39; 'State Cabinet', *Age*, 20 August 1912, 9; State Parliament', *Age*, 4 September 1913, 9; Victorian Hansard 1913, vols. 133, 134, 135, 'Cash Order System Abolition Bill'. First Reading, 29 July 1913, 456; Second Reading and Debate, 3 September 1913, 1109–23; 15 October 1913, 1904–1907.
24. 'Multiplying Middlemen', *Age*, 22 September 1913, 10.
25. K.W. Jackson, 'Cash Order System', *Age*, 12 August 1912, 4.
26. The director of Dimmey's Model Store in Melbourne claimed that the cash order companies charged higher interest rates than 'any business firm' and led to many bad debts: 'The Mysteries of Shopping: Do Cash Orders Help or Fine the Working Class', *Geelong Advertiser*, 8 May 1918.
27. Brett, *Australian Liberals and the Moral Middle Class*, 89–94.
28. 'Cash Order Agencies', *Age*, 12 July 1918, 6.
29. 'Cash Orders', 11 October 1921, 9; Harold Burston, 'Merits and Abuses of Cash-Orders', *Herald*, 21 September 1927, 12; 'The Cash Order System', *Age*, 3 May 1918, 8. W
30. 'Cleric', 'Those Cash Orders', *Herald*, 18 October 1921, 4; 'Abolishing Cash Orders', *Argus*, 7 October 1921, 6.
31. 'Cash Order System and the Workers', *Gippsland Mercury*, 3 May 1918, 3; 'Cash Order System: Favoured by Women', *Daily Standard*, 4 May 1918, 7.
32. Beverley Kingston, *Basket, Bag and Trolley A History of Shopping in Australia* (Melbourne: Oxford University Press, 1994), 118–19; Robert Crawford, *But Wait, There's More* (Melbourne: Melbourne University Press, 2010) 19, 152–53.

33. Matthew McCormack, *The Independent Man: Citizenship and Gender Politics in Georgian England* (Manchester: Manchester University Press, 2005), 3–6.
34. 'Cash Orders', *Age*, 11 October 1911, 9; 'Cash Order System', *Argus*, 18 October 1921, 4. For an example of this urban myth, see Victorian Legislative Council, Wages Attachment Bill, 12 October 1927, 1872.
35. J.A. La Nauze, 'The Inter-State Commission', *The Australian Quarterly* 9, no. 1 (Mar. 1937): 48–58.
36. '"Cash Order" System', *Argus*, 1 May 1918, 6.
37. '"Cash Order" System', *Argus*, 1 May 1918, 6.
38. 'Only Had An Idea', *Daily Telegraph*, 16 March 1928, 6.
39. 'Luxuries Not Bought', *Age*, 26 October 1921, 14; 'Cash Orders Controversy', *Herald*, 13 October 1911, 3.
40. 'The Mysteries of Shopping?' *Geelong Advertiser*, 3 May 1918, 5. See Stephen Gageler, 'Chapter IV: The Inter-State Commission and the Regulation of Trade and Commerce under the Australian Constitution', *Public Law Review* 28 (2017): 205–218.
41. 'The Mysteries of Shopping'.
42. 'Is There Profiteering in Clothing? *Worker*, 10 November 1926, 9; *The Cash Order System*, 16 pages, s. n. [S.I. :1926?], National Library of Australia (NLA) RIL 2101, 1.
43. 'Cash Orders', *Age*, 11 October 1911, 9.
44. 'Consumer Credit: Canada Suspends Regulations', *Herald*, 6 May 1952, 6.
45. 'Cash Orders', *Warwick Daily News*, 28 March 1927, 4; 'Why Pay Cash?' *Age*, 1 November 1932, 4.
46. 'Cash Orders', *Queensland Times*, 14 October 1927, 6.
47. 'Cash Orders', *Queensland Times*, 14 October 1927, 6.
48. 'Is There Profiteering in Clothing?' *Worker*, 10 November 1926, 9; 'Cash Orders', *Queensland Times*, 14 October 1927, 6.
49. 'Debate on Cash Orders', *Herald*, 19 September 1927, 5.
50. 'New Act to Curb Money-Lenders', *Herald*, 14 July 1927, 21.
51. 'Social Problems', *Age*, 5 October 1927, 15.
52. It was practice in Victoria for members and former members to be appointed occasionally as Honorary Ministers, an unpaid position. See, for example, 'Mr Irvine an Honorary Minister', *Leader*, 13 February 1904, 23; 'Protecting Workers' Wages', *Herald*, 15 September 1927, 39; Victorian Legislative Council, Wages Attachment Bill, 12 October 1927, 1872; 1 December 1927, 3069.
53. Victorian Legislative Council, Wages Attachment Bill, 12 October 1927, 1872.
54. Timms, *Time-Payments*, 191–96.

55. Victorian Legislative Council, Wages Attachment Bill, 12 October 1927, 1873.
56. '"A Blessing:" Cash Order Praise, Labor Women Move', *Sun News-Pictorial*, 15 September 1927, 21.
57. 'A Word for Cash Orders', *Herald*, 9 June 1927, 8.
58. Harry Thomson, 'Cash Orders', *News*, 22 October 1927, 4.
59. 'Woman's Way', *Worker*, 21 September 1927, 19.
60. 'Cash Orders and Moneylending', *Herald*, 2 September 1927, 2; 'State Parliament', *Argus*, 9 September 1927, 6; 'Opinions Differ', *Labor Daily*, 9 September 1927, 1; 'Merits and Abuses of Cash Orders', *Herald*, 21 September 1927, 12; 'Cash Order System', *Age*, 10 October 1927, 13. The Money Lenders Bill was discussed in the Victorian Parliament across the fourth quarter of 1927, especially on 6, 8 and 15 September and 30 November 1927.
61. 'Edward Arnold's Cash Order System', *Labor Daily*, 23 August 1935, 13.
62. 'Cash Order Criticism', *Daily Telegraph*, 3 November 1936, 2; 'The Bible and Cash Orders', *Age*, 23 April 1936, 11.
63. Australia. Royal Commission Appointed to Inquire into the Monetary and Banking System in Operation in Australia. Canberra: Commonwealth Govt. Printer, 1937.
64. 'Sydney Cash Order Companies', *Barrier Miner*, 24 December 1937, 5.
65. 'Cash Order Social Credit', *Labor Daily*, 5 February 1937, 4. Victoria included cash orders in the Money-Lenders Act passed in December 1938: 3 Geo. VI, Act no. 4625, 22 December 1938, 790.
66. NSW Hansard, 23 May 1939.
67. NSW Hansard, 23 May 1939.
68. 'War Measure: Hire Purchase and Cash Orders Federal Inquiry', *Maitland Mercury*, 14 February 1941, 1;
    'Danger of Free Spending', *Chronicle*, 6 November 1941, 25.
69. 'Retailers and Cash Orders', *Age*, 1 May 1941, 4.
70. 'Cash Orders Defended. "The Poor Man's Overdraft."', *Sydney Morning Herald*, 30 April 1941, 6; 'Company Registered', *Age*, 7 March 1936, 27.
71. Timms, *Time-Payment*, 45–7.
72. Timms, *Time-Payment*, 46.
73. 'Cash Orders Defended'; John Hinde, 'Millions in Cash Orders', *The ABC Weekly* 3, no. 50 (13 December 1941), 10–11.
74. 'Cash Orders Defended'.
75. 'Retailers and Cash Orders', *Age*, 1 May 1941, 4.
76. 'Home Worth £400 Sold to Meet £36 Debt on Piano', *The Age*, 10 July 1941, 6; Hind, 'Millions', 11.
77. 'Cash Orders and Loans', *Age*, 15 May 1941, 8.

78. 'Canvassing for Loans', *Argus*, 15 May 1941, 5.
79. 'The Mysteries of Shopping', *Geelong Advertiser*, 3 May 1918, 5.
80. 'Cash Order System and the Workers', *Gippsland Mercury*, 3 May 1918, 3.
81. 'Cash Order System and the Workers'.
82. 'Cash Order System', *Argus*, 30 June 1927, 18; 'Workers' Cash Order and Finance Co.', *Age*, 17 October 1933, 13.
83. 'Discounts and Cash Orders', *Age*, 13 May 1941, 8; 'Cash Orders and Loans', *Age*, 15 May 1941, 8.
84. 'Snows Unbeatable Offer', *Herald*, 5 December 1953, 29.
85. State Library of Victoria, Records of Coles-Myer Ltd. and its predecessors, ca. 1840–ca.1990 (hereafter CM), MS 13468, Box F3352, Credit Order Coupon Book, Myer Credit Order Coupons, n.d.; Box 2020, Cash orders used for mail order services, 8 March 1955.
86. CM, Box 1725, 'Economic Coupons Won This Customer', *Myer Store News* 12, no. 4 (June 1952): 14–15.
87. CM, Box 2040, 'Economic Hire Purchase – And How to Deal With It', *Myer News*, March 1957, 3; 'Economic Floats on 10% Basis', *Herald*, 29 September 1954, 6.
88. 'Economic Coupons Won This Customer'; 'The Cash Order System', *Age*, 14 May 1941, 14.
89. 'Economic Floats on 10% Basis'.
90. 'Economic Floats on 10% Basis'; 'Retail Profit Margins Smaller', *Age*, 9 November 1951, 7.
91. 'Retail Profit Margins Smaller'.
92. 'Highlights on 'Change: Economic's First Sale', *Herald*, 8 November 1954, 6.
93. 'Economic Floats on 10% Basis', *Herald*, 29 September 1954, 6; 'Retail Profit Margins Smaller'; 'Highlights on 'Change'.
94. 'Cash Orders Defended', *Argus*, 13 May 1941, 4.
95. 'Cash Order Trade', *Sydney Morning Herald*, 23 March 1948, 6.
96. CM, Box 334, Arthur Andersen & Co. Memorandum for General Manager, Mark Foy's Limited, 'Credit Management, Promotion and Organisation', 14 January 1965, 1.
97. 'Credit Trends in Melbourne Stores: Three-Year Trend Examined', *Retail Merchandiser*, February 1959, 19–20.

References

Alexander, Catherine. 'The Simple Bare Necessities: Scales and Paradoxes of Thrift on a London Public Housing Estate', *Comparative Studies in Society and History* 64, no. 4 (October 2022): 934–65. https://doi.org/10.1017/S0010417522000159

Australia. Royal Commission Appointed to Inquire into the Monetary and Banking Systems at Present in Operation in Australia. Canberra: Commonwealth Govt. Printer, 1937.

Batchford, Alison and Stuart Macintyre, eds. *The Cambridge History of Australia*. Cambridge: Cambridge University Press, 2013.

Brett, Judith. *Australian Liberals and the Moral Middle Class*. Melbourne: Melbourne University Press, 2001.

Butlin, S.J. *Foundations of the Australian Monetary System 1788–1951*. Melbourne: Melbourne University Press.

Crawford, Robert. *But Wait, There's More: A History of Australian Advertising 1900–2000*. Melbourne: Melbourne University Press, 2010.

Davison, Graeme, Tony Dingle and Seamus O'Hanlon, eds. *The Cream Brick Frontier: Histories of Australian Suburbia*. Melbourne: Monash Publications in History, 1995.

Gageler, Stephen. 'Chapter IV: The Inter-State Commission and the Regulation of Trade and Commerce under the Australian Constitution'. *Public Law Review* 28 (2017): 205–218. https://search.informit.org/doi/10.3316/agispt.20174017

Kingston, Beverley. *Basket, Bag and Trolley: A History of Shopping in Australia*. Melbourne: Oxford University Press, 1994.

Johnson, Paul. *Saving and Spending: The Working-Class Economy in Britain, 1870–1939*. Oxford: Oxford University Press, 1985.

La Nauze, J.A. 'The Inter-State Commission'. *The Australian Quarterly* 9, no. 1 (Mar. 1937): 48–58

McCormack, Matthew. *The Independent Man: Citizenship and Gender Politics in Georgian England*. Manchester: Manchester University Press, 2005.

Records of Coles-Myer Ltd. and its predecessors, ca. 1840–1990, MS13468, State Library of Victoria.

Reekie, Gail. 'Decently Dressed? Sexualising Consumerism and the Working Women's Wardrobe'. *Labour History*, no. 61 (1991): 42–4. https://doi.org/10.2307/27509089

Retail Merchandiser: The Official Journal of the Masters Drapers and Traders' Association of Victoria. Melbourne, Vic.: Masters Drapers and Traders' Association of Victoria, 1949–1967.

Smart, Judith. 'Feminists, Food and the Fair Price: The Cost of Living Demonstrations in Melbourne, 1917'. *Labour History* no. 50 (1986): 1–5. https://doi.org/10.2307/27508786

Stephen, Anne. 'Selling Soap: Domestic Work and Consumerism in the Inter-war Years'. *Labour History* no. 61 (1991): 57–69. https://www.liverpooluniversitypress.co.uk/doi/abs/10.3828/27509083?download=true

Timms, J.C. *Time-Payment Trading and Accounts: Hire-Purchase, Instalment Sales, Cash Orders, Lay-Bys.* Melbourne: Sir Isaac Pitman & Sons, 1941.

Van Der Eng, Pierre. 'Consumer Credit in Australia during the Twentieth Century'. *Accounting, Business & Financial History* 18, no.2 (2008) 243–65. https://doi.org/10.1080/09585200802058917

CHAPTER 5

The Account of the Century

Abstract From the late 1920s, middle-class Australians used a metal charge plate to pay for their department store purchases. The plate conferred social status, signifying that its bearer had been judged a reliable credit risk and was the type of person the store welcomed. However, by the 1950s, the success of the charge account (and its status-conferring plate) had undermined its exclusivity, and department stores looked for alternative ways to keep their VIPs feeling special. The answer was the revolving credit account which would gradually replace the cash order. Accounts such as Myer's Permanent Budget Account (PBA) helped normalise revolving credit, preparing working-class consumers for the era of the credit card.

Keywords Credit • Retail • Status • VIPs • Revolving credit • Workers • Consumers • Australian history

'Now you can buy what you want when you want it!' a Myer advertisement promised readers in August 1953. 'Now you can satisfy your love of beautiful things on a modest budget'.[1] The advertisement introduced Myer's new Permanent Budget Account (PBA) to Australians, as 'another great service' from the nation's leading department store. Myer claimed that the PBA was 'the answer to all your family budget problems', offering

J. Dickenson, *Credit and the Australian Department Store Since 1900*, https://doi.org/10.1007/978-3-032-16612-8_5

extended credit to approved customers for a 'small and easily manageable' fortnightly payment.[2] The store established a special office on the fifth floor of its Lonsdale Street Store in Melbourne, where customers were invited to meet with a credit representative, 'quietly, confidentially, and at your convenience', to discuss opening a PBA. Described by Myer as 'practical, dignified and efficient', the new account was above all modern, 'hand-tailored to the needs of to-day'.[3] To administer the PBA, the firm had also acquired a new accounting system, the Burroughs' 'Sensimatic', which was marketed as 'the greatest advance in accounting machines in 25 years'.[4] Myer's investment in the PBA signalled its awareness of the growing importance of credit to Australian consumers and its capacity to transform the retail sector.

Consumer Power

This investment in a new credit facility and its up-to-date technology occurred in the heady atmosphere of the early years of an economic boom that would last for two decades. The deprivations of the interwar Depression and the Second World War were over for most Australians and they were eager to acquire the new products that were now streaming onto the market.[5] Across the first half of the twentieth century, middle-class Australians had progressively learnt to navigate an ever-expanding selection of consumer goods.[6] Now, post-war, the economic boom and a narrowing income gap meant unskilled workers were able to join in the fun. Stability in the form of a reliable income stream meant that credit was no longer simply a means for workers to secure necessities when cash was hard to come by: it might also allow them to purchase small luxuries, to act on an impulse and fulfil their desires on the spot. Retailers such as Myer understood the significance of this shift, and sought to transform consumer attitudes to credit as well as their access to it.

David Graeber has described consumer debt as 'the lifeblood of our economy'.[7] This was certainly the case in the 1950s, when the consumer's shopping activities were central to the nation's economic fortunes. In this period, the concept of the 'consumer-citizen'—'a person who accepts any political situation as long as there is an abundance of consumer goods'[8]—became particularly potent.[9] Frank Trentmann has suggested that the citizen-consumer should be studied by investigating 'the iteration and overlap between ideas and practices of consumption and citizenship'—and the multiple forms of identities this interaction generated.[10] The flow of knowledge between consumption and politics in Australia and elsewhere in this period revolved around preventing pent-up demand, caused in part by the war hiatus, from ushering in inflation.[11] News from the United States pointed to the part the consumer now played in 'checking inflation':

> during the past year [the role of the consumer] seems to have transcended all other means of regulation and control. ... Largely as a result of the lull in consumer buying, the past year had been characterised by a degree of overall stability that few economists had anticipated.[12]

The power of the consumer in either causing or controlling inflation was recognised in Australia. Experts such as the economist and academic Wilfred Prest called for consumer credit control: 'It is important to check that as well as to check credit given by the private banks to business for investment, which the banks are doing'.[13] In 1955, the federal treasurer called for 'restraint in spending', arguing that great rise in the demand for imports was a clear pointer to 'the trend of things' within the Australian economy—'a boom was getting underway, chiefly in consumer spending and private investment'.[14] Personal spending on goods and services had risen by £268,000,000, or 9% in the previous year, and 'on the investment side', it was estimated that 'expenditure on capital equipment was £108,000,000, or 15% greater than in 1953–1954'.[15] The 'formidable upsurge of spending' had been facilitated by 'a far-too-generous expansion of credit on the part of the banking system, together with the rapid growth of hire-purchase finance' and 'unless corrected', this would result in 'open inflation'; 'Demand has thrust ahead much too fast for the growth of our resources'.[16] Only after 1955 would the threat of inflation begin to ease, and the economy settle into 'a pattern of steady growth'.[17]

Revolving Credit

It was in this context that the Myer Emporium introduced the PBA. The new credit plan was based on the 30-day Optional Payment Account (OPA) that had originated in the United States, and which had been hailed there as 'The Account of the Century'.[18] The OPA had gained 'very wide acceptance in the US' because it had simplified billing procedures and because the store was able to impose a small service charge of 1½%. The benefits to the consumer were two-fold and revealed customers' general dissatisfaction with the hierarchy of credit administered by most stores, especially those on lower incomes. First was the customer's ability 'to adjust her repayments in accord with other commitments', but 'most important', she was able to do this 'without any loss of face'.[19] Second, no distinction was made at the point of sale between the customer who had a 30-day account and the one who had previously operated a budget account using store currency (that is, cash orders or coupons). In other words, the OPA was socially more acceptable than the cash-order.[20] A British observer noted in 1953 that, in the United States:

> Large department stores have added a new type of credit service [the OPA] which is a combination of charge account and hire-purchase; the customer is given a 'credit ceiling' and pays an agreed monthly sum regardless of the total amount of purchases.[21]

This description fit exactly the PBA (Myer's name for the OPA) which, once approved, gave the customer a permanent line of credit.[22]

Informed by Myer executives' frequent research trips to the United States, the introduction of the PBA signified the store's response to two business challenges.[23] First, as noted above, the prestige of the charge account was under threat. Before the war, Arthur Hert, a US commentator, drew attention to this problem. Hert emphasised the importance of credit to expanding a business, explaining that the charge customer spent more than other customers, helping to shift luxury goods and build customer loyalty because a charge account customer whose name was recorded by the store enjoyed a closer relationship to the retailer than did 'an unknown buyer' who paid with cash.[24] According to Hert, the privileges enjoyed by charge patrons only, which had been held out alluringly by merchants in an effort to attract new charge customers to their stores, were proving to be a problem for merchants. Charge customers 'generally' felt that they were entitled to more privileges and to more consideration than a customer who paid with cash. As a matter of fact, Hert claimed, the reverse was true:

> There is more profit in a cash sale than a charge sale, burdened as it is by bookkeeping costs, collection expense, and so forth, but the merchants have only themselves to blame for the feeling on the part of charge customers that they are the preferred patrons of the store.[25]

Many US credit executives now believed that a charge account no longer carried the prestige it had 'a few years ago':

> Where once a charge account was carried as a convenience by persons who were accustomed to paying for their accumulated purchases in a lump sum at the end of the month, undoubtedly most of them are now carried by the wage earner as a necessity, many debtors paying 'on account' each pay day instead of taking care of their purchases in full each month, the original intent of the plan.[26]

The wrong people were now using charge accounts in the wrong way, and this undermined the account's prestige. According to these credit executives, 65% of charge customers used the accounts because they had insufficient cash and were forced to buy essential family items on credit, while the other 35% had no problem paying for their purchases in full but used charge accounts as a convenience.[27]

Department store charge accounts (or monthly accounts) had taken off in Australia from the late 1920s, facilitated by the arrival of new technology such as the metal Charga-Plate, as discussed in Chap. 3. There was a clear link between the ways these accounts were used to signify and confer social status and their speedy uptake by middle- and upper-middle-class shoppers. Though small, the plates had presence, made from solid metal and contained in a classy leather-look case. They were individualised with the customer's name embossed on the back of the plate. The individualisation was important, as it provided a feeling of belonging when the shopper presented the plate to the sales assistant and was acknowledged by name: staff training manuals repeatedly asserted the importance of using a charge customer's name during a transaction, as this made the customer feel special.[28] Possession of the plate announced that the customer belonged to a select group, their membership had been approved, recognising them as financially stable and (depending on the store) even well-heeled.

The atmosphere of a store became attached to its charge plate, as it did to other promotional items, such as the bag that stores provided for customers to carry their goods home (also a form of free advertising) for the store. Some stores built on their aura to reinforce their position in the hierarchy of department stores and thus to manage who did and did not feel comfortable in their store, and the charge plate played a role in defining this. The plate was also used to encourage a shopper's loyalty by reinforcing the feeling of belonging to an exclusive club, with the cardholder receiving invitations to special events and access to discounts and special offers. There was even a hierarchy *within* the charge plate system: some Grace Bros' charge accounts were marked with an XX after the name and address, to indicate that the holder was entitled to a 10% discount on their purchases.[29]

As noted above, by 1938 charge accounts in the United States had lost much of their prestige. In Australia, this shift occurred after the Second World War with a big increase in the number of charge accounts between 1946 and 1951.[30] To cope with the number of accounts, Australian department stores moved towards more efficient cycle billing and looked to new forms of credit to deal with increased demand.

The 1950s has been presented by some historians as the era when Australian consumers shifted from embracing an ideology of British thrift to US hedonism. This ignores the long history of thrift activism in America, which had become a worldwide phenomenon with the advent of World Thrift Day in 1929.[31] Nevertheless, something different was going on in the 1950s, which the criticisms of politicians and bankers reveal.[32] An advertisement in Melbourne's *Argus* was telling. The advertisement, which seems to have been an advertorial for the State Savings Bank of Victoria, acknowledged the desire that drove consumption: 'It would be a rare and contented person who wants nothing more in life; who is perfectly satisfied with what he or she possesses. It is practically certain there is something you desire'.[33] However, the advertisement advised the reader to put this desire aside and to practice self-denial for peace of mind.

The advertisement listed the types of items a consumer might currently wish for: a bicycle, a new car, a new suit, a television set, a refrigerator, a radio, a vacuum cleaner, lawn mower, tool kit, even a house. Thousands of people were 'continually pondering' on whether they could afford to spend large sums of money on new or extra equipment for their homes. 'In all their minds' was the question: 'Will it be wise to saddle myself with a loan bearing a high rate of interest?' They realised that if they take on the burden of a loan, they were automatically cutting off 'a large slice' of their weekly wage. It was a hard question to answer, the advertisement concluded, but there was a way out. 'It is that advocated by the State Savings Bank of Victoria: "Save the necessary first." … This may seem a drastic scheme of self-denial … When a person has saved, he goes shopping with a free mind. Because there is no interest to pay on a loan, he is saving …'.[34]

Myer and the Credit Boom

The Myer retail group was at the forefront of this 1950s credit boom. In the 1930s, Myer had offered its customers three forms of credit: the Entry Account (also known at various times as the Monthly Account or the Charge Account), the Credit Order, and Deferred Payment. With an Entry Account, the customer did not pay for merchandise at the time they bought it but needed to settle the account in full each month for goods purchased in the preceding month.[35] A Credit Order (a euphemism for the controversial cash order discussed in the previous chapter) offered approved customers 'very low deposit and extended terms'.[36] The deferred payment (hire purchase or Easy Terms Payment) method was available for merchandise priced from £3 upwards, principally furniture, furnishings, and household goods. The customer paid a deposit (usually not less than 10%), then paid off the balance in instalments over an agreed period.[37]

In January 1949, Myer updated its OK credit approval system in preparation for a new era in retail and retail credit (Fig. 5.1). Designed for Myer by the Standard Telephone and Cable Company, this equipment had previously been available only in America. The first of its kind in Australia, it was the most up-to-minute credit authorisation system in the world.[38] In the 1950s, there were 270 OK phones in use throughout the store; this number could be increased to 600 extensions. The switch board in the office was divided into 10 alphabetical divisions. Twenty operators could be used in busy period; in off-peak periods, the switchboard could be manned efficiently by five women. A queuing device ensured calls were taken in the correct order.[39]

Fig. 5.1 'The New O.K.', *Myer Store News* 19, no. 1, January 1949, 9. MS13468, Box 1725, COM13495, SLV

Staff were encouraged to promote the Credit Order coupons.[40] Staff training material explained that 'No Money Doesn't Necessarily Mean No Sale. Economic Cash Buying Company to the Rescue'. If a customer without a charge account did not have the cash for an item they desired immediately, staff were told to refer them to the Economic Cash Buying Company office 'just around the corner' in Elizabeth Street, where they would find an office 'just like a bank with confidential offices for interviews'. The spiel also included staff assuring the customer that the Economic Cash Buying Company was 'much better' than Thrift Accounts at competitors' stores: interest charged was 'less than 9d. in the £, 3d. less than is charged for most Thrift Accounts'.[41]

By 1953, it had become clear that Australia had embarked on a new, more positive economic era: in his address to shareholders that year, Norman Myer reassured them that 'the insecurity and misgiving prevalent earlier have been replaced by a great measure of confidence'. The chairman also announced the introduction of Myer's new 'continuous' credit account, the Permanent Budget Account (PBA).[42] As we have seen, Myer had long had a charge account system (its Entry or Monthly account) and, as James Brennan showed for America, these charge accounts were popular with customers, with department stores selling large amounts of goods through them, 'often without due consideration of whether or not the individual was a good credit risk'.[43] The PBA solved this problem for Myer, because it allowed cash-strapped customers to defer payments for a longer period and meant Myer had access to more customers with lower risk of bad debts. A Myer staff handbook produced in the 1960s described the PBA as:

> a convenient form of credit which enables the customer to buy goods anywhere in the Store, payable not in a lump sum in a limited time, but by easy fortnightly instalments. The only extra cost for the convenience of PBA is a small charge of 1% on the balance of the account each month to cover accounting expenses.[44]

The PBA also went a long way to removing the stigma associated with use of the cash or credit order, as it was known at Myer. Customers who signed up for a PBA received a charge plate to use 'in the same way as those who had Entry accounts'.[45] The move to the plate and away from the coupon meant that, in service encounters, it would now be harder to identify those using continuing credit, saving these customers from any related embarrassment.[46]

Revolving credit required new, more affordable technology. In 1959, the *Retail Trader* reported on the switch in the United States from metal credit plates to plastic embossed cards that did not require a protective cover and so were cheaper to produce. Each store issued its own plate, which meant there were too many to carry around, and so the cards were now 'issued and controlled by a single agency'.[47] Typewritten 'credit cards' were more commonly used on budget accounts for which the customer had not been issued with a credit plate, although some stores still issued them to 30-day (monthly/entry) account customers.[48]

Also in 1959, a US credit manager outlined the history of revolving credit to give the member of the Retail Association a better understanding of this new phenomenon.[49] The manager began by explaining that 'basically', the principle of revolving credit was no different from that of the instalment selling plans that retailers had used for many years. The only major change was in 'the procedural handling of the account … to avoid the annoyance of [customers'] repeated visits to the credit department after each small purchase'.[50] US department stores had originally had two plans—the 'Regular Charge Account' and the 'Hard Goods Instalment Plans'.[51] However, during the Great Depression, struggling charge account customers had asked for longer than the usual time (just 10 days then) to pay and were awarded extensions of up to three months. This was the beginning of revolving credit. In 1938, John Wanamaker's, the New York department store, advertised its new revolving credit plan, prompting the *New York Times* to comment:

> Many merchants throughout the country have shown interest in the 'revolving credit' plan featured last week by John Wanamaker, New York. Designed to take care of consumers' natural peak-purchasing periods by enabling them to open an account for the total amount of the purchases without carrying charge, an official of the store said customer response had 'exceeded expectations'. The 'revolving' feature of the credit plan arises through the fact that, as the monthly payments are made, additional credit to the amount of the payment is open to the customer.[52]

Wanamaker's Christmas advertising that year spelled out the details of its new credit plan. It was 'a life saver for the family budget at Christmas', devised by Wanamaker's for such times when 'your expenditures are unusually heavy'. It allowed the customer to spread out their repayments and, each time they paid, their credit was good up to the amount of their original purchase. Already 'thousands of people' had opened a revolving credit account, the advertisement claimed:

> Come to the Eighth Floor and let one of our credit men explain Revolving Credit—it's easy, no coupon books, not one penny to pay down, no red tape, no carrying charge; but a passport to a Merry Christmas for your budget.[53]

Despite this supportive commentary for revolving credit, the author also warned retailers that 'revolving credit' was 'by no means a panacea'. On the contrary, it had presented retailers with many 'unusual operating difficulties and financial problems'. 'In evaluating these problems', he advised his audience to bear in mind the change in the concept of the credit selling which had taken place as well as the change in the economic structure. Credit extension was no longer limited to the wealthy; to-day retailers met a broader demand for credit conveniences. Revolving credit required a substantially larger capital investment than charge accounts, which meant that 'in to-day's tight money market' the retailers' number one problem was the operation (of revolving credit).[54]

Encouraged by the uptake of the PBA, Myer sold the Economic Cash Buying Co. (or Economic Holdings, as it was now known) at the end of the 1950s.[55] The PBA had replaced the service offered by the cash-order company, incorporating its customers into a more modern system. However, as we will see, the stigma attached to the cash-order system transferred to the PBA in its early iteration.

Myer adopted 'modern' forms of credit for regular purchases, but customers needed to be convinced of the benefits to them of these new facilities.[56] This is where advertising stepped in. As John Watkins has shown, advertising helped to create desires and, where income was lacking, credit provided the means to act on those desires.[57] Regular newspaper advertisements spelled out the '4 Easy Ways to Buy at Myer's: Lay-By, Charge Account, Pay on Delivery, and the PBA'.[58] These forms of payment were presented to customers with arguments promising money-saving, simplicity, and convenience. Myer's Lay-By plan differed from the forms of credit the store offered because no interest was paid, but this meant that the fulfilment of the customer's desire was deferred for many weeks. Myer told customers that the Lay-By plan helped them save money: they could 'Buy at today's prices and save the inevitable price rise'. Customers paid the listed prices only, there were 'no added charges with Myer Lay-By', in other words, no interest was charged.[59]

The selling points for Myer's credit facilities included rational and emotional appeals. These facilities were described as an 'easy', 'economic', 'simple', 'efficient', 'private', and 'convenient' means of shopping, but they were also 'modern', appealing to the aspirational shopper, and 'dignified', reassuring the shopper that they could buy the goods they wanted 'right now' and remain respectable, despite taking advantage of credit facilities.[60] Permission to use credit without losing respectability was important to what Judith Brett has called 'Australia's moral middle class', that is, the voters represented by Australia's longest-serving Prime Minister, the Liberal Party's Robert Menzies, who served as prime minister (for the second time) from 1949 to 1966.[61]

Myer had launched the PBA, with an advertisement declaring that 'Whatever Your Income the P.B.A. is Best for You!' To illustrate this flexibility, three male workers were depicted: a carpenter, a draughtsman and a delivery man (Fig. 5.2).

Fig. 5.2 Myer used illustrations of men at work to represent diverse household incomes. 'Whatever Your Income', *Age*, 29 August 1953, 4, National Library of Australia

> Whatever you want, just when you want it, is what opening a Permanent Budget Account at Myer's will mean to you! You're charged only 1% on your monthly balance to cover accounting costs, and the amount of credit you want is your decision—£10, £20, £30 or even more if you want it! Continuous, as each payment gives you just that much more credit, and so economical!

Advertising copywriters have long been encouraged to address the consumer directly, to use the second person wherever possible. The 'you' addressed in Myer's PBA advertisements was, in most cases, a women reader not a man, yet the sources of income portrayed in the illustrations were the household income, earned predominantly (though not solely) by men. Women might be the default consumer, but advertisers remained unready or unwilling to acknowledge their full agency as such.

An examination of Myer's PBA advertisements in the mid-1950s challenges the traditional view of 1950s' Australia as an era in which an ideology of domesticity prevailed. With its small deposit and interest charges, the PBA replaced cash orders as a means for those on tight budgets to make small, but necessary purchases. Most of the PBA advertisements targeted women, often for the purchase of small household goods, Manchester and Christmas toys, but also for personal items such as coats, frocks, bags, hats, and shoes. The illustrations and messages in these advertisements emphasised individual expression and modernity, linked, especially, to a United States sensibility (Fig. 5.3).

The PBA message was sometimes incorporated into the advertisement template; placed in the top left-hand corner of the header. The copy read: 'Open a Permanent Budget account at Myer's! You make a fortnightly

Fig. 5.3 The PBA gave Australian women easier access to US 'style', *Herald*, 4 March 1954, 7, National Library of Australia

payment and can immediately buy up to eleven times that amount!' The word 'immediately' worked hard here, linked to the urgency of the main message, for example: 'We've hurried along new US American styles and patterns … a nylon dress is a must in your wardrobe this season!.[62]

An important selling point was the ease of obtaining credit at Myer. Material collected from the US National Retail Merchants Association (NRMA) reminded Myer decision-makers that extending credit was a costly undertaking.[63] Given Myer's efficiency ideology, it was surprising that interview, approval, and payments facilities for the three types of credit were not housed together in one office. All were located in the Lonsdale Street Store (the 'Little Store') but on different floors of that building: the Easy Terms (previously Deferred Payments) Office on the fourth floor, the PBA Office on the fifth floor, and the Charge (previously the Entry or Monthly) Accounts Office on the eighth floor.[64] Perhaps such differentiation was based in part on a desire to avoid exposing middle- and upper-middle-class customers (those using the Charge Account) to the 'lower' types (those using the Easy Terms and PBA). That said, customers in the United States were reported to complain if the credit office was located too high in the building: perhaps Myer's charge card customers were happy to forgo convenience for privacy.[65] No doubt they also appreciated Myer's investment in ensuring that the department was attractive and welcoming. Again, in the United States, attention to such things as décor was considered an investment in 'customer goodwill, customer service and employee morale'.[66]

On its introduction, the new PBA had received special attention including a concerted effort to make those using the facility 'feel special'. Advertisements encouraged customers to 'Shop the PBA Way', by visiting a 'special' PBA office 'where our credit representative will be glad to meet you and give you full particulars—quietly, confidentially, and at your convenience'.[67] The strategy paid off: by 1963, Myer was able to note that the 'general public [were] now more aware of the advantages of a PBA account' and report an increase of PBA sales at its new Chadstone store.[68] The increase at the new shopping centre was put down to a transfer to 'cycle billing' which had 'removed the last stigma from P.B.A.'s [sic]'.[69] This type of account, the report continued, offered the customer the same advantages as a Monthly Charge account.[70] Cycle billing involved a credit check before the customer was approved and a contract between the customer and the supplier.[71] This 'removed the stigma' surrounding risky, unsecured loans given to customers who could not secure credit, which had its roots in cash-order loans.[72] With this move, the PBA became a respectable, middle-class form of credit and was promoted by Myer well into the 1970s.[73]

Revolving credit accounts such as the PBA were not the only indication that a new era of retail credit was on the horizon. In the early 1950s, department stores began to pay increased attention to the opportunities offered by the 'impulse sale'. A US study in 1950 had revealed that 30% of department store business came from 'spur of the moment' purchases.[74] This meant that the Australian 'retailer's postwar ambition number one … must be planned around impulse buying'. Store design and merchandising display and layout needed to encourage impulse buying, with more merchandise exposed to create more sales.[75] Impulse buying also meant stock moved out faster, reducing stock space and damage to the product.[76] This would have implications for the future of revolving credit in Australia. After praising the ease and convenience of using his Potts Brothers credit plate, one commentator pointed out how dangerous the plate actually was: 'It is apt to give a magic wand complex. You feel that by showing it you can get something for nothing—which is far from the truth'.[77] The plastic credit card would make impulse buying even more difficult for the customer to resist.[78]

Hire purchase remained controversial. As we have seen, concerns about its growth had been raised by the federal treasurer in 1955 and these concerns continued to grow. Towards the end of the 1950s, the *Retail Trader* noted the 'meteoric rise' in instalment credit or hire purchase. Such transactions had grown from 6 million in 1945 to 'about 350 million' in 1959, although the rise was in credit overall, not just in hire purchase, which comprised just 10% of the goods sold in Australia compared with 15% in 1934.[79] Despite these concerns, the rise in hire purchase was said to signal 'a revolution' in the thinking and spending habits of consumers, who were now willing to go in to debt to 'acquire durable assets' which had become 'part and parcel of today's high standard of living'.[80] Hire purchase was 'a clean and lovely way of doing business', especially useful for newly married couples looking to furnish a house.[81]

A large of proportion of the people buying goods on hire purchase were migrants or 'New Australians' who were arriving in Australia from post-war Europe without 'very much capital' and needed to access retail credit:

> When we think of New Australians, we wonder how the average migrant family could have established homes in this country without hire purchase. How much more satisfactory for them to pay a few pounds more in hiring charges than to face life without all the amenities that make it worth living.[82]

In 1962, the recently formed Australian Hire Purchase Conference reported that, because of language difficulties, many migrants misunderstood Australia's retail credit systems and found themselves in trouble. The conference announced plans to produce a 'simply worded brochure on hire purchase for distribution throughout Australia and at immigration offices', as well as to provide migrant organisations with speakers on the topic and prepare notes for migrant advisers to help them guide migrants on hire purchase.[83] Calls for more attention to helping migrants understand instalment credit so they avoided over-committing themselves would continue into the 1970s and beyond.[84]

Retail credit gained increasing attention in the retail trade press. A number of papers were delivered on the topic at the annual Residential Conference of Retail Executives organised by the Retail Traders' Association of NSW. At the 1958 gathering, the manager of Buckingham's department store explained that retail credit depended 'principally on the lower income and middle class people on middle and lower class'. He then outlined the change in conditions since the war. With rising wages, there was now less disparity in income between skilled and unskilled labour, and this had increased the demand for household goods: 'this demand had been channelled into the rising credit stream'.[85]

Retailers were shifting their view of credit, observed a speaker at the 1959 conference: 'Credit nowadays is regarded as a mark of character rather than an inability to pay'.[86] It used to be a privilege that retailers granted to consumers, but now, more realistically, retailers understood that credit demonstrated the consumer's own financial power and belonged to the individual; it was now something the retailer had to secure rather than grant. Credit must be treated as merchandise now, the article argued, with advertising that convinced the customer to 'bestow on [the retailer's] store that valued credit possession'.[87] Until recently, the only available forms of retail credit had been 'the 30-day monthly account and hire purchase'. Retailers now had to offer consumers 'a variable credit set-up', in other words, a choice of credit forms. The article went on to describe the mechanics of successful credit management in the 1950s, including accurate recording, duplicate dockets, and the use of microfilm.[88]

Australia's economy faltered in 1960 when the country found itself in a so-called 'credit squeeze'. The squeeze had been caused by the Reserve Bank of Australia's (RBA's) move to curb bank lending in August that year.[89] This time credit forms such as hire purchase escaped much of the blame for the situation, with experts identifying attempts to house Australia's growing population as the cause of much of the nation's present economic woes.[90] Leading economists such as the University of Melbourne's Ronald Henderson and Ernst Boehm argued that the real estate boom was 'the most disturbing feature of the Australian [economic] scene'. In 1959 and 1960, land values in Sydney had 'reached a level nearly twice as high as in 1958'; the position was similar in Melbourne.[91]

As the credit squeeze eased during 1961, Myer's credit sales continued to increase, rising from 37.81% of sales in 1960–1961 to 43.15% in 1962–1963, a 24.44% increase.[92] Consumer credit had begun its inexorable rise. In the United States, retailers moved to expand their in-house credit facilities, encroaching onto the banks' turf. In response, the Bank of America introduced its own, branded revolving credit card, the BankAmericard (renamed Visa in 1976).[93]

Amidst continued coverage of the expansion of credit in the retail press, Australian banks floated the possibility of introducing their own revolving credit card in 1970.[94] Along with other large retailers, Myer came out strongly against the idea, arguing that department stores would struggle to absorb the banks' interest charges. Not mentioned, but perhaps even more concerning for Australian retailers such as Myer was the knowledge that the introduction of bank-branded credit cards, which could be used at any store, had undermined store loyalty in the United States.[95] Despite this resistance, the banks would go ahead with the plan.[96] The era of the revolving credit card had arrived and retail credit would continue its seemingly relentless incursion into the lives of Australians.[97]

Notes

1. 'Myer Emporium Announces Another Great Service', *Herald*, 22 August 1953, 9.
2. 'Myer Emporium Announces Another Great Service'.
3. 'The Myer Emporium', *Argus*, 4 September 1953, 7.
4. 'Myer Emporium Selects Burroughs Sensimatic', *Herald*, 23 August 1953, 9; 'The Myer Emporium', *Argus*, 4 September 1953, 7.

5. Simon Ville, 'The Economy', in *Cambridge History of Australia*, ed. Alison Bashford and Stuart Macintyre (Cambridge: Cambridge University Press, 2013), 378, 394.
6. Ville, 'The Economy', 394; Janet McCalman, 'Private Lives in the Garden Suburbs Between the Wars', in *The Cream Brick Frontier: Histories of Australian Suburbia*, ed. Graeme Davison, Tony Dingle and Seamus O'Hanlon (Melbourne: Monash Publications in History, 1995), 51–61.
7. David Graeber, *Debt: The First 5,000 Years* (Brooklyn, New York, Melville House, 2011), 15.
8. Joel Spring, *Educating the Consumer-Citizen: A History of the Marriage of Schools, Advertising, and Media* (New York: Routledge, 2003), 5; Lizabeth Cohen, *A Consumers' Republic: The Politics of Mass Consumption in Postwar America* (New York: Vintage, 2003), 8–9.
9. Lizabeth Cohen, *A Consumers' Republic; The Politics of Mass Consumption in Postwar America* (New York: Vintage, 2003), 8–9.
10. Frank Trentmann, 'Knowing Consumers', in *Making of the Consumer: Knowledge, Power and Identity in the Modern World*, 1–26 (Oxford: Berg Publishers, 2005), 18; Jackie Dickenson, 'Luxury and the Australian Labour Press, 1890–1918', *Labour History* 124, May 2023, 3–4.
11. G.L. Wood, 'Inflation and the Consumer', *Werribee Shire Banner*, 7 July 1949, 3; 'Inflation', *Construction*, 2 May 1951, 5; 'High Carnival of Spending', *Age*, 1 December 1954, 2; Pierre van der Eng, 'Consumer Credit in Australia during the Twentieth Century', *Accounting, Business & Financial History* 18, no. 2 (2008): 256–58; Judith Brett, 'The Menzies Era', in *Cambridge History of Australia*, ed. Alison Bashford and Stuart Macintyre (Cambridge: Cambridge University Press, 2013), 121–22.
12. Guy Sims Fitch, 'U.S. Consumer A Big Factor, *Queensland Times*, 10 June 1952, 5
13. Wilfred Prest, 'Anti-Inflation Policy Promising', *Sun News-Pictorial*, 20 July 1951, 5.
14. 'Treasurer Calls For Restraint in Spending', *Canberra Times*, 25 August 1955, 2.
15. 'Treasurer Calls For Restraint in Spending'.
16. 'Treasurer Calls For Restraint in Spending'.
17. Brett, 'The Menzies Era', 124. See John Murphy, *Imagining the Fifties: Private Sentiment and Political Culture in Menzies' Australia* (Sydney: UNSW Press, 2000), 186–89.
18. R.B. Purser, 'The Mechanics of Credit', *Retail Trader*, October 1959, 48.
19. Purser, 'The Mechanics of Credit', 48.
20. 'Budget Accounts', *Retail Trader*, December 1962, 40–41.
21. William Stafford, 'The Never-Never Purchase is Booming', *Brisbane Telegraph*, 7 October 1953, 5.

22. Myer oscillated between using PBA and OPA: State Library of Victoria, Records of Coles-Myer Ltd. and its predecessors, ca. 1840–ca.1990 (hereafter CM), MS 13468, Box 3523, '30 Day Charge or Optional Payment Account', c.1970s. Farmer's credit offer included both a Budget Account (cash-order equivalent) and an OPA, CM, Box 1370, 'Farmer's: Give Yourself Credit'.
23. See, for example, CM, Box F3352, 'Better Basement Selling', *Myer Store Bulletin*, 7.
24. Arthur H. Hert, 'Charge Accounts of Retail Merchants', *Annals of the American Academy Political and Social Science* 196, no.1 (1938): 111–20, 112.
25. Hert, 'Charge Accounts of Retail Merchants', 112.
26. Hert, 'Charge Accounts of Retail Merchants', 111.
27. Hert, 'Charge Accounts of Retail Merchants', 111.
28. CM, Box F3352, *Myer Store News*, 'How You Can Please Customers', 28 August 1941, 1; CM, Box 80, Grace Bros, Mount Druitt, 'Summary of "We Care" Committee Minutes', 1980, 1–2; CM, Box 2881, 'We Take Steps Every Day to Improve What We Do: Using a Customer's Name', *Myer Grace Bos: Customer Service Matters*, 16 August 1993, 3
29. CM, Box 1510, Grace Bros. Retail-Eze, 1980s, x.
30. Bovis, 'New Efficiency in Cycle Billing'; 'New Accounts System Praised', *Retail Merchandiser*, September 1956, 22.
31. Andrew L. Yarrow, *Thrift: The History of an American Cultural Movement*. Amherst: University of Massachusetts Press, 2014.
32. 'Savings Key to Growth', *Argus*, 4 June 1955, 10.
33. 'Save First And Then Buy', *Argus*, 6 July 1956, 11.
34. 'Save First And Then Buy'.
35. University of Melbourne Archives (UMA), Myer Emporium (hereafter ME) 1979.0180, Unit 141, Sales System Guide Book (Melbourne: 1935 [1929]), 51.
36. Sales System Guide Book, 75.
37. Sales System Guide Book, 113.
38. CM, Box 1725, 'The New O.K.', *Myer Store News* 19, no. 1, January 1949, 8–9.
39. ME, Unit 141, 'Souvenir Booklet, 1956–1957'.
40. CM, Box 3523, Credit Order Coupon Book, n.d.
41. CM, Box 1725, 'Economic Coupons Won this Customer', *Myer Store News* 12, no. 4, June 1952, 14–15; 'The Cash Order System', *Age*, 14 May 1941, 14.
42. 'Company Meeting', *Argus*, 7 November 1953, 6. 'Myer Emporium Chose Burroughs', *Herald*, 22 August 1953, 9.

43. James T. Brennan, 'Securing Department Store Charge Account Sales', *Connecticut Bar Journal* 39, no. 1 (1965): 33–71.
44. CM, Box 1725, *Myer Hand Book for Staff*, 40.
45. CM, Box 3523, 'Fancy That! ... A Permanent Budget Charge Plate Gives You $100 to Spend Immediately', c. 1970s.
46. CM, Box 3523. 'Fancy That!'; 'PBA Credit Card Operations, Continuous Credit - $50– $200, Uniform Monthly Instalments', c. 1970s.
47. 'The Mechanics of Credit', *Retail Trader*, October 1959, 44.
48. 'The Mechanics of Credit', 46.
49. A.L. Trotta, Revolving Credit', *Retail Trader*, March 1959, 8.
50. Trotta, 'Revolving Credit', 10.
51. Trotta, Revolving Credit', 8.
52. 'Watch "Revolving Credit" Plan', *New York Times*, August 28, 1938, 8.
53. 'Today John Wanamaker', *Philadelphia Inquirer*, 16 November 1938, 12, https://cdn.theconversation.com/static_files/files/3587/, accessed 22 June 2025.
54. 'Revolving Credit', *Retail Trader*, March 1959, 12.
55. 'Economic Floats on 10% Basis', *Herald*, 29 September 1954, 6.
56. 'PBA is the Modern Way', *Argus*, 4 September 1953, 7.
57. John P. Watkins, 'Corporate Power and the Evolution of Consumer Credit', *Journal of Economic Issues* 34, no. 4 (December 2000): 909.
58. 'The Myer Emporium', *Herald*, 16 October 1954, 20; CM, Box 3127, *National Retail Merchants Association, Study of Customer Credit Costs in Department Stores 1963* (New York, 1963).
59. *Advertiser*, 3 April 1951, 9.
60. 'Open A Permanent Budget Account', 22 August 1953, 9; 'Talking Big', *News*, 12 September 1951, 19; 'Permanent Budget Account', *Herald*, 4 September 1953, 15.
61. Judith Brett, 'The Menzies Era, 1950–66', *Cambridge History of Australia* (Cambridge: Cambridge University Press, 112), 112–34, 112.
62. 'It's Magic, It's Nylon', *Herald*, 3 October 1953, 23; CM, Box 3523, 'Trust Myer, The Myer Promise'.
63. CM, Box 3127, 'Study of Customer Credit Costs in Department Stores 1963' (New York, 1963), 14.
64. 'Study of Customer Credit Costs'.
65. Thelma A. Farison, 'Sales Appeal in the Credit Office', *Retail Trader*, 10 January 1952, 22.
66. Farison, 'Sales Appeal', 22
67. 'Myer Emporium Announces Another Great Service', *Herald*, 22 August 1953, 9.
68. CM, Box 1429, 'Annual Credit Report For the Year Ended 31st July 1963', 2.

69. 'Annual Credit Report', 2.
70. 'Annual Credit Report', 2.
71. Malcolm Tatum, 'What is Cycle Billing?' https://www.wise-geek.com/what-is-cycle-billing.htm, accessed 31 October 2022.
72. 'Annual Credit Report', 2.
73. 'Have Up to $100 Now to Spend', *Herald*, 2 May 1970, 9; 'Stigma of Instalment Credit Has Now Gone', *Australian Retailing*, August 1970, 11–17.
74. 'Spur-of-the-Moment Purchasing', *Retail Merchandiser*, May 1950, 21.
75. 'Provide for More Buying on Impulse', *Retail Merchandiser*, January 1951; 'Impulse Sales', *Retail Merchandiser*, September 1950, 40.
76. 'Impulse Sales'.
77. Ross Campbell, 'Impulse Buy', *Australian Women's Weekly*, 8 September 1965, 33.
78. 'Spur-of-the-moment Purchasing'.
79. 'Growth Since War', *Retail Trader*, September 1959, 42.
80. 'Growth Since War'.
81. 'No Interference with Hire Plan', *Age*, 12 September 1951, 7.
82. 'Growth Since War'.
83. 'Guide on Hire Purchase', *Good Neighbour*, 1 December 1962, 2.
84. 'Consumer Credit', *Retail Trader*, April 1964, 6–7.
85. J.B.J. Lawler, 'Buy Now–Pay Later', *Retail Trader*, January 1959, 30–42, 30.
86. 'The Mechanics of Credit', *Retail Trader*, October 1959, 42–48.
87. 'The Mechanics of Credit'.
88. 'The Mechanics of Credit'.
89. 'Big Fall on London Stock Market', *Canberra Times*, 26 February 1960, 7; Reserve Bank of Australia Annual Report – 1961, Monetary Policy, https://www.rba.gov.au/publications/annual-reports/rba/1961/monetary-policy.html, accessed 22 June 2025.
90. 'Important Role in Development'; 'Institute's Beginning In 1910', *Sydney Morning Herald*, 17 October 1960.
91. Ronald F. Henderson, 'Monetary Policy in Australia 1960/61', *Economic Record* 37, no. 79, September 1961, 294–307.
92. Reserve Bank of Australia Annual Report – 1963, Monetary Policy: Problems of Policy, https://www.rba.gov.au/publications/annual-reports/rba/1963/monetary-policy.html, accessed 22 June 2025; CM, Box 1429, 'Fuller, King & Co., Chadmyr Proprietary Ltd. 31 July 1963', 22.
93. 'The Little Bank that Began It All', *Australian Retailing*, September-October 1972, 10–11; https://www.forbes.com/advisor/credit-cards/history-of-credit-cards, accessed 19 June 2025.

94. 'Revealing Study of Bank Credit Card Plans', *Australian Retailing*, September 1970, 19. 'Growth of Credit Cards', *Australian Retailing*, January 1971, 20; 'Huge Increase in Bank Credit Cards', *Australian Retailing*, November 1971, 8–9; 'Towards A Money-Less Society', *Australian Retailing*, September-October 1972, 8–9.
95. 'Credit Cards: Retail Opposition', *Bulletin*, 17 January 1970, 44; Eng, 'Consumer Credit in Australia', 17.
96. 'Myer Accepts Bankcard', *Sydney Morning Herald*, 6 May 1978, 29; 'From the Myer Boutique', *Sydney Morning Herald*, 9 July 1978; 'Myer Special Purchase', *Sun Herald*, 25 June 1978, 18; Eng, 'Consumer Credit in Australia', 17.
97. Margaret Griffiths, 'The Sustainability of Consumer Credit Growth in Late Twentieth Century Australia', *Journal of Consumer Studies & Home Economics* 24, no. 1 (March 2000): 23–33.

References

Australian Retailing. Sydney: Australian Council of Retailers, 1967–1973.

Bashford, Alison and Stuart Macintyre, eds. *Cambridge History of Australia*. Cambridge: Cambridge University Press, 2013.

Brennan, James T. 'Securing Department Store Charge Account Sales Under the Uniform Commercial Code'. *Connecticut Bar Journal* 39, no. 1 (1965): 33–71.

Cohen, Lizabeth. *A Consumers' Republic; The Politics of Mass Consumption in Postwar America*. New York: Vintage, 2003.

Davison, Graeme, Tony Dingle, and Seamus O'Hanlon, eds. *The Cream Brick Frontier: Histories of Australian Suburbia*. Melbourne: Monash Publications in History, 1995.

Dickenson, Jackie. 'Luxury and the Australian Labour Press, 1890—1918'. *Labour History* 124 (May 2023): 1–29. https://doi.org/10.3828/labourhistory.2023

Graeber, David. *Debt: The First 5,000 Years*. Brooklyn, New York: Melville House, 2011.

Griffiths, Margaret. 'The Sustainability of Consumer Credit Growth in Late Twentieth Century Australia'. *Journal of Consumer Studies & Home Economics* 24, no.1 (March 2000): 23 33. https://doi.org/10.1046/j.1365-2737.2000.00117.x

Hert, Arthur H. 'Charge Accounts of Retail Merchants', *Annals of the American Academy Political and Social Science* 196, no.1 (1938): 111–20.

Henderson, Ronald F. 'Monetary Policy in Australia 1960/61'. *Economic Record* 37, no. 79, September 1961, 294–307.

Murphy, John. Imagining the Fifties: Private Sentiment and Political Culture in Menzies' *Australia*. Sydney: UNSW Press, 2000.

Records of Coles-Myer Ltd. and its predecessors, ca. 1840–1990, MS13468, State Library of Victoria.

Retail Merchandiser. Melbourne: Masters Drapers and Traders' Association of Victoria 1949–1967.

Retail Trader. Sydney: Retail Traders' Association of NSW, 1921–2006.

Spring, Joel. *Educating the Consumer-Citizen: A History of the Marriage of Schools, Advertising, and Media.* New York: Routledge, 2003.

Trentmann, Frank. *Making of the Consumer: Knowledge, Power and Identity in the Modern World.* Oxford: Berg Publishers, 2005.

Van Der Eng, Pierre, 'Consumer Credit in Australia during the Twentieth Century'. *Accounting, Business & Financial History* 18, no. 2 (2008) 243–65, https://doi.org/10.1080/09585200802058917

Watkins, John P. 'Corporate Power and the Evolution of Consumer Credit'. *Journal of Economic Issues* 34, no. 4 (December 2000): 909–32.

Yarrow, Andrew L. *Thrift: The History of an American Cultural Movement.* Amherst: University of Massachusetts Press, 2014.

CHAPTER 6

Plastic Fantastic

Abstract Responding to the imminent arrival of revolving credit cards from the United States, a consortium of Australian banks launched Bankcard in October 1974, using the new technology of the mass mailout. Every Australian with a bank account received a Bankcard, which helped normalise the credit card in Australia. Bankcard's flat 'democratic' offer contrasted with the tiered systems of the US credit cards, which were set up to confer status on the biggest spenders. Its introduction also coincided with significant steps in the economic liberation of Australian women. Some department stores were slow to introduce Bankcard to their customers, but by the early 1980s, it became clear that they needed to respond to a rapidly evolving credit environment.

Keywords Credit • Retail • Revolving credit • Bankcard • Status • Women • Australian history

In 1973, nine of Australia's leading banks came together to form the Bankcard Association of Australia.[1] The new consortium aimed to introduce Australia's first revolving (or continuing) credit card, in response to the imminent arrival of US credit cards.[2] Despite the rapid spread of revolving credit cards in the United States and Europe in the 1960s, they were slow to arrive in Australia. The convenience of credit on a card had

J. Dickenson, *Credit and the Australian Department Store Since 1900*, https://doi.org/10.1007/978-3-032-16612-8_6

been limited to department store charge cards and, from 1965 and 1970, respectively, the US charge cards, Diners Club and Carte Blanche, all of which had to be paid in full after one month and so were considered to be 'for the wealthy'.[3] However, this was poised to change and Australian banks wanted to ensure that the profits earned from revolving credit remained in Australia.

In October 1974, the normalisation of revolving credit in Australia took a significant step forward. Every Australian with a bank account was issued with a pre-approved Bankcard whether they wanted one or not, with an average credit limit of $300 and—unlike the US charge cards—no initial fee or yearly subscription.[4] The banks distributed the new card through a mass mailout, using database marketing, a recent innovation, which, like most of the developments in the technology and marketing of retail credit, had emanated from the United States.[5]

From the late 1950s, the application of computer technology had allowed direct marketers to better handle their lists of current and potential customer names. They were now able to collect data on millions of customers, store transactional and behavioural information in a database, analyse the performance of various tactics, and manipulate data to maximise the return on investment, all of which gave them the ability to target customers more precisely.[6]

By the 1970s, the precise targeting of customers had become increasingly important to those seeking commercial success. With the social and political upheaval of the 1960s and the weakening of class allegiances, the parameters of mass marketing had also shifted, with the 'one-size-fits-all' approach no longer an effective way to reach customers.[7] Charge cards had led the way in personalising direct marketing, in particular, the world's most popular business charge card American Express (Amex), which launched in 1958 but arrived in Australia only in early 1974, in anticipation of the Bankcard launch.[8] Like its rivals Diners Club and Carte Blanche, Amex offered its 'upscale' cardholders 'an illusion of membership—more like a private country club than a mere retail business',[9] with a payment model of convenience rather than credit that charged users an annual fee instead of interest and required them to pay the account in full after one month. Amex was considered to have 'mastered' the art of direct marketing and, in 1982, planned to use its 'top-notch, built-in mailing list' to 'narrowcast' and target its offer to specific audiences.[10] By 1986, it would become the fifth largest direct marketing merchandiser in the United States.[11]

A Hierarchy of Revolving Credit

According to Maurizio Lazarretto, consumers carry the debtor-creditor relationship in their pockets and wallets encoded in the magnetic strip on their credit cards.[12] I would add to this that the *form* of that credit card signals to others the consumer's status in the debtor-creditor relationship, which, far from being binary, operates on a nuanced spectrum of indebtedness, class, and social standing. As Lara Swartz has noted, payment is 'a vector of identity', an example of what Michel Foucault called 'technologies of the self', through which identity is performed and policed.[13] Charge card companies clearly understood the importance of payment as a tool through which customers could signal their identity, as well as determine and compare the identities of others.[14] They created advertisements that emphasised the aura their cards bestowed on the holder, showing 'fashionably-dressed people in luxurious surroundings' and using words such as 'exclusive, refined, by invitation only, and prestige'.[15] Moreover, by narrowcasting through personalised mailouts, these companies were able to appeal to the status anxiety of individual customers, offering them the reassurance of knowing they sat at the very top of the hierarchy of payment—if they could afford it.[16]

American Express again led the way in developing this 'card class system'.[17] In 1966, it introduced the Amex Gold Card for 'big spending members', with a product name and design that reinforced a message of exclusivity and prestige.[18] However, by the 1980s, the Gold Card's popularity (now with half a million cardholders in the United States) had started to undermine its promise of prestige and exclusivity. After briefly trying a more exclusive black card service, Amex responded in 1984 with the invitation-only Platinum Card, which was billed as an 'ultra-exclusive' credit card with a $250 annual fee.[19] Then, in the late 1990s, with the Platinum Card losing exclusivity in its turn, Amex introduced the Centurion Card, popularly known as the Black Card, which was (and is) aimed at the 'ultra-wealthy'.[20] Long associated with power and prestige—think James Bond in his black tuxedo—the use of black gave the card an aura of luxury and sophistication.[21]

American Express's move to the Black Card responded to the fact that, by the mid-1990s, gold and platinum cards were no longer unique to Amex. The revolving credit cards Mastercard and Visa had also begun to offer their customers markers of exclusivity and prestige, adding gold cards to their offers in 1981 and 1989, respectively; platinum cards followed in the mid-1990s.[22] In 1998, each of the eight largest US banks issued a gold credit card and three of the eight issued a platinum card.[23]

By using the words 'gold' and 'platinum', the card companies sought to associate themselves with the prestige level of valuable metals that were no longer used to make money.[24] However, there was more to the choice of these words. The credit card system was hierarchical, with three levels—platinum above gold and gold above plain or, in the case of Amex, green, the colour of money—that corresponded to the upper, middle, and working classes in the stratification of debt in America.[25] This also reinforced the popular conception that different precious metals represented an individual's social, economic, or political status. This idea has deep historical roots, going back to Plato's 'Myth of Metals' (c320 BCE), which itself riffed on Hesiod's 'Five Ages of Man' (eighth century BCE) and influenced Ovid's 'Four Ages of Man' (c.8 CE). In *The Republic*, Plato has Socrates explain that:

> While all of you in the city are brothers … yet God in fashioning those of you who are fitted to hold rule mingled gold in their generation, for which reason they are the most precious—but in the helpers silver, and iron and brass in the farmers and other craftsmen.[26]

In other words, each human being has a metal in them: those 'naturally suited' to be rulers have gold, those suited to be guardians have silver, and those suited for farming and the other crafts have iron and brass (an alloy of copper and zinc). The marking of hierarchy and status using metals had been further reinforced in popular culture when the organisers of the 1904 Olympic Games introduced gold, silver, and bronze medals for first, second and third place respectively.[27] This hierarchy reflected the position of each element on the periodic table, with copper (the main component of bronze) the most abundant of the three and gold the rarest.

Using the names of precious metals might have attached an aura of luxury to the credit card, but this was undermined by the fact that they were made from plastic. Plastic occupies a complex place in popular culture. After a rocky start in the post-war period, it gained acceptance in the 1960s in part through the promotion of Tupperware home products, only to become endowed with an aura of shoddiness, emerging as a cultural metaphor for superficiality and excess, and becoming synonymous with 'counterfeit'.[28]

This ambiguity towards the value of plastic was discernible in the commentary about credit cards, in particular, the dismissive term, 'Plastic Fantastic'.[29] On the one hand, informally 'fantastic' means 'great', which acknowledges the convenience of the 'plastic' credit card and marks it as a welcome addition to everyday life. On the other hand, the formal meaning of 'fantastic' is 'not real', 'fantasy', 'illusory', 'extravagantly fanciful', and 'unrealistic'—in other words 'plastic' was counterfeit and something less than 'real' money.

Some customers continued to use their 'real' metal charge plates until well into 1980s. Alastair Graham, a manager at Walton's in the 1970s, recalls the respect shown to those with a metal card at David Jones, presumably because they were customers of long-standing:

> if you were a special type of customer of David Jones [you] used to have a metal credit card [a charge plate]. The common plastic one was just starting to spring up into the marketplace. And if you had a metal card you were, or you should have to be, addressed by your name. So, you know, Good morning, Sir David, or whatever your name was and if you wanted a cup of tea they'd go and get one for you. And they will look after you.[30]

Given society's ambivalence towards the material, a plastic credit card was never going to cut it at the luxury end of the market. Simply labelling a plastic card as 'gold' or 'platinum' could not provide the aura of luxury this segment of the market desired. Again, American Express took the lead in responding to this 'problem', when they introduced the Black Card, which was made not from plastic but from anodised titanium. Although not a precious metal, titanium has the highest strength to weight ratio of any metal and offered a weight and durability that cheap, crack-prone plastic could not.[31] Since then, the weight of the metal card has become a marker of status and luxury. For example, the Mastercard Gold, Black, and Titanium Cards (like the Amex Black Card, now made from brushed stainless steel) are marketed as 'outweighing the competition' with a 'card weight of 22 grams'.[32]

A Card for Every Australian

Australia's homegrown credit card resisted the move to differentiate between the status of its customers in the manner of the US charge cards. 'Aimed mainly at shoppers' rather than 'businessmen on expense accounts',

Bankcard was for every Australian (with a good enough credit rating) no matter their social or economic status, and so was unapologetically plebian in its design.[33] Unlike Amex with its Roman centurion that utilised the distant past for status representation and reinforcement, Bankcard used a contemporary colour palette and design that reflected the simple, contemporary designs of the basic Visa and Master Charge (as Mastercard was then known), against which it would soon be competing on its home turf. One commentator described it as 'a shiny rectangle of plastic decked out in nauseous shades of red, yellow, orange, and green' (Fig. 6.1).[34] As we will see, Bankcard's resistance to a tiered membership (alongside the fact that it could not be used overseas) would impact its success and longevity.[35]

With its mass unsolicited distribution, Bankcard was off to a controversial start: one report began with the line 'I need a Bankcard like I need the Black Death'.[36] The card's introduction caused concern on a number of fronts, including inflation, security, and privacy, all of which had been discussed in the retail press as the arrival of credit cards loomed, with some of this discussion emanating from the United States. Politicians concerned about the card's inflationary potential were at the forefront of the attack. The New South Wales Labor Opposition leader Neville Wran criticised the 'sloppy' Bankcard scheme, calling it 'another great credit coup' that 'could be inflationary' and 'put up prices', as retailers might incur extra costs that

Fig. 6.1 Grace Bros staff training Bankcard, 1980s. MS13468, COMY02405, Box 347, SLV

they would then pass on to consumers.[37] The issue divided the Australian Labor Party, with Wran's deputy Jack Ferguson attacking the Federal Treasurer, Frank Crean, for failing to obstruct the introduction of Bankcard. Crean had approved the card in June 1973.[38]

The response to the launch picked up on the long history of unease in Australia about the pitfalls of using credit. Bankcard's rollout instigated yet another moral panic with commentators warning about the impact of credit cards being sent out 'indiscriminately'. The day after the rollout, there were reports that cards had been sent to 'unreceptive people'—the dead—and to children.[39] Another concern was that the mass mailout would allow unsavoury characters to get their hands on someone else's Bankcard. Within days of the mailout, a man who had 'falsely used a Bankcard to buy clothes and a wristwatch' was remanded in custody in Sydney and later received an 18-month good behaviour bond.[40] A second man, charged with attempting to buy a rifle with a stolen Bankcard, was fined $120 and also placed on an 18-month good behaviour bond.[41] Linked to this was the concern about who might be liable for money spent on a card, if it were lost or stolen. Bankcard reassured the public that in the case of a lost card, the cardholder would only be liable for funds up to $50 and, if a card had been stolen, 'the person whose name had been forged on the card would not be liable for the costs of goods or services purchased'.[42] Consumer groups such as the Australian Consumers Association (ACA) were worried that the data collected for the mailout could be misused by bad actors, foreshadowing significant concerns in the present, digital age.[43] On this point, the Federal Attorney-General Lionel Murphy moved to outlaw the practice of making unsolicited offers through the mail, noting his concern about 'the confused way' in which 'the Bankcard offer' had been made.[44] The churches described the card as 'an invitation to get into debt', with one representative condemning the scheme as 'a purely commercial enticement' and 'an unpleasant expression of capitalism'.[45]

Bankcard's launch was expected to bring 'many newcomers into the field of credit buying',[46] an expectation that revived familiar tropes from Australia's credit history, such as the possibility of 'easy credit' encouraging people to spend what they did not have. One group of 'newcomers' was particularly problematic. As we have seen, women shoppers had long taken the brunt of society's concerns about the injudicious use of credit, and the old trope that women might use credit irresponsibly would gain fresh momentum in this period.[47] An exchange between a reporter and

Australia's Prime Minister Gough Whitlam in October 1974 showed the resilience of interest in women's financial activities:

> Questioner: What is your view about the unsolicited distribution of bank cards, and do you feel that they could add to inflation? And also, did you receive one?
> Whitlam: Yes, I did. I did.
> Questioner: Did Mrs Whitlam receive one?
> Whitlam: Yes, she did. In recent months she has got an account of her own actually. So, we received bank cards. Now at last, when I don't have to establish my bona fides as a creditor, credit is being foisted on me. I am not sure that we will use them or destroy them or return them. I think that is the interesting order of probability.
> Questioner: Can you say which one has the greater credit, or is that too personal?
> Whitlam: Oh, I think it is, but you are an old friend, and I will talk to you afterwards. I mean you and I both married well.[48]

Whitlam sidestepped the question about the inflationary possibilities of the new cards, underlining the Federal Government's support for the banks' move. This contrasts with his willingness to engage on the subject of Margaret Whitlam's banking arrangements, which should be viewed in the context of recent changes to the financial independence of women, especially married women.[49] An Australian woman recalled her experience in the 1960s, as the co-owner (with her husband) of a motel:

> One day I went to the bank to get a loan for television sets for the motel. The bank wanted my husband to sign and take responsibility. … It was my money and my responsibility, and the bank treated me as though I scarcely knew how to tie my shoes.[50]

Such discrimination began to change in 1971, when the Australian women's liberation movement lobbied successfully for women to be able to access bank loans without a male guarantor, although married women could still 'come up against resistance in opening a trading bank account in her own name or be asked for evidence of her husband's agreement to make a major purchase'.[51]

Nevertheless, credit was gradually shifting away from its ambiguous past and becoming an essential part of life for many Australians, including women. In 1966, Australia's most popular women's magazine, the

Australian Women's Weekly, had given its readers permission to embrace credit enthusiastically:

> There's no need to run your life on a 'strictly cash' basis and deny yourself something you really want until you have the full price. Credit, used wisely, can be a useful part of the family's spending and saving plan. The old rule (great-grandfather's day) was pay or go without. But people today live in a credit-oriented society.[52]

Two years later, the NSW Rural Bank launched a marketing device aimed solely at women: a cheque book cover in 'an attractive two colour design with emphasis on a very feminine pink'. Because of 'the extensive use of credit today', women were 'as much in need of a cheque account as men', and the pink cover was expected to attract even more women to open an account at the bank. In designing this special 'for women only' cover, the bank's general manager explained, the bank was 'extending the personalised nature of banking'.[53]

The move to appeal to women in the late 1960s and 1970s was part of a general shift away from targeting broad economic and social classes to aiming more specifically for 'identity' groups, one of which was newly liberated women. Swartz has noted that the personal liberation that inclusion in the credit society seemed to offer US women was, in fact, 'a kind of pseudoliberation', because fulfilling their desire for immediate gratification came at a significant cost, in the form of high interest rates.[54]

Perhaps Australia's delayed embrace of revolving credit made Australian women warier of the 'pseudoliberation' it offered. As they were gradually accepted into the 'credit-oriented society', many had absorbed the message to use credit 'wisely', fully aware of the dangers of credit use. Using her Grace Bros credit card was a temptation that Ella Tilbrook, a widowed pensioner, resisted, 'because I'd really let myself go if I did'. She saved her Bankcard for emergencies: 'I don't think I can trust myself spending money I don't have'.[55] Interviewees who were asked about their memories of the Bankcard launch recalled their resistance to using credit cards, citing warnings from family members about the pitfalls of credit.[56] Asked whether she remembered the launch, Lizzie Bartlett replied:

> Yes. I think I was very aware of this brand new thing that my father warned me was the highway to hell with these credit cards ... I remember when Bankcards arrived. ... I could hear these warnings ringing in my ears from

> my father ... you know, 'can't pay for it, you can't have it'. But that technology, I think, made a big difference. I think a lot more people started purchasing stuff. ... it was the very beginning of what I now see as the sort of abject consumerism and throwaway fashion and stuff like that. And I seem to link those two things, with the advent of Bankcards and the increase in a lot more people shopping and buying stuff.[57]

Michele Matthews has never had a credit card, 'because I've got such an aversion to them ... if I haven't gotten the money, I don't buy it'.[58] Elizabeth Pallet has also avoided credit: 'I never have [liked it]. I've always believed in paying for what I get, rather than putting it on credit and then having to pay it off over time. Because you never know what's going to happen'.[59] Sofia Russo recalled that: 'We always had cash. ... You had to use cheques [and] lay-buy only occasionally. Never been card. Not in those days, [that's] only recent use'.[60] Only one interviewee remembered the Bankcard launch favourably. Asked if she recalled it, Laura Peden replied:

> Yeah, I do. Definitely. Because I moved to Melbourne to go to [university] around about the time that the first Bankcards came in. They weren't called credit cards ... Bankcards. And my dad helped me organise the Bankcard through the National Bank ... I definitely got a Bankcard. That was part of being an adult, I think.[61]

With the exception of Sydney's David Jones, the leading department stores were also reluctant to get involved with Bankcard, concerned about its impact on the profitability of their own credit facilities.[62] 'Unlike its competitors', David Jones' credit card was 'perceived as prestigious' and, given the loyalty and economic status of their clientele, the store trusted their customers would be able to absorb the financial impact of an additional card without affecting its own profits.[63] Early in December 1974, David Jones became the first major retail store organisation to adopt the Bankcard system.[64]

When, just three months after its introduction, 'multi-million dollar spending' had guaranteed Bankcard's future, other department stores began to follow suit.[65] In March 1975, Grace Bros agreed to accept it across its 10 Sydney stores and, when Bankcard signed up Walton's the following month, it was said to have 'now almost cornered the Sydney department store scene'.[66] By May 1976, Bankcard had extended to all parts of New South Wales.[67] Major retailers Myer and Adelaide's John Martin's held out against introducing Bankcard, finally succumbing in 1978.[68] Discount department stores were particularly concerned about the costs of the new scheme. The board of Kmart, for example, sent two executives to the United States, the United Kingdom, and Europe to study credit cards and report back, and then took another 18 months to agree to accept Bankcard.[69]

By 1979, one in five Australians used Bankcard—a total of two million cardholders. The leader of the Federal Opposition accused the banks of operating as a cartel, arguing that the Bankcard system was generating 'exploitative profits'.[70] Bankcard was said to have taken about $90 million in interest from its users in 1978 and about $60 million from the 75,000 stores and outlets which accepted it, making a yearly profit of $150 million.[71]

Despite such profits, Bankcard operated under significant constraints. A major drawback of Bankcard had long been that it could not be used overseas; Australians who wanted to use 'plastic' money when they travelled had to take their American Express or Diners Club cards with them. In 1978, Bankcard had tried to solve this by signing a co-branding agreement with the US credit cards Visa and Mastercard to enable international usability, but this proved a false start, with the agreement quickly dissolving.[72] Six years later, Visa and Mastercard launched internationally, including in Australia. These new credit cards could be used at home and abroad and, with their arrival, Bankcard's long decline began.[73] As the *Sydney Morning Herald* observed at the time, 'with the launch of Westpac's Mastercard the death of Bankcard had begun'.[74]

By 1987, the banks and other financial institutions had issued 1.5 million Visa cards and 1.3 million Mastercards to Australian customers, a trend that was said to be 'fast eroding Bankcard's market slice'.[75] Banks were keen to win support for the Visa/Mastercard combination, because, unlike Bankcard, they could put their names on these cards and use them to promote themselves. Bankcard might be past its use by date, but it had paved the way for the acceptance of credit card use, which was now firmly entrenched in Australia. 'Don't bother saving, just buy anything you want on a plastic card', wrote one journalist. 'If your credit limit is used up, simply take out another card'.[76]

Modernising Retail Credit

In 1984, *Business Review Weekly* (*BRW*) published a consumer panel's ranking of credit and charge cards, set out from the most to the least prestigious. Amex headed the list, followed by Diners Club, Mastercard, David Jones/Georges, Bankcard, and, finally, Myercard.[77] The position of David Jones/Georges store cards at the top of the local offerings reflected the position of each store in the long-established hierarchy of Australian department stores, in terms of image and pricing. Myercard's position towards the bottom of the list (followed only by the moribund cash order) reflected Myer's own analysis of the store's status: 'We aren't upmarket, but we also don't compete with the discounters such as Kmart, Target or Big W'.[78]

Two years before the publication of this ranking, Myer had undertaken a major review of its credit facilities. Together with the store's recent acquisition, Grace Bros Sydney, Myer's credit operations were, at the time, the single biggest charge card operation in Australia after Bankcard, with 2.9 million cards on 1.4 million accounts. We might take this to mean that Myer would be fairly sanguine about its lowly position on the prestige ladder, but developments in 1982, in particular, news of the impending arrival of Visa and Mastercard in Australia, had compelled Myer to review its credit processes.[79]

Early in 1982, the retailer set up a Financial Services Task Force to conduct a review and report back by the end of the year.[80] The Chair of the Task Force noted that providing a line of credit had always been a necessary feature of department store business because 'customers had few if any alternative sources of credit and retailers needed to develop sales'.[81] With the entry of Bankcard and US cards into the market, that was no longer the case and Myer needed to take steps to improve and modernise its credit system.[82]

In September 1982, the store shifted its Entry Account to the revolving credit Optional Payment Account (OPA) to bring their 'entry accounts into line with current practices in the retailing industry':[83] *Retail Trader* had recommended the shift to its subscribers as far back as1959.[84] Myer's slow uptake of automation such as data processing compared with its competitors meant that any errors made by Myer's system were less acceptable to consumers than they had previously been. Myer's General Manager Kevin Fuller observed that 'we receive so many complaints ... it is time we did something about it'.[85]

After surveying 3000 respondents, the Financial Services Review task-force reported in December 1982.[86] They found that, after Bankcard, Myer's card operations, which included Grace Bros, were the biggest in Australia with 2.9 million cards on 1.4 million accounts in 1982. However, Bankcard was eroding Myer's credit base, despite being more costly to use. Once seen as 'a pacesetter', Myer credit was now seen as outdated and many of those surveyed perceived Myer's 'plastic' as 'nothing'.[87]

Designated the 'Credit Project', the restructuring of Myer Credit Operations was launched in November 1983 with a document entitled 'Credit—The Future'.[88] The document briefly outlined the history of the Myer system—Myer Entry Accounts dated back to the early 1920s, it reported, with the first plastic credit card introduced in the early 1970s, although the 'occasional steel plate is still seen'.[89] Some automation had occurred at Myer, but the majority of functions were 'still labour intensive'.[90]

The researchers had studied approaches to credit by overseas management, finding a 'more liberal attitude to credit granting' than in Australia.[91] Other findings included the importance of target marketing and positioning credit 'in a way that was compatible with the image and position of the retailer'; the need for swifter customer updates; and the 'integration, liaison, cooperation, and coordination of credit operations with merchandising policy makers'. On the existing credit arrangements, the study found those under 30 were reluctant to use store credit.[92]

Respondents gave two reasons for preferring Bankcard to Myercard. First was Bankcard's mobility, the fact that it could be used across a range of stores, rather than being restricted to one store. Second, Bankcard offered customers a higher credit limit than that offered by retail store cards such as Myer. This made Bankcard a popular choice for larger items, which was impacting Myer's hire purchase business—Bankcard's flexibility enabled customers to pay off their debt more quickly than did Myer's fixed payment system.

Finding that 'there were no real barriers' to the general acceptance of revolving credit, the study argued that Bankcard had a key role in a store's 'acceptability' and that its continued rejection by Myer would drive away some customers 'at least as much from resentment as from financial necessity'.[93] However, with the arrival of Visa and Mastercard, the study expected Bankcard's growth 'to remain stagnant', which would open up 'unprecedented opportunities in 1984 and beyond' for a new national card to fill the gap between Amex (400,000 users) and Bankcard (4 million users), although Roberts 'didn't think Myer could make money by entering the Credit Card business—nobody does'.[94] That said, the revolution in retail technology offered 'a new business opportunity, building logically on existing assets and skills', and there were 'many other prospects' available to Myer 'including owned in-store ATMs, which could be prospered [sic]'.[95] Also, by moving to data processing, Myer hoped to reduce the cost of its credit operations from 6 % [of its profit margin] to 5%.[96]

The taskforce had also been charged with exploring the replacement of Myer's in-house credit operations (The Myer Limited or TML) with a partnership with an outside credit provider such as Visa, Amex, or HFC Financial Services, in the hope that a Myer-Visa card could be used by Myer customers 'to satisfy their travel and entertainment needs'.[97] Indeed, in 1982, Visa had approached Myer, offering to partner with the store so it might issue a credit card with the Myer logo and a small Visa symbol that would provide Myer customers with 'all Visa services'.[98] However, the study did not recommend partnering with an outside credit provider because it would cost Myer an extra 2% on every transaction to use the Visa brand; Amex was 'not an attractive option' for the same reason.[99] Myer Credit Ltd was established in May 1984, and Myercard—'in its present form'—launched, replacing the 30-day Entry Account and the PBA.[100] Myer Credit Ltd changed its name to Australian Retail Financial Network Ltd (ARFN) in 1987 and the following year it integrated its financial services with those of Grace Bros Sydney, creating one of Australia's largest financial services operations.[101]

Behind Myer's credit review was the barrage of complaints the store continued to receive about its existing credit facilities.[102] The recent merger with Grace Bros Sydney had led to confusion and customer complaints, particularly about the lack of flexibility of Myer's credit offering.[103] Alan J. Robison—a Myer account holder and shareholder—spelled out the problems the merger had caused. His main complaint was that the stores that 'had been sold to Grace Bros' would not accept his Myer charge account, because Myer's computer program was not compatible with Grace Bros program. 'Surely one does not have to rely on computers even though it is 1984', he observed. Faced with the rejection of his Myercard, Robison had been told that, if he wished to apply for a Grace Bros account, he would have 'no trouble obtaining one'. 'I don't want an account with Grace Bros', he told Myer. Clearly frustrated, he pointed out that 'your opposition store', David Jones, seemed to have been able to cope with the

Georges merger very easily. 'I have been able to use my George's [sic] credit card throughout Australia on travels'.[104] Robison was also unhappy with the administration of his account, as were other Myer customers.[105] The Myer monthly statement was 'very badly designed', according to Robison. In particular, it was 'very confusing to the uninitiated'. On two occasions, he recalled, members of his staff had paid the minimum monthly balance by mistake.[106]

Any hope that shifting to the new, centralised system might stem the tide of customer complaints was misplaced, at least in the short term. The new card offered the approved customer entry to an exclusive club with access to special offers and item information unavailable to the general customer. Approval was concrete evidence of their financial security, and the cardholder felt trusted and valued by the store. However, these positive emotions were precarious. They depended on card authorisation procedures operating swiftly and flawlessly, and on the aura of security and wellbeing surrounding possession of the card being reinforced across every transaction.[107] If a problem arose with the card, especially instore (and, therefore, in public), it could lead to feelings of rejection, embarrassment, and shame:

> when I presented my card to charge a purchase, I suffered the acute embarrassment of being told that my card was no longer able to be used. ... The immediate implication to customers standing within earshot is that my credit is unsure! Whilst this was handled with courtesy, the sales assistant had no option but to advise me of the situation BUT this does little to change the raised eyebrows of nearby customers! I felt both humiliated and angry ....[108]

Complaints about the new system also reveal a hierarchy within 'the exclusive club'—the store valued some cardholders more than others. At the top sat the shareholders, especially those who were personally acquainted with Myer's chairman, Baillieu Myer. When Sydney shareholder Peter R. Graham Q.C. wrote in to complain about the credit changes, he included a hand-written note to 'Dear Bails': 'If shareholders don't talk up the company, customers might in a different way!', he warned the chairman.[109] Graham saw the changes as a shift away from Myer's core business: 'It surprises me that Myer should choose to prefer money lending to the provision of retail facilities for which it has been renowned'.[110] It was left to the credit manager to explain to Graham that the growing demand for and widespread use of credit facilities had forced Myer to consider the overall cost of providing these services. The store had chosen to accept third-party credit facilities and introduce an in-house credit facility, Myercard. Addressing the accusation of moneylending, the manager assured Graham that a 'usurious approach' would be in conflict with the store's intentions.[111]

Other shareholders took their complaints directly to the chairman. Julie Lidgett of Toorak, for example, leveraged her friendship with 'Dear Baills' when she raised the administration of her credit account in June 1984. 'Dear Julie', Baillieu Myer replied, 'There are still some bugs in our new system and one of them seems to have found its way to you'.[112] The following month, he explained to Sir Richard Eggleston Q.C. that 'a new accounting system has recently been introduced which has created several unexpected problems which we are making every effort to overcome'.[113] In July, Brian D. Marks wrote to Baillieu Myer after receiving a statement for his recently closed Entry Account. 'I always believe that when matters get to a silly state, then one is entitled to advise the Chief Executive with a view to having inefficient areas rectified', he wrote. Marks had been told by a manager that the mistake had occurred because the credit department was 'snowed under'.[114]

Complaints from non-shareholder customers were copied to Baillieu Myer. These tended to emphasise the customers' lengthy relationship with the store and linked problems with the new card operations to the general demise of Myer's customer service.[115] As a loyal customer of the store since 1971, P.V. Subramaniam was disappointed that anomalies with his credit account had not been resolved:

> Probably the loss of my custom may not affect the operations of Myer, but I am very disappointed with the service I receive in any Myer store these days. ... I look for service when I am in a store, and above all, a hassle-free accounts department. If you value my custom here is the opportunity to show it.[116]

The report came out in the context of major changes to credit legislation with the passing of the Credit Act 1984, which introduced uniform laws across New South Wales, Victoria, Western Australia, and the ACT.[117] According to the second reading of the Bill in the Victorian Parliament, 'Australia was the third most credit orientated country in the world after the United States of America and Canada', and, given the major developments in the credit industry in recent years, amendments to the previous Act (1981) were necessary. When that was being developed, Bankcard had been the only widely available form of revolving credit, but now new credit cards had emerged. The new legislation reflected this, with 'one of the most important changes' being 'a much broader definition of what constitutes continuing credit'.[118] Myer continued to work to modernise its credit offering.

In their investigation of what they call 'networks of desire', Kozinets et al. argue that technology can increase the passion to consume, that 'networks of desire create a passionate new universe of technologically enhanced desire'.[119] Australian consumers' response to the technology of the new credit systems of the 1970s and 1980s supports this thesis. Alastair Graham recalls that for 'a majority of people who had never had a credit card, it was something that was convenient and was issued as such, as a convenience to make shopping easier and lively and dynamic, and all these sorts of things'.[120] With shopping rituals energised by innovative machinery that facilitated instant gratification, as well as an object—the credit card—that gave the consumer the chance to signal their place in the consumer hierarchy on a daily basis, Australian shoppers' 'passion to consume' reached new levels. Grace Bros picked up on this more pleasurable emotion attached to using credit, reminding its staff of the store's motto: 'Credit is a pleasure at Grace Bros'; Myer told its 'VIP' card holders 'Want it? Charge It'.[121]

Moreover, participation in new credit systems (including the revamped department store cards) became a means of delivering to consumers a sense of belonging to an exclusive club of like-minded shoppers. An example of this was Grace Bros' GeeBees card, which was targeted towards women under 30. Like other department stores (Myer's Miss Shop, for example), Grace Bros identified women aged 18–30 as a burgeoning market and opened a fashion department aimed solely at them. To shop at GeeBees, as the department was named, young women could use their GeeBee's charge card, which was designed differently from the standard Grace Bros charge card and marketed to young women as 'A Girl's Best Friend'.[122] Instant gratification was at the forefront of the marketing appeal. 'Nail Liberation. Why Wait?' the application form asked, as it promoted savings on a manicure using the language of the women's movement.[123] Another example from this period was Grace Bros' promotion of the Presidential Card, one of Australia's earliest loyalty programmes. Aimed at business executives and with links to the Sheraton Hotel chain, the Presidential Card offered individual Grace Bros customers savings on travel, dining, and entertainment, as well as the status reassurance of belonging to a club of successful business leaders—'presidents'—with Tony Ingleton, the founder of the loyalty programme, as the model.[124]

One hundred years before the launch of the GeeBee's card, 'A Storekeeper' had observed that 'Once a person has opened an account with a retailing house, it is generally taken for granted by both parties that the more business done between them the better'.[125] With the introduction of Bankcard, such loyalty could no longer be assumed. More working Australians than ever before now had the means and the desire to buy on credit, but they also had the freedom to shop around. The following chapter will examine how those managing retail credit and its marketing geared up to ensure that a department store's customers would keep coming back.

Notes

1. Peter Weekes, 'Bankcard Checks Out', *Age*, 3 February 2006.
2. Michael J. Etzel, 'Revealing Study of Bank Credit Card Plans', *Australian Retailing*, September 1970, 19; 'Huge Increase in Bank Credit Cards', *Australian Retailing*, November 1971, 8; 'Charging By Card', *Sydney Morning Herald*, 14 November 1973, 3; 'American Express to Introduce Credit Card', *Sydney Morning Herald*, 11 January 1974.
3. Irwin Ross, 'The Credit Card's Painful Coming of Age', *Australian Retailing*, April 1972, 10–17.
4. Alastair Graham interviewed by Robert Crawford, 7 July 2023; Wallace Crouch, 'Bankcard Opens the Door to Instant Credit', *Sydney Morning Herald*, 4 October 1974; Weekes, 'Bankcard Checks Out'.
5. Lisa A. Petrison, Robert C. Blatterberg, Paul Wang, 'Database Marketing Past, Present, and Future', *Journal of Direct Marketing* 11, no. 4 (Fall 1997): 109–25, 110; Daniel Snyder, 'From List Fatigue to Relationship Marketing', *Direct Marketing* 60, no. 7 (Nov. 1997): 57–60.
6. Petrison, Blatterberg, and Wang, 'Database Marketing Past, Present, and Future', 112; Sally Harridge-March, 'Direct Marketing and Relationships', *Direct Marketing* 2, no. 4 (2008): 192–98, 193.
7. Snyder, 'From List Fatigue to Relationship Marketing', 59.
8. 'Bank Card Conference', *The American Banker* 16 October 1985; Jason Crisp, 'Cut-price Solution for Faster Mails', *Financial Times,* 24 July 1985.
9. Jack Weatherford, *The History of Money: From Sandstone to Cyberspace* (New York: Crown Publishers Inc., 1997), 229.

10. Cynthia Rigg, 'Amex Veteran to Direct Mail Order Business', *Crain's New York Business*, 8 September 1986, 7; Michael P. Sullivan, 'Direct Response', *The American Banker*, 25 August 1982. See Andrew N. Case, '"The Solid Gold Mailbox:" Direct Mail and the Changing Nature of Buying and Selling', *History of Retailing and Consumption* 1, no. 1 (2015): 28–46.
11. Rigg, 'Amex Veteran to Direct Mail Order Business', 7.
12. Maurizio Lazaretto, *The Making of the Indebted Man: An Essay on the Neoliberal Condition* (Los Angeles: Semiotexte, 2012), 20.
13. Lana Swartz, 'Gendered Transactions', *Women's Studies Quarterly* 42, 1 & 2 (Spring/Summer 2014) 140; Michel Foucault, 'Technologies of the Self', in *Technologies of the Self: A Seminar with Michel Foucault*, ed. Luther H. Martin, Huck Gutman and Patick H. Hutton (London: Tavistock Publications, 1988).
14. Robert Gottleibsen and David Lindorff, 'Identity Is The Name of the Game', *Business Review Weekly*, 20–26 October 1984, 84, 86.
15. Weatherford, *The History of Money*, 228–29. https://journals.sagepub.com/doi/full/10.1177/2053951720907632
16. Weatherford, *The History of Money*, 228–29.
17. Weatherford, *The History of Money*, 229; Claire Tsosie, 'How "Platinum" And "Gold" Credit Cards Lost Their Shine', *Forbes*, 12 May 2016, https://www.forbes.com/sites/clairetsosie/2016/05/12/how-platinum-and-gold-credit-cards-lost-their-shine/.
18. Weatherford, *The History of Money*, 229; Tsosie, 'How "Platinum" And "Gold" Credit Cards Lost Their Shine'.
19. Tsosie, 'How "Platinum" And "Gold" Credit Cards Lost Their Shine'; https://www.americanexpress.com/en-us/newsroom/articles/amex-for-business/american-express-celebrates-172-years-of-powerful-backing.html.
20. 'The Complete History of Credit Cards, from Antiquity to Today', The Points Guy. https://www.forbes.com/sites/clairetsosie/2016/05/12/how-platinum-and-gold-credit-cards-lost-their-shine/.
21. https://www.verywellmind.com/the-color-psychology-of-black-2795814,
22. 'MasterCard: The Future of Money', 84, www.brandsearch.superbrands.com; Richard Brass, 'Visa to Offer "Gold Card" Credit Facility', *AFR*, 23 May 1989; Weatherford, *The History of Money*, 229
23. Tsosie, 'How "Platinum" And "Gold" Credit Cards Lost Their Shine'.
24. Tsosie, 'How "Platinum" And "Gold" Credit Cards Lost Their Shine'.
25. Weatherford, *The History of Money*, 229.
26. Plato, *Republic*, Book 3, 415.

27. Mike Szydlowski, 'Why are Olympic Medals Gold, Silver and Bronze?' *Columbia Daily Tribune*, 11 February 2014.
28. Jeffrey I. Meikle, *American Plastic: A Cultural History* (New Brunswick, N.J.: Rutgers University Press 1995); Mary Warner Marien, 'How the Word "Plastic" Became a Complex Metaphor', *The Christian Science Monitor*, 23 May 1996; 'The Exciting World of Plastics', *The Retail Trader*, January 1964, 26.
29. 'The Fantastic Plastic Maze', *Sydney Morning Herald*, 14 November 1984, 51; Jane Hutchinson, 'The Best Credit Card Deals In the Plastic Jungle', *Sydney Morning Herald*, 15 April 1987, 30; Beverley Head, 'EFTPOS Triples In A Plastic-Happy Country', *The Australian Financial Review*, 26 October 1987, 49; Yvonne Preston, 'Paying With Plastic Isn't So Fantastic', *Sydney Morning Herald*, 20 April 1988, 18; Tony Kaye, 'Slippery Plastic Path To Youth Bankruptcy', *The Australian Financial Review*, 6 July 1988, 1; Peter Weekes, 'Bankcard Bound for the Shredder', *Sydney Morning Herald*, 3 February 2006.
30. Alastair Graham, interviewed by Robert Crawford, 22 July 2023.
31. 'Who Offers Metal Credit Cards in Australia', https://www.canstar.com.au/credit-cards/metal-credit-cards/#are-there-really-metal-credit-cards?, accessed 26 July 2025; 'Is the American Express Platinum Card Metal?', https://wallethub.com/answers/cc/is-the-american-express-platinum-card-metal-1000529-2140781879/#:~:text=The%20American%20Express%20 Platinum%20card%20is%20made %20of%20stainless%20steel,it%20will%20be%20more%20durable, accessed 26 July 2025.
32. https://www.luxurycard.com/titaniumcard, accessed 26 July 2025; https://www.qantasmoney.com/credit-cards/premier-titanium/features-and-benefits#titanium-status-credits, accessed 26 July 2025.
33. 'American Express to Introduce Credit Card', *Sydney Morning Herald*, 11 January 1974.
34. Ian Hicks, 'Making a $700 Foray with a Bankcard', *Sydney Morning Herald*, 11 October 1974.
35. In 1975, there was discussion about the scheme 'going international', 'Bankcard Likely To Go "Abroad"', *Sydney Morning Herald*, 9 November 1975.
36. 'Making A $700 Foray with A Bankcard', *Sydney Morning Herald*, 11 October 1974, 7.
37. 'Wran Attacks "Sloppy" Bankcard Scheme', *Sydney Morning Herald*, 12 October 1974, 3; Wallace Crouch, 'A Bankcard Can Buy A Hat', *Sydney Morning Herald*, 5 October 1974; A.E. Carson, 'Supplying Credit Costs Cash', *Australian Retailing*, May 1970, 14–15.

38. 'Wran Attacks'; 'Bankcard Opens the Door to Instant Credit', *Sydney Morning Herald*, 4 October 1974.
39. 'Bankcards Galore, Even for the Dead', *Sydney Morning Herald*, 10 October 1974.
40. 'Bankcards: Youth Charged', *Sydney Morning Herald*, 11 October 1974; 'Bankcard', *Sydney Morning Herald*, 16 October 1974, 17; 'Cleaner Fined for Bankcard Fraud', *Sydney Morning Herald*, 18 October 1974; 'Bankcard Charge', *Sydney Morning Herald*, 20 October 1974.
41. 'Bankcard Charge'.
42. 'Bankcard Liability Ad Infinitum?', *Sydney Morning Herald*, 14 October 1974, 6; 'Making A $700 Foray with A Bankcard', *Sydney Morning Herald*, 11 October 1974, 7; 'Bankcards Galore, Even for the Dead', *Sydney Morning Herald*, 10 October 1974.
43. 'Bankcard How One Could Hit Your Pocket', *Sydney Morning Herald*, 15 October 1974; 'A Bankcard Can Buy a Hat, Coat, Dress but Not Groceries'; 'World's First Data Bank Control Law', *Australian Retailing*, December 1973, 23–24.
44. 'Bankcards Criticised: "Hamhandedness By Banks"', *Sydney Morning Herald*, 16 October 1974, 14.
45. 'Wran Attacks "Sloppy" Bankcard Scheme', *Sydney Morning Herald*, 12 October 1974, 3.
46. Wallace Crouch, 'Bankcard Opens the Door to Instant Credit', *Sydney Morning Herald*, 4 October 1974.
47. 'American Express to Introduce Credit Card', *Sydney Morning Herald*, 11 January 1974; 'America's New Social Issue: Women Now Want Credit Liberated …', *Australian Retailing*, June–July 1972, 15–16; Jackie Dickenson, '"The Poor Man's Overdraft": A Longer History of Retail Credit in Australia', *History Australia* 21, no. 4 (June 2024): 546–65.
48. Prime Minister's Press Conference, Canberra, Tuesday 15 October 1974, 4–5.
49. 'America's New Social Issues: Women Now Want Credit Liberated …' *Australian Retailing*, June-July 1972, 15-16; Marilyn Lake, *Getting Equal: The History of Australian Feminism* (Sydney: Allen & Unwin, 1999) Chapters 9 and 10.
50. Jane O'Reilly, 'Women and Money', *Australian Women's Weekly*, 22 March 1978, 148.
51. 'Double Bed and Separate Bank Accounts', *Australian Women's Weekly*, 30 October 1974, 35.
52. 'Facts About Credit', *Australian Women's Weekly*, 3 August 1966, 11.
53. 'Smart Cheque Book Cover', *Western Herald*, 9 February 1968, 5.
54. Swartz, 'Gendered Transactions', 147.

55. Ruth Dewsbury, 'The Day the Nibbles Become A Bite', *Sydney Morning Herald*, 19 August 1986, 17; State Library of Victoria, Coles-Myer [hereafter, CM], MS 13468, Box 1370, A.J. (Tony) Roberts (Chief Executive) File – Credit, 1982–1983, 'Financial Services: Environmental Conditions', 1; Financial Services Review, December 1982, Survey, 3000 respondents.
56. Jen Nolan interviewed by Robert Crawford, 13 July 2023.
57. Lizzie Bartlett, interviewed by Robert Crawford, 13 July 2023.
58. Michele Matthews, interviewed by Robert Crawford,13 July 2023.
59. Elizabeth Pallet, interviewed by Robert Crawford,13 July 2023.
60. Sofia Russo, interviewed by Robert Crawford, 13 July 2023.
61. Laura Peden, interviewed by Robert Crawford, 13 July 2023.
62. 'A Bankcard Can Buy a Hat'.
63. CM, Box 1370, A. J. (Tony) Roberts (Chief Executive) File – Credit, 1982–1983, 7.
64. 'David Jones to Accept Bankcard', *Sydney Morning Herald*, 3 December 1974, 3; CM, Box 1370, A.J. Roberts, Financial Services, 6 July 1982, 7.
65. Maurice Dunlevy, 'Multi-million Dollar', *Sydney Morning Herald*, 2 February 1975, 10.
66. 'Grace Bros to Accept Bankcard', *Sydney Morning Herald*, 6 March 1975, 23; *Sydney Morning Herald*, 8 April 1975, 16.
67. 'Bankcard Extends to All Parts of NSW', *Sydney Morning Herald*, 4 May 1976, 12.
68. 'Myer Accepts Bankcard', *Sydney Morning Herald*, 6 May 1978, 29; Paul Flavel, *John Martin's: the Story of South Australia's Beloved Department Store* (Melbourne: Broadcast Books, 2024), 108.
69. CM, Box 4203, 'Bankcard File: Date Range 1973–1980', 1–2.
70. 'Bankers Defend Bankcard Rate', *Sydney Morning Herald*, 10 July 1979, 9.
71. 'Labor Pledge to Cut Bankcard's 18pc Interest', *Sydney Morning Herald*, 9 July 1979, 1.
72. Amy Bradney-George, 'Credit Card History – A timeline from the 1900s to now', *Finder*, 22 December 2023, https://www.finder.com.au/credit-cards/credit-card-history, accessed 1 August 2024.
73. Ruth Ostrow, 'American Distress', *AFR*, 4 December 1987, 1; Bradney-George, 'Credit Card History'.
74. Colleen Ryan, 'Personal Finance', *Sydney Morning Herald*, 4 March 1984, 83.
75. Ostrow, 'American Distress'.
76. Michael Laurence, 'Spend Today, Regret It Tomorrow', *Sydney Morning Herald*, 10 January 1987, 11; Jane Hutchinson, 'The Best Credit Card Deals in the Plastic Jungle', *Sydney Morning Herald*, 15 April 1987, 30.

77. Robert Gottleibsen and David Lindorff, 'Identity Is The Name of the Game', *BRW*, 20–26 October 1984, 84, 86. Visa was not mentioned in the list, but it is safe to assume that it ranked alongside Mastercard.
78. Neil Shoebridge, 'A New Togetherness Comes to Myer and Grace Bros', *AFR*, 19 January 1990.
79. State Library of Victoria, Records of Coles-Myer Ltd. and its predecessors, ca. 1840–ca.1990 (hereafter CM), MS 13468, Box 1370, A.J. Roberts, Wallet 4; 'Higher Bid in Offing As Myer Shares Leap', *Sydney Morning Herald*, 30 July 1985, 14.
80. CM, Box 1370, A.J. Roberts, Wallet 4, 3.
81. CM, Box 1370, A.J. Roberts, Wallet 4.
82. CM, Box 1370, A.J. Roberts, Wallet 4, Financial Services, 6 July 1982.
83. CM, Box 1370, Draft 4, September 23, 1982, 'Advertisement to Myer Entry Account Customers', No. 1.
84. 'The Mechanics of Credit', *Retail Trader*, October 1959, 48.
85. CM, Box 1370, Kevin W. Fuller Memorandum, 'Analysis of Credit Customer Complaints', 21 July 1983.
86. CM, Box 1370, A.J. Roberts, 'Financial Services: Environmental Conditions', 1
87. CM Box 1370, A J. Roberts, Wallet 4, 'Credit: The Future', 6.
88. CM, Box 1370, Fuller to Whyte (Grace Bros), Subject Myer Credit Ltd setting up. 'Restructuring of Myer Credit Operations'; Interoffice Memo, Whyte to Michael Grace on changes, 15 November 1983, 1.
89. CM, Box 1370, 'Factsheet. Myer Entry Account', 23 September 1982, 2; CM, Box 4203, 'Australian Retail Financial Network Ltd Company Milestones', 15 July 1992, 1.
90. CM, Box 4203, 'Australian Retail Financial Network Ltd Company Milestones', 1.
91. CM, Box 1370, Fuller to Whyte (Grace Bros). Subject Myer Credit Ltd setting up; 'Restructuring of Myer Credit Operations', Interoffice Memo, Whyte to Grace on changes, 15 November 1983, 1.
92. 'Credit: The Future'.
93. CM, Box 1370, A.J. Roberts, Wallet 4, 6.
94. CM Box 1370, Memo, A.J. Roberts to S.B. Myer, 10 November 1983, 1.
95. Memo, A.J. Roberts to S.B. Myer.
96. CM, Box 1370, A.J. Roberts, Wallet 4, 3.
97. CM, Box 1370, A.J. Roberts, Wallet 4, 12.
98. CM, Box 1370, 1982, Introduction, 1.
99. CM, Box 1370, A.J. Roberts, Wallet 4, 12.
100. CM, Box 4203, 'Australian Retail Financial Network Ltd Company Milestones', 1–2; CM, Box 2881, Myer Credit Ltd, On-line Computer Systems,15, n.d.

101. https://casetext.com/case/paysys-intl-inc-v-atos-se-worldline-sa-atos-it-servs-ltd/, accessed 15 August 2024.
102. CM, Box 1370, 'Report on Credit – VICTAS', 11 March 1983, 1–7.
103. Mark McGinness, 'Born To Run the Grace Bros Empire', *Sydney Morning Herald*, 26 August 2009.
104. CM, Box 3469, 'Customer Complaints Regarding Myer Credit Cards and Other Matters: 1983–1984', Wallet 1, Alan J. Robison to Baillieu Myer, 28 February 1984.
105. CM, Box 1370, Kevin W. Fuller, Memorandum, 'Analysis of Credit Customer Complaints', 21 July 1983.
106. CM, Box 3469, 'Customer Complaints Regarding Myer Credit Cards and Other Matters: 1983–1984', Wallet 1, Alan J. Robison to Baillieu Myer, 28 February 1984.
107. CM, Box 1370, 'Australian Retail Financial Network Ltd Company Milestones', 15 July 1992, 2; Berndt to Roberts, 20 September 1982; Wallet 2, Baillieu Myer decisions.
108. CM, Box 3469, June Uski, to Baillieu Myer, 22 September 1984.
109. CM, Box 3469, Peter R. Graham Q.C. to Baillieu Myer, 23 May 1984; CM, Box 3469, Peter R. Graham Q. C. to R.B. Mudgway, 23 May 1984.
110. CM, Box 3469, Graham to Mudgway, 23 May 1984.
111. CM, Box 3469, R.B. Mudgway to Peter R. Graham Q.C., 17 May 1984.
112. CM, Box 3469, Baillieu Myer to Mrs Julie Lidgett, 4 July 1984.
113. CM, Box 3469, R.B. Mudgway to Sir Richard Eggleston Q.C., 5 July 1984.
114. CM, Box 3469, 'Customer Complaints Regarding Myer Credit Cars & Other Matters: 1983–1984', Brian D. Marks to Baillieu Myer, 6 July 1984; Philomena Kaarma to Baillieu Myer, 13 July 1984; W.G. Kent to S.B. Myer, 27 July 1984.
115. CM, Box 3469, Reg Mitchell, 14 May 1984; Hodgetts, 17 April 1984.
116. CM, Box 3469, P.V. Subramanian to Accounts Manager, 12 July 1984.
117. Victorian Government, Hansard, Assembly, Credit Bill 'Uniform Laws', 22 March 1984, Credit Bill, 3402–3407. Second Reading, Credit Acts 1978, 1981, and 1984; Victoria, Credit Act, No. 10097 of 1984.
118. Victorian Government, Hansard, Assembly, Credit Bill 'Uniform Laws', 22 March 1984, Credit Bill, 3402–3407. Second Reading,
119. Kozinets, Patterson, and Ashman, 'Networks of Desire', 659.
120. Graham, interview.
121. CM, Box 3214, 'Grace Bros. and Service', n.d., 4; CM, Box 2966, 'Want It? Charge It', c.1980–1990; Fiona Guthrie, 'Debt is Our Drug and Credit Pushers Are to Blame', *Courier Mail*, 5 July 2004, 13.
122. 'Shape Up with Helancyl', *Sydney Morning Herald*, 20 November 1983, 136.

123. CM, Box 6, Wallet 1, n.d.
124. CM, Box 6, Wallet 2, Leaflet 'The Presidential Card', 1988; Tony Gray, 'Disney A Winner for President', *BRW*, 17 March 1989, 72.
125. 'Limiting Retail Buyers' Credit', *Goulburn Herald*, 9 November 1889, 3.

References

Australian Retailing. Sydney: Australian Council of Retailers 1967–1973.

Case, Andrew N. '"The Solid Gold Mailbox:" Direct Mail and the Changing Nature of Buying and Selling in the Postwar United States', *History of Retailing and Consumption* 1, no. 1 (2015): 28–46. https://doi.org/10.1080/2373518X.2015.1012863

Flavel, Paul. *John Martin's: The Story of South Australia's Beloved Department Store* (Melbourne: Broadcast Books, 2024).

Harridge-March, Sally. 'Direct Marketing and Relationships: An Opinion Piece', *Direct Marketing* 2, no. 4 (2008): 192–98. https://doi.org/10.1108/17505930810931008

Kozinets, Robert, Anthony Patterson and Rachel Ashman. 'Networks of Desire: How Technology Increases Our Passion to Consume', *Journal of Consumer Research* 43 (2017): 659–82. https://doi.org/10.1093/jcr/ucw061

Lake, Marilyn. *Getting Equal: The History of Australian Feminism*. Sydney: Allen & Unwin, 1999.

Lazaretto, Maurizio. *The Making of the Indebted Man: An Essay on the Neoliberal Condition*. Los Angeles: Semiotexte, 2012.

Magarey, Susan. 'Beauty Becomes Political: Beginnings of the Women's Liberation Movement in Australia', *Australian Feminist Studies* 33, no. 95 (2018): 31–44. https://doi.org/10.1080/08164649.2018.1498738

Marien, Mary Warner. 'How the Word "Plastic" Became a Complex Metaphor: From Environmentally Safe, To Counterfeit, To Adaptable'. *The Christian Science Monitor*, 23 May 1996. https://www.csmonitor.com/1996/0523/052396.feat.books.1.html

Martin, Luther H., Huck Gutman and Patick H. Hutton, eds. *Technologies of the Self: A Seminar with Michel Foucault*. London: Tavistock Publications, 1988.

Meikle, Jeffrey I. *American Plastic: A Cultural History*. New Brunswick, N.J.: Rutgers University Press 1995.

Petrison Lisa A., Robert C. Blatterberg and Paul Wang. 'Database Marketing Past, Present, and Future', *Journal of Direct Marketing* 11, no. 4 (Fall 1997): 109–25. https://doi.org/10.1002/dir.4000070306

Records of Coles-Myer Ltd. and its predecessors, ca. 1840–1990, MS13468, State Library of Victoria.

Retail Trader. Sydney: Retail Traders Association of NSW, 1921–2006.

Snyder, Daniel. 'From List Fatigue to Relationship Marketing: the Credit Card Industry is Reassessing Its Direct Mail Strategies', *Direct Marketing* 60, no. 7 (Nov. 1997): 57–60. link.gale.com/apps/doc/A20242697/AONE?u=unimelb&sid=bookmark-AONE&xid=be42b5e7

Swartz, Lana. 'Gendered Transactions: Identity and Payment at Mid-century', *Women's Studies Quarterly* 42, 1 & 2 (Spring/Summer 2014) 140. https://www.jstor.org/stable/24364916

Tomlinson, Alan. *Consumption, Identity and Style*. London: Routledge, 1990.

Vihma, Susann, ed. *Objects and Images: Studies in Design and Advertising*. Helsinki: University of Industrial Art, 1992.

Weatherford, Jack. *The History of Money: From Sandstone to Cyberspace*. New York: Crown Publishers Inc., 1997.

CHAPTER 7

The Loyalty Ladder

Abstract The wide acceptance of Bankcard undermined loyalty to a single department store. In response, department stores geared up to ensure their customers would keep coming back. Coupons, stamps, and branded charge cards had long been used to build customer loyalty, but the schemes of the 1990s were unprecedented. Facilitated by technological innovations such as mass data processing, the new loyalty culture engaged more Australians than ever in the pleasures and pitfalls of retail credit. Loyalty programmes became an additional means for retailers to exploit status anxiety for profit and a significant feature of 'aspirational' Australia. The promise of rewards encouraged consumers to shop using their linked credit card, drawing more Australians into credit card use and the debt this might incur.

Keywords Credit • Retail • Relationship marketing • Loyalty • Data processing • Status anxiety • Australian history

The history of retail credit in the last decade of the twentieth century is inseparable from the history of the loyalty programme. The shift to credit cards that could be used across stores—Bankcard, Visa, and Mastercard—drove department stores to explore new ways of connecting with and holding on to customers. They turned to the Flybuys model that offered

J. Dickenson, *Credit and the Australian Department Store Since 1900*, https://doi.org/10.1007/978-3-032-16612-8_7

members free points towards air travel when they made purchases at participating outlets using a National Australia Bank (NAB) credit card.[1] The model enabled the special treatment that department stores once reserved for their charge card clients and extended it to the growing mass of credit card users, especially those who spent up big. The more members spent with their linked credit card, the more rewards they earned. This helped entrench credit card use in Australia, as well as the debt such use might incur.

The new emphasis on loyalty programmes emerged from a significant development in the marketing industry. In 1983, Leonard L. Berry, a US marketing academic, delivered a paper to the American Marketing Association's (AMA's) 'Services Marketing' conference entitled 'Relationship Marketing'.[2] Defining 'Relationship Marketing' as 'attracting, maintaining and … enhancing customer relationships', Berry argued that attracting new customers was only an intermediate step in the marketing process and the primary objective should be retaining the customers that businesses already had.[3] Berry's intervention constituted 'a major shift in marketing theory and practice', and relationship marketing had 'undeniably become the hot topic of the marketing discipline during the 1990s'.[4]

Relationship marketing was not a new phenomenon, however. As we have seen, from the introduction of charge cards at the end of the 1920s, high-end stores used the promise of exclusive benefits to attract and reward loyal customers. Moreover, from at least the turn of the twentieth century, the lower end of the market used loyalty schemes too, in the form of coupons and trading stamps. Before examining the explosion of loyalty programmes in the 1990s, this chapter returns to the early years of the department store in Australia to explore how stores used these sales promotion devices to hold on to their customers. These devices helped build consumers' expectations that their loyalty to a store would be rewarded, and, at the same time, led them to question the value of such rewards.

Coupons and Trading Stamps

By the turn of the twentieth century, consumers were enthusiastically collecting coupons every time they made a purchase, and, when they had collected enough, they would be rewarded with a discount or free gift. These early loyalty schemes were often cooperative enterprises, meaning organisations could buy in bulk, keep costs down, and pass the savings on to customers; some also rewarded customers for paying with cash.[5] The Green Coupon Scheme was one popular example of this cooperative model. Customers received one coupon for every sixpence spent at participating shops, which they then pasted in a booklet. Once the booklet was full, they took it to a Green Coupon Office where they could exchange the coupons for household goods, such as small appliances, Manchester, crockery, and cutlery.[6]

Competing retailers (including the Retail Traders' Association and the Anti-Coupon Leagues that formed in NSW and Western Australia) lobbied to ban coupon/trading stamps because they considered them 'a hindrance to ordinary trading operations'.[7] They were a hindrance for two reasons: (1) Coupons disadvantaged the small trader who has 'not the resources to carry stock for the sole purpose of giving it away in return for worthless pieces of paper'; (2) the public were forced to pay more for the original article than necessary because the trader offering the coupons recovered the cost of the subsequent 'gift' in the price of the original purchase.[8]

Influenced by this retail lobby, governments across Australia moved against these schemes, introducing legislation either to regulate or abolish them. In 1902, Victoria and Tasmania followed New Zealand's lead (the NZ Trading Stamps and Coupons Abolition Bill, Act No. 65, 1900) and passed laws prohibiting the issue of trade coupons.[9] When South Australian merchants failed to convince the government to introduce a Coupon Abolition Bill, they took matters into their own hands and 'formed a coupon company of their own, on co-operative principles, so that if profit had to be made by this system, the money would be returned to their own pockets in the shape of dividends'.[10] The South Australia government introduced an Act to regulate the use of Trading Stamps or Coupons (the Trading Stamp Act, no. 859) in 1904.[11]

In New South Wales, coupons and trading stamps found a more supportive legislative.[12] From 1901, delegations of NSW retailers regularly approached politicians requesting they act to contain the coupon industry.[13] The delegations claimed the system was 'pernicious' and 'a serious interference with the retail traders' business',[14] the scheme forced traders to reduce their range of goods or increase prices. Either way, 'the consumer suffered'. [15] If the system was such a threat to their business, why did they continue to take the coupons, one delegation was asked.[16] A 1904 libel action provided the answer. The proprietor of the Co-operative Coupon Company—the firm spearheading the defence of the coupon system—took out a libel action against the manager of a tea company, who was accused of making detrimental statements about the system, claiming it was a fraud.[17] In his summing up, the judge spelled out the bind that retailers who opposed the scheme found themselves in: 'Evidence had been given that tradesmen had to combine and start coupon companies in order to protect themselves and even one witness called on behalf of [the] plaintiff admitted that it would be a good thing if the system were abolished'. The judge's summing up made it plain that he objected to the schemes 'which affected the poorer classes of the community'.[18] The jury found for the defendant; the plaintiff's appeal for a new trial was later granted, but the parties appear to have then settled out of court,[19] and New South Wales would not introduce legislation to control coupons and trading stamps until 1972.[20]

The labour press condemned moves to legislate against coupons, arguing that their abolition would cause the greatest loss to the poorest section of society, as they were favoured by grocery stores and used by those on lower incomes to buy food staples. Coupons were also useful for those who had insufficient cash to access the discounts many firms offered for cash payments.[21] As the socialist paper the *Tocsin* put it, 'If the rich man is entitled to his 5% discount on a £1 cash purchase, why not the poor man on a 6d. cash purchase?'[22] In October 1929, just days before the Wall Street Crash, the Victorian state government moved to amend its coupon legislation to match that of South Australia, outlawing coupons that entered the state from New South Wales, where the measures against them were laxer.[23] Again labour opposed the legislation because it would punish local stores and the communities that frequented them. The Labor MP Tom Tunnecliffe claimed that the Premier had introduced the legislation to placate his friends in 'certain influential business firms' whose profits were 'weakening' because they were unable to keep up with 'modern business methods'.[24]

In the context of escalating unemployment and restricted incomes, the battle over the use of these 'modern' business methods was unrelenting. On the one hand, the business lobby continued to organise against coupons, despite the fact that many coupons were issued by manufacturers and all were distributed by retailers. The businessman and politician William Angliss, a director of the Mutual Store, declared hyperbolically that 'the coupon system is one of the greatest evils ever connected with business ... I know of many a good man who has been ruined by it'.[25] Victorian retailers formed their own Anti-Coupon League and Victorian grocers claimed coupons and trading stamps added 15–20% to the cost of groceries.[26] On the other hand, the Amalgamated Engineering Union (AEU) argued against stricter measures on coupons, as this would seriously affect employment because those involved in producing the stamps would lose work.[27] In 1940, women's organisations, including Labor women, urged the government to leave the coupon system alone. They also pointed out the impact of abolition on unemployment, but added that it would also deprive housewives of the benefits that coupons offered, since 'no reduction of prices would occur'.[28]

From June 1942, discussion around the benefits or otherwise of coupons and stamps came to an abrupt halt, as third-party trading stamps were banned and coupons of a very different kind became central to department stores' business.[29] The government introduced clothes rationing as part of the wartime economy, and clothing could now only be bought using coupons issued by the Commonwealth Rationing Commission (CRC). Department store advertising carried information on these coupons, letting the consumer know how many coupons they needed to buy a dress or hat, as well as the services they offered for the exchange of coupons.[30]

After the war, Western Australia revived the debate about discount coupons, introducing a bill to prohibit the reintroduction of the 'free' gift coupons which had developed into 'quite a conspicuous feature of pre-war retail trading'.[31] Some manufacturers had been forced into 'this gift form of advertising' by competition between the wars, a report noted, and the arguments against coupons remained the same. The appeal of coupons to housewives was 'undeniable', but the belief that the gifts were free was 'illusory'. Moreover, the system contained a danger of unfair trade practices as it benefited 'the large concern' and disadvantaged 'the small manufacturer'.[32]

Criticisms continued, but the post-war economic boom with its pent-up spending splurge, rise in discretionary income, increased interest in shopping as a leisure activity, and surge in the number of products that businesses need to shift pushed any doubts into the background. Indeed, by the end of the 1950s, coupons (now in the form of trading stamps) had undergone a miraculous renaissance, including in the United Kingdom where the Green Shield Stamp phenomenon captured households across the country. In the 1960s and 1970s, British children (including this author) studiously pasted the stamps into booklets, then pored over the Green Shield catalogue to choose a 'free' gift. Similar schemes operated in

Australia from the early 1960s, examples included Blue Shield Stamps, Gold Shield Stamps, and Tiki Green stamps.[33] These 'sticky little persuaders' were well established overseas, the *Western Herald* noted in 1971, but from time to time they had come under 'the most severe criticism'. Despite this, they had proved themselves 'as singularly the most effective means of retail promotion'.[34]

As the report indicated, not everyone was enamoured of the stamps: an 'anti-trading stamp movement' in the United States had erroneously blamed the stamps for retail failures.[35] In Australia, the *Bulletin* noted the problems caused by 'third party' trading stamps—those offered not directly by a retailer but by independent operators such as Gold Shield and Tiki.[36] Once again, pressure started to mount for their abolition and the NSW government moved to ban them in 1971. When the ban was announced, a Mrs Stephen wrote into the *Canberra Times*:

> As the mother of six children, anything that will bring prices down, even a small item such as eliminating trading stamps, is of interest to me. But is trading stamps the only thing that is a hidden cost to the consumer, passed on by the retailer? ... If the stamps are to be banned, then why not all the other hidden costs such as competitions and particularly the 'plastic junk' and picture cards manufacturers enclose in packets of cereals, etc, to 'get the kids to tell Mum to buy'. [37]

Conscious consumers such as Mrs Stephen understood that there was a both reward and a cost to their brand loyalty. They also understood that, ultimately, it would be the retailer who would come out on top in the deal.

As for the department stores, their use of sales promotion devices such as stamps and coupons depended on the status of their clientele. The lower to mid-end of the market, and especially those that sold food (as Myer and Grace Bros did),[38] used manufacturers' discount coupons to draw in customers.[39] Myer's Bendigo store, also at the lower to mid-end, used discount stamps to stimulate sales. Known as Cash Coupons, these operated in the same way as third-party trading stamps, with the stamps collected in a Coupon Book, except these coupons were only redeemable from Myer.[40] The upper end of the market—David Jones, for example—eschewed discount coupons but they did offer 'free' gifts through regular competitions that matched their image and the interests of their patrons, such as needlecraft competitions, art competitions, and word games, as well as competitions aimed at children.[41]

This brief history of coupons and trading stamps provides valuable background to the loyalty programme boom of the 1990s in which department stores would be enthusiastic participants. It shows that Australian consumer society was ambivalent towards the use of sales promotion devices. Retailers and their associations were divided over them and, though households found them a useful way to stretch their budgets, they were increasingly conscious that these 'free' gifts had to be paid for somehow, and it would probably be them who would pay. Despite such misgivings, the new loyalty programmes would be embraced enthusiastically, including by Australia's department stores.

Relationship Marketing

Backed by a new, higher level of research and analysis, marketing's reimagining of relationship marketing from the early 1980s offered increased insight and strategic reliability to retailers. This was great timing for Australian department stores. The success of the Bankcard rollout threatened to undermine their hard-won customer loyalty because the new credit card could be used easily across competing stores and customers no longer needed to sign up for an exclusive, branded charge card. Although some charge accounts were beginning to introduce extended or revolving credit, Bankcard had made it available to everyone.

The new marketing showed department stores that, while many customers might appreciate the convenience offered by using Bankcard across a number of stores, many others valued a continuing, high-quality relationship with their brands. It gave department stores a way forward. Building this relationship and ensuring it lasted meant building trust and delivering satisfaction, and stores were advised to use the strongest possible strategies for customer bonding, to market to employees and other stakeholders, and to work on building trust as a marketing tool. Trust takes years to build in any context and Australia's department stores had invested heavily in ensuring their customers found them to be competent and reliable, two aspects of the four pillars from which trust is built. The other two components—honesty and openness—are connected and more problematic for retailers, as business considerations required them to withhold information from consumers and competitors alike.[12]

Significantly for this study, stores were also advised to target their most profitable customers. As the *Financial Review* noted, in most markets, there was a group of hard-core loyal buyers who only ever bought one brand. These loyal buyers were a profitable group for the stores because they were heavy or frequent buyers and numerically large. In the era of relationship marketing, the goal was to make these buyers even more committed to the store, encouraging them to climb the 'loyalty ladder'.[43]

Marketing scholars highlighted the complexity of relationship retailing, identifying multi-level relationships between customers and stores and exploring how these relationships were linked to store loyalty.[44] The first step on the loyalty ladder for the consumer was the 'person-to-store relationship', in which store loyalty was encouraged by the aura and attitude of the store in general, its merchandise, its atmosphere, its service style, and its design. However, this did not have a direct impact on purchase intention. That took the second step on the loyalty ladder: the development of interpersonal relationships between retail salespeople and customers. This was why stores such as Myer put so much effort into training and retaining staff. Encouraged to think of their employment as being part of a big family, staff were able to purchase shares in the store, to join staff clubs, and attend staff events. It was also why stores placed so much emphasis on prompt and respectful service. When sales staff trusted their employers and had been trained in customer service, they were more likely to perform successful service encounters which would then build trust between the sales staff and the customer and encourage future purchases. As a Grace Bros training manual put it 'When service fades so do customers'.[45]

The emphasis on relationship marketing grew through the 1980s and 1990s, made possible by the take-up of computers and the improvements in data collection this allowed. By the turn of the millennium, department stores had more information on their customers to work with than ever before, as this *Sydney Morning Herald* article showed:

> In the old days, an exclusive store would hire a doorman to stare down the riff-raff. Now, thanks to ever-growing computer data bases, companies can use more subtle means to seek out their valued customers and direct the marketing effort towards them.[46]

The article went on to imagine the valued customer experience at an Australian department store in the very near future:

> It is 2001. You walk into a Grace Bros department store. At the door, you swipe your Fly Buys [sic] card at a kiosk. A screen at the kiosk welcomes you and offers a 25 per cent discount on any shirt you buy that day. A receipt is printed for you to take to the shirt counter.

> Your marketing profile has just been identified. You have not been classified according to old-fashioned demographics, by age, suburb or profession, but in a way that's much more interesting to Coles Myer, the retailing giant that owns Grace Bros.
>
> You have just been pigeon-holed according to the profits you have delivered to Coles Myer in the past. That's lucky for you if you've got a track record as a big spender with expensive tastes. You will pay less for your shirts today, whether you choose Christian Dior or the cheapest home brand. But it's not so lucky if you always buy the generic. You will pay full price again.[47]

Although overtly hierarchical loyalty programmes were more common in hospitality and travel, all loyalty programmes were, in fact, hierarchical.[48] This was the new world of marketing delivered by 'ever greater computing power married to the ubiquity of the plastic card', the report continued. Information about consumers could now be 'sliced, diced and neatly arranged for the delectation of companies with any imaginable product or service to sell'.[49]

The future imagined here did not come to pass, but it came close. Customers were increasingly classified by their profitability. The improved means of accessing information on valued customers—the big spenders—made the management of tiered rewards far easier than previously, which also made delivering the interpersonal element of a loyalty programme easier to achieve:

> It's important to identify everything about the individual. These days it's no longer 80 per cent of your profit coming out of your top 20 per cent of customers, it's more like 150 per cent of profit coming out of your best 20 per cent of customers.[50]

This was a risky approach for the department stores to take. They might acknowledge that every customer deserved to be treated fairly but they also knew that there was more profit to be made by treating 'special' customers (the big spenders) differently from those who were unable or unwilling to spend up big. The more money you had the more you were able to save on your purchases or receive as rewards and, as with charge card users, those customers rewarded for their big spending felt recognised and valued for their loyalty. On the other hand, if your limited income meant you could not be a big spender, you knew through advertising campaigns and in-store promotion that you were on the outside of the club and missing out in some way. The discomfort of the less-well-off when confronted by the credit hierarchy had been spelled out to Australian retailers back in 1959 when a US credit manager explained the factor in the shift from the coupon (or cash order) system to revolving credit, including the 'unfavourable psychological reaction of the [coupon] customer feeling she was an inferior credit risk particularly when shopping with a friend who had a 30 day charge account'.[51]

Did this 'missing out' affect the store loyalty of those who were not able to spend up big? Looking at the political discourse abroad in Australia around the turn of the twenty-first century, the answer is probably no. It is, perhaps, no coincidence that Australian political rhetoric of the time emphasised the dreams of the 'aspirational' voter.[52] Politicians such as then Labor leader Mark Latham and later the Coalition Prime Minister Malcolm Turnbull exploited this type of rhetoric to try and connect with uncommitted voters.[53]

In this broader context, the department stores might have assumed (perhaps correctly) that every Australian aspired to be a big spender and dreamt of climbing to the top of the loyalty ladder. The evolution of loyalty programmes needs to be viewed in the context of decades of neoliberal policies in Australia. Supported by both the ALP and the Coalition, the rhetoric of the market encouraged shareholding ('mum and dad investors') to stimulate investment in public floats of government instrumentalities, such as that of Telstra from 1997.[54]

One loyalty programme was instrumental in this shift to minor shareholding: the Coles Myer shareholder discount card. First introduced in 1993, the programme encouraged Australians to buy a minimum of 500 shares in the Wesfarmer conglomerate that owned Coles Myer. The card provided shareholders with an average of $400 in savings per year through discounts of between 3% and 10% at participating outlets.[55] Programmes such as this might have offered 'ordinary' Australians the 'opportunity' to participate in the market, but as we will see, they were also expensive to maintain and did not always provide the desired outcomes.

When Myer launched its Myer One loyalty programme in 2004, the store made plain its commitment to treating customers differently depending on their capacity to spend.[56] The first members of the programme would be those customers who had 'high spend rates ($1,500 or more a year)'. Other customers could sign up for a Myer One card in-store then 'build to attain the membership qualifying spend'. Myer would implement a tiered system to convert credits to 'rewards' and offered 'personalised product specials' based on 'in-house information', using Coles-Myer's Flybuys programme to identify those with high spend rates.[57]

Launched in September 1994 amongst 'a plethora of customer loyalty-come-rewards-come relationship marketing programs', the Flybuys programme represented, arguably, the single most significant tool for classifying retail customers developed in Australia.[58] 'Loyalty' had 'been around for a while', a report noted, but now it was 'seriously going mass market'.[59] As with coupons and trading stamps, the primary motivation to start a loyalty programme was 'fear' with 'every Australian marketer in the top 200' asking 'What's the potential damage to our business if we don't get involved?' [60] The brainchild of Dr Peter Langkamp, an agricultural scientist and business executive, Flybuys was managed through Loyalty Pacific, a company set up by Coles Myer (the parent company of the Myer department store at the time), the NAB, and the international oil and gas company, Shell, and run by Langkamp.[61] Before the introduction of Flybuys, loyalty programmes such as the frequent flyer programmes of the Australian airlines Qantas and Ansett were exclusive clubs that frequent flyers paid to join. The only rewards given out were points for flying and no credit facility was attached.[62] The Flybuys programme offered consumers free points towards air travel based on spending at participating outlets and purchases using an NAB credit card.[63]

Flybuys was an immediate success. The programme was heavily promoted and in just four weeks a million households signed up. By September 1994, more than 2.5 million Australians were collecting points towards flights.[64] Conceived as 'no ordinary sales promotion'—not the usual 'steak knives, fluffy toys, sweepstakes or scratchies', Flybuys was to be managed as a product, more structured than a sales promotion and there for the long term.[65] 'The longer it goes on, the more opportunity the customer has of success', Langkamp asserted, stating the obvious.

Langkamp's claims about the programme's longevity were immediately questioned.[66] Marketing experts pointed out that there was little hard evidence that customer loyalty could be maintained over the longer term. Most people were loyal over the short term, but over time they became disloyal for all sorts of good reasons, such as moving house so they were 'no longer able to shop at Myers or wherever'.[67] The proportion of customers who could choose to be loyal was fairly small, so, in the long run, the scheme would impact just a small number of people. Moreover, if every retailer had a frequent buyer programme, then any competitive advantage would be negated.[68]

However, the main criticism of the scheme concerned data collection.[69] The level of data collection (and its potential for invasive data-mining) involved with the Flybuys programme drew fears that customer privacy would be threatened.[70] Experts argued that, if any value were to be found in frequent buyer schemes, it would be in the huge amounts of data that companies would be able to collect via every application form.[71] Customers became 'members' of the programme, but there was a cost (beyond the financial) to membership. The programme's terms and conditions required members to consent to the gathering, retention, and use of information, which included names, addresses, and dates of birth; members also consented to this information being used by 12 participating retailers, as well as by Loyalty Pacific. The programme made no promises that this information would remain with Loyalty Pacific and not be passed on to outside parties, and critics feared that the company could on-sell the information to direct mail or telephone companies.

Loyalty Pacific rejected this criticism and denied that its programme would result in an invasion of customer privacy. Nevertheless, critics called for an upgrade in Australia's privacy laws, given the rapid changes in technology and in the marketplace. The problem was only going to grow, they argued; following 'an international trend which had seen frequent-buyer programs mushroom'; several of Australia's biggest companies were now 'banding together to set up customer loyalty programs'.[72]

'You must ask how they will use that information', critics argued, now that firms would be able to analyse the consumption and purchasing behaviour of a wide range of people.[73] One answer to that question was that they would use the information to target a specific group of consumers, as 'it was important to have the right customer base to start with'.[74] The 'right' customers were invariably the most profitable, the 'revolvers'. Some sectors of the community—especially small business owners—tended to pay off their credit card entirely each month, which severely diminished the amount of money that could be made from that card. In credit jargon, these consumers were known as 'transactors'. 'Revolvers' were those who did not pay off their account at the end of the month but allowed the debt to build and thus accrue interest. This was a far more profitable group than the 'transactors', and it was crucial to identify and target as many of these as possible.[75]

Slater and Hornery drew attention to the power of data-mining as a targeting tool and warned consumers about giving away too much information:

> In the old days, an exclusive store would hire a doorman to stare down the riff-raff. Now, thanks to ever-growing computer data bases, companies can use more subtle means to seek out their valued customers and direct the marketing effort towards them. … It's all part of the new world of marketing delivered by ever greater computing power married to the ubiquity of the plastic card. Information about consumers can be sliced, diced and neatly arranged for the delectation of companies with any imaginable product or service to sell. [76]

As hierarchies of consumption became easier to enforce (and more furtive), the 'riff-raff' (low-income customers) could now be excluded before they even reached the doors of the store.

Stores soon found that their ability to cut out the 'riff raff' was not necessarily good news for their bottom lines. They wanted to attract the big spenders, but big spenders were more likely to be big earners and so were more able to pay off their accounts on time. The money was actually in the 'revolvers', those who failed to pay their accounts off at the end of the month and who then accrued interest. If stores could attract this group and hold on to them, they were on 'a winning ticket'.[77] Reward programmes could help with this, some argued, as they provided low-income customers with a sense of continuing value. However, as a customer's relationship with the retailer changed over time, they needed to be reminded of this value at regular intervals, so they were able to justify the interest rates and fees they were being asked to pay.[78] Once a store landed a customer, the challenge was to hold on to them.[79] Direct mail continued to play its part, allowing for highly personalised communication with the shopper—addressing them by name and making the mailout look as though it was prepared just for them—and taking customer service to the next level. Moreover, sending out a bill allowed the company to include targeted promotional leaflets in the envelope.

Loyalty Tested

As Australia's loyalty programmes matured, data-mining continued to be viewed as 'a double-edged sword'.[80] Although it could deliver 'a lot of benefits' to 'middle-class, wealthy consumers' who could afford to pay the fees and charges involved in loyalty programmes, for low-income consumers those same fees and charges could present 'a real problem'.[81] A representative from the Australian Consumers' Association (ACA) outlined the implications for low-income customers:

> This technology allows you to target the needs of people because you see how they behave; but on the other hand, if you don't like what you're seeing, you can do things to get rid of the undesirable customers, like pricing services out of their range, no delivery in that neighbourhood or demanding a minimum purchasing requirement.[82]

This was beginning to happen with banking services, she explained. Banks were withdrawing physical access to their premises, which 'removed the cross-subsidies' that once 'forced' the wealthy to create 'a slightly more even offer' to those less well-off. The landscape was rapidly shifting away from those who offered little profit to those who offered a great deal, and data-mining made it that much easier.[83] Hierarchy remained important with the members of loyalty programmes divided into similar status levels as credit card holders—bronze, silver, gold, and platinum. As with earlier credit systems, status would be based on a customer's cumulative spending with those who exceeded the threshold level promoted to higher status and receiving special recognition and preferential treatment. However, those who failed to exceed the required threshold results would be demoted to a lower tier (what Shanta Banik calls 'status demotion') and lose all the associated rewards. Banik draws attention to the threat to the social identity of those customers who suffer 'status demotion'.[84]

In June 1995, loyalty programmes took a new turn when the telecommunications company Telstra (previously Telecom) launched Australia's first mass market company-branded credit card, to counter the success of Flybuys. Telstra joined with the ANZ Bank and Visa to launch the Telstra Visa credit card to a potential market of six million phone users.[85] These types of 'coalitions' would become the norm for loyalty programmes, with at least a bank involved as it became commonplace to link the programmes to a credit card.[86] The Telstra card offered 'no fees and big rewards' to a potential market of six million phone users and was welcomed as a point of difference in the 'increasingly cluttered and confusing credit-card and loyalty-marketing categories'. [87] Its bonus-points scheme covered 15,000 outlets in 200 product and service categories. Consumers had been 'very smart' about the various loyalty programmes, a spokesman said: 'They have ... figured out which ones offer maximum value'.[88] Industry sources claimed that Telstra had to work hard—and offer incentives—to persuade some of the retailers to participate. 'Call it loyalty or call it greed. Whatever it is, it's generating sales growth for our merchants'.[89] Big spenders continued to receive the most benefits. Telstra eschewed marketing its credit card to its entire customer base of six million. Instead, it offered the new credit card to its most valuable customers, that is, 'people with above-average expenditure' on STD, IDD, and mobile telephone calls.[90]

Trouble was on the horizon. When Flybuys was launched, the only reward had been points towards flights, which were out of the reach of many members. Unused points expired after three years, which made it challenging to save enough points for a flight.[91] Overall, too many points were required for too little reward, which led to growing customer dissatisfaction.[92] The ACA warned people that they may have to spend a lot of money before they receive benefits: 'People should be very careful not to get too deep into credit just because (they think) there's some sort of pot of gold at the end of the rainbow'. Victoria's Office of Fair Trading and Business Affairs had received five complaints about frequent-flyer programmes since their inception. The complaints were about the allocation of points with people claiming that they had been cheated out of points they had earned.[93]

Competition, high costs, and choosy customers had left many card reward programmes failing to meet the expectations for customer numbers and revenue targets. Many customers had become 'locked in' to rewards programmes, which were often viewed by companies as simply effective barriers to customers leaving the organisation: 'They do not promote true brand loyalty'.[94] Another problem was the low collection of rewards. Only 2% of Flybuys cardholders claimed their free flights. When all other loyalty programmes were counted, only 8% claimed rewards. Even the programme that had started it all, Flybuys—'not a credit card but a loyalty scheme linked to purchases from some retail outlets'—had been rejigged in a bid to ignite growth.[95]

Loyalty programmes came under increased pressure in March 2002 when the domestic airline Ansett collapsed along with its massively subscribed loyalty programme, Global Rewards. Thousands of members were left holding points they were unable to redeem. In response to Ansett's demise, rival reward programmes were 'quietly' tidied up. The banks, for example, including ANZ, Citibank, and Westpac, adjusted their loyalty programmes, withdrawing or rebranding cards, and 'winding back' rewards.[96] The pressure on the programmes increased almost immediately when Coles Myer announced that it was phasing out its popular shareholder discount card.[97] Shareholders were given two years grace before the card was no longer honoured, but investors reacted to the announcement immediately by wiping $300 million from the company's market value.[98]

The commentary around these two developments revealed the difficulties that loyalty programmes faced. They had 'lured' millions of Australians during the past decade, according to the commentary, but 'corporate collapses, regulatory scrutiny, and an old-fashioned concern for the bottom line' were now 'conspiring against them'.[99] A market researcher noted that customers had 'probably' always been sceptical about reward schemes, but 'the more things go wrong for them the more people are going to be resistant'.[100] Moreover, he added, 'the mid-1990s obsession with developing large customer databases to facilitate savvy direct marketing schemes was behind many of the reward programs. ... In reality that strategy never really worked. It was just too big and too clumsy'.[101]

Coles Myer began to withdraw its shareholder discount card in 2002 to the consternation of many Australian 'mum and dad investors'. Melbourne's *Herald Sun* explained the motivation for withdrawing the card: 'The decision to phase out the program was made ... because it cost about $170 million a year in gross profits but failed to provide the loyalty incentives of rival schemes'.[102] The demise of the shareholder card freed Myer to revamp its existing loyalty programme. The following chapter will explore this new direction in the context of three factors—the growing fragmentation of society; economic crisis and the resultant reframing of credit legislation; and the emergence of new technologies of credit—examining the pressures these developments placed on a retail sector already under siege.

Notes

1. Tony Featherstone, 'Fears For Privacy Grow As Fly Buys Gather Speed', *Australian Financial Review*, 23 September 1994, 5.
2. Leonard L. Berry, 'Relationship Marketing of Services Perspectives from 1983 and 2000', *Journal of Relationship Marketing* 1, no. 1 (2002): 59–77, 60.
3. Berry, 'Relationship Marketing of Services Perspectives', 60; L.L. Berry and L.G. Gresham. 'Relationship Retailing; Transforming Customers into Clients'. *Business Horizons* (November/December 1986), 43.
4. Robert M. Morgan and Shelby D. Hunt. 'The Commitment-Trust Theory of Relationship Marketing'. *Journal of Marketing* 58, no. 3 (July 1994): 20; Kristian Möller and Aino Halinen, 'Relationship Marketing Theory: Its Roots and Direction', *Journal of Marketing Management* 16 (2000): 29.
5. 'The Coupon System', *Balmain Observer and Western Suburbs Advertiser*, 13 October 1906, 3.
6. 'The Granville Guardian', *Journal of the Granville Historical Society* 11, no. 8 (August 2004): 3, https://ehive.com/collections/4907/objects/507717/green-coupon-collecting-book, accessed 17 July 2025.
7. 'The Trading Coupons Abolition Act', *Table Talk*, 8 September 1899, 12; 'The Trade Coupon System: No. 11', *Brisbane Courier*, 5 February 1902, 8; South Australia, Trading Stamp Act, No. 859 of 1904; Lex, 'The Jurist. Interesting Decisions, Trading Coupons', *Australasian*, 21 November 1914, 47.
8. 'Trading Stamp Act, 1924–1935: Coupons and Cut Prices', https://classic.austlii.edu.au/au/journals/AdelLawRw/1963/8.pdf, accessed 6 June 2025.
9. Trading Stamp Act, 1924–1935.
10. Trading Stamp Act, 1924–1935.
11. The Trading Stamp Act, no. 859, 1904.
12. ' Trading Stamps', *Australian Retailing*, September/October 1971, 3.
13. 'NSW', *North Western Advocate and the Emu Bay Times,* 20 August 1903, 3; 'The Coupon System', *Goulburn Herald*, 28 September 1903, 2; 'The Coupon System. Delegation to the State Treasurer', *Sydney Morning Herald*, 22 October 1903, 4; 'Coupon System. Grocers' Attitude. Legislation Urged', *Sydney Morning Herald,* 2 March 1926, 9.
14. 'Coupon Trading: Protest in New South Wales', *Argus*, 20 August 1926, 16.
15. 'Anti-Coupon Petition', *Daily Telegraph,* 26 January 1907, 6.
16. 'The Coupon System', *Goulburn Herald*, 28 September 1903.

17. 'New South Wales', *Mercury*, 23 March 1904, 3; 'In Chambers: The Coupon System', *Sydney Morning Herald*, 1 December 1903, 7.
18. 'Supreme Court of New South Wales', *Sydney Morning Herald*, 1 April 1904, 3; 'Law Report', *Sydney Morning Herald*, 2 December 1904, 7.
19. 'Supreme Court of New South Wales'; High Court of Australia, Godhard v. James Inglis, 1905, 78–93; 'Law Report', *Sydney Morning Herald*, 2 December 1904, 7.
20. 'The Coupon System', *Balmain Observer and Western Suburbs Advertiser*, 13 October 1906, 3; 'Trading Stamps', *Australian Retailing*, September/October 1971, 3.
21. State Library of Victoria, Records of Coles-Myer Ltd. and its predecessors, ca. 1840–ca.1990 (hereafter CM), MS 13468, Box 1510, Myer Bendigo, 'Pay Cash and Get a Discount', n.d.
22. 'Trading Coupons', *Tocsin*, 2 November 1899, 2.
23. 'Trading Coupons: The Proposed Prohibition. Opposition to Measure', *Argus*, 8 October 1929, 14.
24. 'Trading Coupons: The Proposed Prohibition', 14; 'Coupon Trading. The Proposed Prohibition. Further Opposition to the Bill', *The Age*, 23 October 1929, 13.
25. 'Coupons and Gifts. Legislation for Abolition. Council Passes Bill', *Argus*, 23 November 1933, 4.
26. 'Trading Stamps Illegal; Move to Stop Practice', *Herald*, 6 September 1930, 4; 'Coupons and Gifts. Alleged Unfair Trading', *Age*, 30 May 1933, 1; 'Free Gifts and Coupons. Prohibitive Legislation Urged', *The Age*, 24 August 1933, 12; 'Attracting Trade. Free Gifts and Coupons', *Age*, 7 September 1933, 11.
27. 'Goods (Trading Stamps Bill). Effect on Employment', *Age*, 22 November 1933, 15.
28. 'Favour Gift Coupons', *Argus*, 20 June 1940, 5.
29. Trading Stamps, *Australian Retailing*, September/October 1971, 3.
30. 'Issue of Ration Books, System Introduced Smoothly', *Western Star and Roma Advertiser*, 19 June 1942, 2.
31. 'Trading Stamps', *West Australian*, 7 December 1948, 2.
32. 'Trading Stamps'.
33. 'Inside the Trading Stamp-Ede', *Western Herald*, 9 July 1971, 2.
34. 'Inside the Trading Stamp-Ede'.
35. Charles Franklin Phillips, 'Trading Stamps and Retail Failures', *Journal of Marketing* 22, no. 3 (Jan. 1958): 304–305.
36. 'Who is for Stamp Trading?' *Bulletin*, 23 Nov 1963; *Bulletin*, 21 December 1963; A.C. Nielsen, Jr., 'The Impact of Retail Coupons', *Journal of Marketing* 29, no. 4 (Oct. 1965): 11–15.
37. 'Trading Stamps', *Canberra Times*, 23 November 1971, 2.

38. '"Cash and Carry" Myer's New System for Grocery Department', *Herald*, 21 June 1926, 4; 'Cash and Carry Store', *Herald*, 23 June 1926, 4.
39. CM, Box 2020, Myer Cash and Carry; 'Cash and Carry: Myer's New System for Grocery Department', *Herald*, 21 June 1926, 4; 'Cash and Carry: Myer's New Department', 21 June 1926, 5; 'Can There Be Larceny in a Self-Service Store?', *Herald*, 21 November 1929, 3.
40. CM, Box 1510, Myer (Bendigo) Pty. Ltd. Coupon-Book, n.d.
41. 'A Sewing Competition for Clever Little Girls', *Watchman*, 5 October 1922, 7; 'Battle of the Emotions: Photomaton Competition Votes Pour In', *Daily Telegraph*, 8 June 1929, 5; 'D. Jones' Prize-winners', *Daily Telegraph*, 24 June 1933, 8.
42. Jackie Dickenson, *Trust Me: Australians and their Politicians* (Sydney: NewSouth Press, 2013), 8.
43. 'Pros and Costs on Loyalty Ladder', *Australian Financial Review*, 2 September 1994, 55.
44. Gerrard Macintosh and Lawrence S. Lockshin, 'Retail Relationships and Store Loyalty: A Multi-level Perspective', *International Journal of Research in Marketing* 14 (1997) 487–97.
45. CM, Box 3124, 'Grace Bros and Service', n.d. See also, CM, Box 3124 'Customer Service and You', n.d., 22; CM, Box 3059, 'Winning Back Customers: Myer Stores', 1984, 17.
46. Elisabeth Sexton and Andrew Hornery, 'The Baiting Game', *Sydney Morning Herald*, 17 July 1999, 59.
47. Sexton and Hornery, 'The Baiting Game'.
48. Shanta Bantik, 'Exploring the Effects of Status Demotion in Hierarchical Loyalty Programs', *Journal of Strategic Marketing* 31, no. 5 (2023): 1087–106. doi:10.1080/0965254X.2022.2050781
49. Sexton and Hornery, 'The Baiting Game'.
50. Sexton and Hornery, 'The Baiting Game'.
51. Trotta, 'Revolving Credit', 11.
52. 'Transcript of the Prime Minister The Hon. John Howard MP at the Aston Electorate Dinner, Melbourne, 16 July 2002', 2, *PM Transcripts*, https://pmtranscripts.pmc.gov.au/release/transcript-12916, accessed 3 June 2025; Robert Corcoran and Jackie Dickenson, *A Dictionary of Australian Politics* (Sydney: Allen & Unwin, 2010), 8–9.
53. Evatt Foundation, 'Aspiration & Inequality', 30 June 2018, accessed 3 June 2025. See Judith Brett, 'If the Liberals want to appeal again to aspirational Australians, they could start by taxing wealth', *The Guardian*, 27 June 2025, accessed online 8 June 2025.
54. Tony Kaye, 'The Stock Market: Small Investors Benefit', *Australian Jewish News*, 26 December 1997, 7.

Telstra Share Offer: Public Offer Document, 1997, https://www.telstra.com.au/content/dam/tcom/about-us/investors/pdf%20A/t1-telstra-share-offer.pdf, accessed 21 June 2025.
55. Anthony Marx, 'Card Hits Use-By-Date', *Herald Sun*, 31 July 2004, 87.
56. Ruth Williams, 'Myer Launches New Card Aimed At Well Heeled', *West Australian*, 21 July 2004.
57. Matt Wade, 'Loyalty Gets Its Just Deserts', *Sydney Morning Herald*, 29 March 2002, 37. MYER one still uses a 'tier benefits' system: Platinum, Gold, Silver, Member, https://www.myerone.com.au/home, accessed 3 June 2025.
58. Paul McIntyre, 'Loyalty Can Have Its Own Rewards', *Australian Financial Review*, 22 November 1994, 46. Tony Featherstone, 'Fears For Privacy Grow As Fly Buys Gather Speed', *Australian Financial Review*, 23 September 1994, 5.
59. McIntyre, 'Loyalty Can Have Its Own Rewards'.
60. McIntyre, 'Loyalty Can Have Its Own Rewards'.
61. Arlene Cullen, 'Big Fly Buys Push Leaves Small Business Up', *The Age*, 2 October 1994, 19.
62. Phil Hawkins, 'Loyalty Blinks: Fly Buys at 30 – Loyalty Lessons', https://australianloyaltyassociation.com/flybuys-at-30-loyalty-lessons/, accessed 17 June 2025.
63. Tony Featherstone, 'Fears For Privacy Grow As Fly Buys Gather Speed', *Australian Financial Review*, 23 September 1994, 5.
64. Featherstone, 'Fears For Privacy Grow As Fly Buys Gather Speed'.
65. Cullen, 'Big Fly Buys Push Leaves Small Business Up'.
66. David Elias, 'Queue for Frequent Flyer Seats', *Age*, 21 May 1994, 1; Tom Ballantyne, 'Fliers Taken for Ride, Says Consultant', *Sydney Morning Herald*, 14 July 1994, 5.
67. Elias, 'Queue for Frequent Flyer Seats'; Ballantyne, 'Fliers Taken for Ride, Says Consultant'.
68. Elias, 'Queue for Frequent Flyer Seats'; Ballantyne, 'Fliers Taken for Ride, Says Consultant'.
69. Featherstone, 'Fears For Privacy Grow As Fly Buys Gather Speed'.
70. Featherstone, 'Fears For Privacy Grow As Fly Buys Gather Speed'; David Elias, 'Queue for Frequent Flyer Seats'; Ballantyne, 'Fliers Taken for Ride, Says Consultant'.
71. Tom Allard, 'Doubts Remain As Fly Buys Takes Off', *Sydney Morning Herald*, 29 September 1994, 34.
72. Featherstone, 'Fears For Privacy Grow As Fly Buys Gather Speed'.
73. Allard, 'Doubts Remain As Fly Buys Takes Off'.
74. 'Scoring Points : A Money Investigation', *Sydney Morning Herald*, 12 November 2003, 8.

75. Sexton and Hornery, 'The Baiting Game'.
76. Sexton and Hornery, 'The Baiting Game'; 'Your Share of the Action: Stocks Bearing Perks ', *Age*, 31 January 1994, 15.
77. 'Scoring Points'.
78. 'Scoring Points'.
79. 'Scoring Points'.
80. 'Doubts Dog Reward Schemes', *Age,* 30 March 2002, 1.
81. 'Doubts Dog Reward Schemes'.
82. 'Doubts Dog Reward Schemes'.
83. 'Doubts Dog Reward Schemes'.
84. Shanta Bantik, 'Exploring the Effects of Status Demotion in Hierarchical Loyalty Programs', *Journal of Strategic Marketing* 31, no. 5 (2023): 1087.
85. 'Co-Brand New Credit Cards: No Fees and Big Rewards', *Australian Financial Review*, 6 December 1994, 1; Neil Shoebridge, 'Telstra Tries to Weigh the Costs and Benefits of 'Loyalty Schemes', *Australian Financial Review,* 19 May 1997.
86. Anna Patty, 'AMEX Targeted Over David Jones Credit Card Taken for Loyalty Card', *Sydney Morning Herald*, 6 December 2022; Pauline Hatch, 'David Jones Launches Mastercard Partnership with Latitude Financial', 28 May 2025, creditcard.com.au, accessed 15 June 2025.
87. 'Co-Brand New Credit Cards: No Fees and Big Rewards', *Australian Financial Review*, 6 December 1994, 1; Shoebridge, 'Telstra Tries to Weigh the Costs and Benefits'.
88. Shoebridge, 'Telstra Tries to Weigh the Costs and Benefits'.
89. Shoebridge, 'Telstra Tries to Weigh the Costs and Benefits'.
90. Shoebridge, 'Telstra Tries to Weigh the Costs and Benefits'.
91. Hawkins, 'Loyalty Blinks: Flybuys At 30 – Loyalty Lessons'.
92. Melissa Fyfe, 'Frequent Flyers Point Out A New Trend In Spending', *Age*, 7 October 1996, 4.
93. Fyfe, 'Frequent Flyers Point Out a New Trend in Spending'.
94. 'Customers, Business Failing to Cash in Loyalty', *Australian Financial Review*, 28 June 1999, 26.
95. 'Customers, Business Failing to Cash in Loyalty'.
96. 'Doubts Dog Reward Schemes'.
97. Wade, 'Loyalty Gets Its Just Deserts'; 4 March 2002; 'Doubts Dog Reward Schemes'; Anthony Marx, 'Card Hits Use-By-Date'.
98. 'Doubts Dog Reward Schemes'.
99. 'Doubts Dog Reward Schemes'.
100. 'Doubts Dog Reward Schemes'.
101. 'Doubts Dog Reward Schemes'.
102. Anthony Marx, 'Card Hits Use-By-Date'.

References

Australian Retailing. Sydney: Australian Council of Retailers 1967–1973.

Bantik, Shanta. 'Exploring the Effects of Status Demotion in Hierarchical Loyalty Programs'. *Journal of Strategic Marketing* 31, no. 5 (2023): 1087–1106. https://doi.org/10.1080/0965254X.2022.2050781

Berry, Leonard L. 'Relationship Marketing of Services Perspectives from 1983 and 2000', *Journal of Relationship Marketing* 1, no.1 (2002): 59–77. https://doi.org/10.1300/J366v01n01_05

Berry, L.L. and L.G. Gresham. 'Relationship Retailing; Transforming Customers into Clients'. *Business Horizons* (Nov./Dec.1986), 43–47. https://doi.org/10.1016/0007-6813(86)90036-4

Bongiorno, Frank. *Dreamers and Schemers; A Political History of Australia.* Melbourne: Black Inc. 2022.

Corcoran, Robert and Jackie Dickenson. *A Dictionary of Australian Politics.* Sydney: Allen & Unwin, 2010.

Dickenson, Jackie. *Trust Me: Australians and their Politicians.* Sydney: NewSouth Press, 2013.

Harker, Michael John and John Egan. 'The Past, Present and Future of Relationship Marketing'. *Journal of Marketing Management* 22 (2006): 215–42. https://doi.org/10.1362/026725706776022326

Macintosh, Gerrard and Lawrence S. Lockshin. 'Retail Relationships and Store Loyalty: A Multi-level Perspective', *International Journal of Research in Marketing* 14 (1997) 487–97. https://doi.org/10.1016/S0167-8116(97)00030-X

Möller, Kristian and Aino Halinen. 'Relationship Marketing Theory: Its Roots and Direction'. *Journal of Marketing Management* 16 (2000): 29–54. https://doi.org/10.1362/026725700785100460

Morgan, Robert M. and Shelby D. Hunt. 'The Commitment-Trust Theory of Relationship Marketing'. *Journal of Marketing* 58, no. 3 (July 1994): 20–38. https://doi.org/10.1177/002224299405800302

Phillips, Charles Franklin. 'Trading Stamps and Retail Failures'. *Journal of Marketing* 22, no. 3 (January 1958): 304–305. https://doi.org/10.1177/002224295802200308

Records of Coles-Myer Ltd. and its predecessors, ca. 1840–1990, MS13468, State Library of Victoria.

CHAPTER 8

Fragmentation

Abstract Department stores have struggled with market fragmentation since at least the 1980s, as consumers turned to alternative retailers such as discount and specialty chains, at first in 'real life' but now increasingly online. Accordingly, department stores embraced new forms of retail credit in attempts to hang on to their market shares, including Buy Now Pay Later (BNPL) platforms, a mode of payment made possible by technological change. Charging late fees rather than interest, BNPL platforms have further fragmented the market as Gen Y and Gen Z consumers embrace the new, more flexible, and convenient schemes, while baby boomers and Gen X hang on to their credit cards. Despite this innovation, retail credit is as hierarchical today as it ever was.

Keywords Credit • Retail • Market fragmentation • Indebtedness • Disruption • BNPL • Luxury • Australian history

In 2025, Australians are the third most indebted consumers in the OECD, after Switzerland and the Netherlands. Most of that debt is 'good debt' (mortgage loans), but 54% of Australians have a credit card ('bad debt') and the average credit card debt is A$3306.[1] Nevertheless, Australians are now generally in control of their debt, and unpaid credit card balances have fallen from their peak in 2011.[2] These unpaid balances have fallen, at

The original version of the chapter has been revised. A correction to this chapter can be found at https://doi.org/10.1007/978-3-032-16612-8_10

J. Dickenson, *Credit and the Australian Department Store Since 1900*, https://doi.org/10.1007/978-3-032-16612-8_8

least in part, because of a new mode of payment made possible by technological innovation.[3] Introduced in 2014, Buy Now Pay Later (BNPL) platforms have changed the face of retail shopping, fragmenting the market as Gen Y and Gen Z consumers embrace the new, more flexible, and convenient schemes, while baby boomers, Generation Jones, and Gen X hang on to their credit cards.[4] Department stores, too, have struggled with market fragmentation since at least the 1980s, as mass and mid-market shoppers turned increasingly to discount and specialty chains, at first in 'real life' but now increasingly online. This shift results from growing inequality, the hollowing out of the middle class, and the consolidation of wealth in the hands of the few. Accordingly, department stores embraced these new forms of retail credit and loyalty programmes in attempts to hang on to their market share.

Fragmentation and Indebtedness

The beginnings of market fragmentation can be traced back to the late 1970s, but US marketing scholars acknowledged its impact on department stores from the mid-1980s.[5] As a range of new retailers, including discount stores and specialty chains, carved out market niches for themselves, department stores failed to share in the growth of retail sales.[6] They had changed little in the past two decades except to cut service levels while trying to maintain high margins, and had neglected to develop new strategic positions in response to a more competitive retail environment and 'the changing consumer'.[7] The decline has continued. In 2024, when Macy's of New York closed 150 of its stores, a report noted decades of decline, blaming the gradual demise of the US department store on a range of factors, including competition from chain store retailers and the shift to online shopping.[8]

The same period has seen an explosion in indebtedness, as the disposable incomes of individuals and families across Western democracies have declined.[9] This decline began with the imposition of the neoliberal state in response to the economic crises of the 1970s and a repudiation of the Keynesian post-war consensus.[10] Neoliberalism has had a significant impact on the middle class in Western democracies. In the same way that working-class women used cash orders to make it through to payday in the 1920s, millions of formerly middle-class families living under neoliberalism, what Michael Sousa has called financialised capitalism, now go into 'heavy' debt to avoid economic marginality and to maintain some semblance of financial security in what's left of a welfare state.[11] In the United States, credit is required to inflate otherwise stagnant wages so as to eke out an existence in the vanishing middle class, replacing earnings as the major sources of middle-class purchasing power: consumer debt is now the defining feature of modern capitalism with debt operating as 'a social power and a class relation of domination and exploitation between creditors and debtors'.[12] Christopher Payne has described how consumers came to be viewed as producers—'both enterprising and entrepreneurial'.[13] Consequently, from the early 1980s, credit rationing ended and consumers and households were encouraged to use debt to expand their personal assets.[14]

The same can be said for Australia where for more than a century governments have been slow to act to regulate credit.[15] As elsewhere, governments of all political persuasions have passively encouraged the growth of consumer indebtedness and appear relatively sanguine about growing inequality here and across the globe.[16] In their discussion of the decline of department stores, David Rachman and Keith Fabes draw attention to the impact of organisational changes, including declining customer services, the increased cost of reaching customers, and the erosion of consumer trust in the institution, as well as environmental factors, including changing consumer attitudes towards mass marketing, demographic changes forcing a suburban focus, and increased competition.[17] They also emphasise the role played by new store social class distinctions that reflect the increasing inequalities in Western democracies: 'the retail industry has been split in two as inflation has taken its toll'.[18] The hollowing out of the middle class and its loss of purchasing power has meant that the mid-level retail sector, formally the largest sector by far, has come under increasing pressure and the market has polarised towards the lower and top ends, that is, discount and luxury stores.[19] Discount stores selling inexpensive items are successful, as are the luxury brands that cater to consumers who still have the means to afford expensive items. Focused on the disappearing middle class of the United States as they are, department stores are on the wane.[20]

Similar changes have occurred in Australia with the success of discount chains such as Kmart and the consolidation of the luxury market, as inequality has increased and the 'middle' has shrunk.[21] The decline in inner city department stores accelerated in the early 2000s with closures and contractions in part because of the popularity of destination shopping centres,[22] but also because of the arrival of the internet and a gradual shift to online shopping, a shift that accelerated again during the global pandemic (2020–2023). Department stores responded in different ways to this decline, including with the introduction of in-store specialty shops and, eventually, a move to online shopping. However, consumer interest in shopping in department stores has continued to decline, along with staff/customer ratios and customer service, and it is uncertain how long these physical stores can survive as the market continues to fragment.

Department stores have tried to navigate these developments in part by improving their rewards offerings. In 2004, Myer launched a new department-store-only loyalty programme to replace its shareholder discount card, confident that the new scheme would cost much less than the old scheme's $170 million.[23] The new programme aimed at luring shoppers back to the store with tailored offers rather than across-the-board discounts, thereby rewarding customer loyalty.[24] The advantage of the programme for shoppers was that they received benefits whether they owned shares or not: shoppers who spent more than $1500 a year were rewarded with points redeemable for gift vouchers.[25] Two years later, Bankcard disappeared from Australia's banking scene after more than 30 years in Australians' wallets, defeated by the fact that it could not be used overseas and by its lack of a rewards programme. Myer took the opportunity of Bankcard's demise to introduce its own branded credit card, known as the Black Card, then, in 2018, introduced a co-branded Myer/Visa credit card.[26]

Loyalty and Luxury

Despite claims that consumerism and credit were democratised after the Second World War, the recent history of retail credit shows that access to credit and its rewards remains as hierarchical as ever.[27] Myer One's structure, for example, reveals that loyalty programmes continue to exploit status anxiety and promote a hierarchy of members.[28] The scheme is geared to reward heavy shoppers telling customers that the more they shop the more rewards they will earn, and uses the hierarchical language that we saw in Chap. 5—Silver, Gold, and Platinum—to differentiate between members.[29] Although rewards are relatively small and vary little across the levels, with just a few dollars difference in the birthday and anniversary rewards, for example, the amount a member needs to spend to move up the loyalty ladder varies greatly: $0–$1499 for basic offers membership; $1500–$5999 for Silver, and $6000 plus for Gold. The 'secretive'

Platinum tier offers similar rewards to the other levels—a $30 birthday voucher, $20 membership anniversary reward, and free 'big and bulky' online deliveries.[30]

So what draws consumers to strive for the pinnacle of this undeniably modest rewards system? A 2011 study on the social benefits of luxury brands provides some insight into the mindset that drives this behaviour. It found that luxury brands act as 'costly signals of wealth and status' with luxury consumption enhancing status and producing benefits in social interactions. Displays of luxury brands elicit different kinds of preferential treatment, which can even result in financial benefits to people who engage in conspicuous consumption. The study concluded that luxury consumption can be a profitable social strategy because conspicuous displays of luxury elicit 'status-dependent favourable treatment in human social interactions'.[31] Myer's Platinum level delivers on this 'costly signal of wealth and status', rewarding 'big spenders' and aiming to make them feel 'extra special'.[32] This feeling starts with the invitation-only membership which in itself signals wealth and status: no one—including 'your closest besties'[33]—will ever know how much you had to spend to get there, they will just assume that it was a hefty amount and more than they could afford to spend. Also designed to make the Platinum member feel extra special are the exclusive invitations to curated experiences that showcase their favourite designers, launch exclusive products, or celebrate a special occasion.[34] As the luxury market shifts from an emphasis on possessions to indulgent experiences in an attempt to reinvent itself, exclusive events are more important than ever.[35] Platinum members enjoy VIP in-store shopping nights, beauty and perfume masterclasses, celebrity masterclasses, and personal shopping suites, all of which confer status.

Retail credit is now inextricably linked to such loyalty programmes, which are more popular in Australia than ever, with most major retailers running some form of programme that rewards loyal customers with discounts, special offers, and exclusive previews, often for purchases made on nominated credit cards. That said, Australian loyalty programmes are dominated by a small group of major players, such as Woolworth's Everyday Rewards (which was introduced in 2016), Qantas Frequent Flyer (Australia's largest programme), and, more recently, Amazon Prime. While loyalty programmes are immensely popular and can seem like a bargain, customers are trading their data in exchange for meagre benefits. A recent report revealed that 55 per cent of customers felt comfortable sharing their information with loyalty programmes to enhance their shopping experience. Meanwhile 26% of shoppers said data collection was an invasion of their privacy and 20% felt indifferent about the process.[36] Flybuys remains in the top three programmes. As we saw in the previous chapter, this programme was envisaged as a long-term proposition rather than a short-term sales promotion. That vision has been realised. Besides Coles supermarkets, the programme is used across the Wesfarmers 'retail family', which now includes a number of Australia's retail giants, such as the supermarket giant Coles, whose private-label credit cards are linked to Flybuys.[37] However, it no longer includes Myer: when Coles sold Myer in 2007, the store immediately left the Flybuys programme to concentrate on developing its Myer One programme. Already linked with the CommBank Awards credit card, the programme has recently been extended to allow members to link their Visa or Mastercard credit cards. With 4.7 million active members, Myer One consistently ranks as one of Australia's top 10 loyalty programmes.[38]

Loyalty programmes have continued to attract criticism, the themes of which have remained constant: customers complaining that they receive too few points for the money they have spent with the store and that they are uncomfortable about the collection of their private information. A 2012 report explained that the information collected through the Myer One programme included when and where a cardholder shopped and how they paid, as well as any information they disclosed over the telephone or online. This was a 'financial windfall' for the department store, as it led to repeat customers and 'potentially lucrative' data. About 70% of sales were to Myer's 4.5 million loyalty cardholders. One young cardholder told the reporter that he was not happy that Myer was able to build a detailed profile of him by keeping track of his purchases.[39] The same report speculated that the rewards that members earned through the programme justified the data collection and its potential invasion of their privacy: a clear quid pro quo. A later report questioned this assertion, asking whether this free reward obsession was really worth it. 'Does anyone ever get to use the points? And if they do, is the reward worth the effort?', the author asked. Given that Myer credit cardholders now have to spend $2000 to receive a modest $20 shopping voucher, it is reasonable to conclude that this complaint endures.

For those on limited incomes, loyalty programmes are even more problematic. As Chenzi Zu and Jeffrey Repucci reported in 2023, poorer consumers pay for the credit card points earned by the comfortably off through the payment of interchange fees: the money it costs merchants to accept noncash payments. A Stanford University study found that, as credit card rewards increased, so did the interchange fees that everyone, no matter their status, had to pay. Credit card rewards are, in essence, a tax on less affluent consumers, who are much more likely to pay for their goods with cash, debit cards, or standard credit products that accrue no such rewards.[40] Moreover, the poor have limited access to rewards credit cards in the first place. With high credit scores needed to qualify for a premium card, those cards with the highest value rewards are usually available only to the rich.[41]

Another department store recently joined the ranks of the 'points for rewards' loyalty programme retailers. David Jones had long resisted introducing a points system to their instant rewards programme but in June 2025, the store launched its new co-branded Mastercard credit card and loyalty programme.[42] The new card continues the practice of hierarchal lending, with its appeals to aspiration and status anxiety, offering two levels of membership, Premiere and Prestige, with higher annual fees and minimum credit balances for Prestige status. The department store was pushed to reconsider introducing points for rewards by events concerning its co-branded American Express (Amex) credit card. In 2022, Amex became embroiled in a court case after complaints that its Amex DJ credit card misled customers into thinking the card was a loyalty card, which it was not.[43] This case highlights the fuzzy line between loyalty programmes and credit cards, and the confusion this can cause consumers. The Federal Court ordered American Express to pay $8 million in penalties for breaching design and distribution obligations.[44] After terminating its contract with American Express in 2023, David Jones signed an exclusive 10-year agreement with Latitude Financial (formerly GE Finance).[45]

Department stores' high-end sales remain moribund everywhere with the physical multi-brand retail environment facing continued sluggishness; Australian department store sales declined by between 2 and 4% in 2024 and, although they recovered early in 2025, they remain unstable.[46] Loyalty to a particular department store, often passed down through generations, has weakened accordingly. We have seen how class allegiance played a major role in maintaining store loyalty in the past, encouraged by the store's promotional activities, as well as by the family's shopping history. As class identification has broken down, customers have expanded their range of shopping locations and now are able to consume in numerous spaces and in numerous ways. Moreover, digital technology has made it easier to set up a small business, so niche interests and groups have mushroomed, and the market now consists of 'a mosaic of new entrants catering to different micro-segments, or fragments'.[47] This scattering of consumers across myriad retailers should make them harder for retailers to target, but, in fact, online surveillance, especially on social media, has counteracted this, making potential customers easier to target than ever before. Social media's algorithms might make it easier to target customers, but they are harder to hold on to than ever. Individuals now embody multiple identities of which class is just one. 'Traditional' loyalties to a social class, for example, have been undermined and subsumed in the past half century, by an infinite number of overlapping (sometimes competing) identities, such as race, gender, disability, and sexual orientation.[48]

The weakening of class allegiances has had significant implications for retail credit and, in particular, for department stores.

When the world economy crashed in 2008, consumer credit performed as it always does in economic chaos: it contracted.[49] With banks reluctant to lend money and consumers equally reluctant to spend, tighter credit conditions and reduced demand led to a sharp decline in business and household credit.[50] Though banking reforms introduced as a result of the crisis did not go as far as some might like, there was some tightening of the rules, particularly around bank loans and risk assessment.[51] In 2009, Australia moved to overhaul and standardise the rules covering consumer credit and the federal parliament passed the National Consumer Credit Protection Act No. 134, 2009, to 'modernise Australia's consumer credit laws'. Moving the bill in June 2009, Australia's then financial services minister said: 'This piece of legislation will—for the first time in our country's history—provide for one, single, standard and uniform regime for consumer credit regulation and oversight'.[52] Regurgitating a familiar argument for limiting the regulation of credit, lobbyists such as the former CEO of the Australian Banking Association subsequently argued that the reforms threatened to 'crush the aspirations' of customers.[53]

The push for reform trickled through to the loyalty industry, which moved to professionalise. In 2014, the Australian industry established the Australian Loyalty Association (ALS), which aims 'to provide thought leadership, education and networking opportunities to those working in the loyalty industry'.[54] The ALS now has over 3500 members and an Advisory Board consisting of 22 loyalty experts from top brands and loyalty services.[55] The launch of an international industry magazine is further evidence of professionalisation. *Loyalty* magazine covers all global markets and business sectors, including retail, financial services, travel and hotels, telecoms, and online commerce and reports on a range of loyalty issues, including customer retention initiatives, loyalty schemes, reward programmes, customer insight, and social media developments, as well as technology as a 'loyalty enabler', for example, developments in AI, AR, automated customer interaction, and advanced data management.[56]

Disrupting Credit

The rapid advance of technology has meant banks are able to access more data than ever to better understand consumers without forensic examination of income and expenses.[57] Retail payment options have changed accordingly. Perhaps of most significance has been the move to debit cards, which involve no credit or interest charges, just customers using the money they already have in the bank.[58] More recently, new forms of digital payment schemes, or FinTech, have come into use. These include virtual and single-use credit cards, and the Buy Now Pay Later (BNPL) schemes, which do not usually involve interest charges and are popular with younger generations who are less financially secure than their parents and grandparents.[59] BNPL schemes such as Australia's Afterpay have made spending without having ready cash at hand easier than ever.[60]

Launched in 2014, Afterpay was praised as a fantastic retail innovation, joining the 'rarefied air' of Visa, Mastercard, and American Express (alongside EFTPOS and cash) as a widely accepted way of paying for shopping.[61] As Australia's first successful homegrown consumer payment option since Bankcard, Afterpay's aim was to disrupt the global credit card market, which was dominated by the banks.[62] The promise was simple: it's like lay-by, but you get the goods upfront.[63] The customer was now able to purchase a good or service immediately and pay off the debt in four equal fortnightly instalments over eight weeks. The new scheme took Australian retail by storm; the uptake was rapid, 'almost breakneck'.[64] Launched in the United States in 2018, Afterpay was reported as rapidly building a global BNPL platform.[65] In the United States, its app was downloaded 640,000 times in May 2021, double the previous May's number and up about 50% on the first two months of 2021. With the platform taking the credit risk and charging just a 'small fee', there seemed to be no downside for the retailer. The data were clear: accepting Afterpay meant more sales and more profit.[66] It was 'a clear win-win'.[67]

The platform now pitches itself as the modern way to shop, in contrast to revolving credit, with a strap line telling consumers that old money does not like the way new money works. According to the advertising, the revolving credit card—old money—is designed to keep consumers paying, whereas Afterpay is designed to be paid off. 'Say no to revolving debt spirals', the sales-pitch concludes.[68] Australia's *Inside Retail* reported a downward trend in credit card use with half a million consumers getting rid of their credit cards by July 2019 and shifting to BNPL.[69] Although these schemes do not charge interest to consumers, most do charge a flat fee on a missed payment and a further flat fee a week later if the scheduled payment has still not been made.[70] However, as a survey of more than 1000 users of BNPL found, also in 2019, the platforms' messaging has not always been as clear or as successful as the industry might like: more than 64% of those surveyed thought BNPL services were a form of credit, despite the suppliers' insistence that their scheme was not credit, but rather a form of budgeting.[71]

The survey also found that, unsurprisingly, the promise of credit without incurring spiralling debt worked best on those on low incomes. Customers who used BNPL schemes were significantly more likely to have other debts than those who did not, with 26% of those surveyed using BNPL because otherwise they were unable to afford the purchase. Eleven per cent of those surveyed had already reached their credit limits and were incurring late fees.[72] Two years later, a consumer insight report found that consumers with incomes below $35,000 per annum were more likely to hold multiple BNPL accounts. The growing use of BNPL by vulnerable customers 'will be an area to watch', an executive warned, noting, however, that 'multiple accounts could also be explained by different retailers offering different BNPL options'.[73] In terms of customer loyalty, the executive concluded, the question would be whether the consumer was loyal to the BNPL brand or to where they shop.[74] BNPL is indeed undermining brand loyalty with consumers' allegiances now shifting from brands to payment methods.[75] Forty-two per cent of shoppers say that they will abandon an online shopping cart if they do not see their preferred payment method available at checkout.[76]

Consumer advocates drew attention to the reasons financially vulnerable consumers were attracted to BNPL schemes. First, the BNPL companies did not conduct credit checks, so those consumers who were unable to get a personal loan or credit card were more likely to be able to access BNPL. Second, using a BNPL service could be cheaper than a credit card or other forms of credit, as long as you pay the instalments on time. However, missing repayments made the consumer vulnerable to a default on their credit report and could affect their credit rating. Given the gendered history of consumer debt, it is no surprise that these indebted consumers are now more likely to be women than men.[77]

Responding to concerns about the exposure of vulnerable consumers, the Australian authorities conducted two investigations into the BNPL industry. Reporting back in 2018, they found that BNPL was 'different' and should not be considered a traditional credit provider. Nevertheless, the government moved to streamline consumer protection, forced to intervene because of the increased availability of payday and fast loans charging extortionate interest rates which were embroiling low-income Australians in significant debt, as well as continuing problems with debt collection practices.[78] In 2020, Australia's consumer credit watchdog, the Australian Securities and Investments Commission (ASIC), reported that one in five consumers were missing BNPL payments.[79] Calls for regulation increased.[80] Two years later, Zip Co, Afterpay's Australian competitor, announced that it would be more conservative in its lending as bad debts had increased beyond its target range; a similar trend was seen at Afterpay.[81]

A UK study in 2023 identified a significant problem with the BNPL model. The schemes might not charge interest, but shoppers could choose to put BNPL purchases onto their credit card, which typically charged upwards of 20% interest and often took decades to pay off. Increasingly attractive credit card rewards made it especially tempting for consumers to charge their BNPL transactions to their credit card, and this was most prevalent among younger consumers and those living in the most deprived neighbourhoods.[82] This exposure of vulnerable consumers prompted a regulatory question as to whether consumers should be allowed to refinance their unsecured debt.[83] In June 2025, Australia introduced new regulations covering BNPL services. BNPL platforms must now follow the same laws as other forms of consumer credit (the NCCP Act 2009), including credit cards. The new regulations have been prompted by concerns about rising late fees in the BNPL industry: the number of Australians paying BNPL late fees increased significantly between January 2020 and July 2023, from 5% to 7%.[84]

What does this all mean for retail stores, including what is left of the department store sector? Besides there being less money to be made by the stores and their financial partners from providing credit to their customers, the schemes also compromise the store's ability to connect with the individual customer over the long term. BNPL schemes now do one quarter of their business in-store, and department stores have moved to piggy-back off this in order to grow their in-store sales. David Jones launched its own BNPL programme, called Mastercard Instalments, in 2018. This programme allows banks, lenders, BNPL providers, and wallets to offer BNPL experiences across the Mastercard network, and David Jones also offers a BNPL platform as a payment option in-store and online.[85] For its part, Myer launched a BNPL platform in April 2017, to which customers responded positively. As part of its plan to draw customers back in-store, Myer began implementing the platform in-store in 2020 in an effort to attract its 2.7 million active customers to visit its retail locations. As the BNPL platforms link up with major retailers, these instalment schemes are likely to gradually replace revolving credit.[86]

We have seen how credit cards and loyalty programmes are tiered, but brands are too, and, as the market fragments, brand tiers have become further entrenched into four broad divisions: mass-market, mid-market, premium, and luxury. BNPL schemes are impacting vulnerable consumers from the mass and mid-market tiers via late payment fees and compromised credit ratings. But they are also affecting the other half of the now heavily polarised consumer market —the high-end, cashed-up customer who sits in either the premium or luxury tier. The obsession with classifying consumers extends to communicating the subtle differences between these two distinct tiers. According to 'brand experts', premium and luxury brands do things differently from the mass and mid-market brands—'they communicate differently, and they operate differently. They attract different clientele, and they never need to justify their pricing'. But they also do things differently from each other with premium brands focusing on high-quality work, innovation, and customer-centric experiences and luxury brands emphasising prestige, lifestyle perception, heritage, and exclusivity.[87]

After a string of economic shocks and their aftermath—the GFC, the COVID-19 pandemic, stubborn inflation, and increasingly unaffordable housing—high-end brands have had to adjust their strategies. For example, many have raised prices to make up for lower profits, which has pushed many luxury aspirants towards 'dupes'—products made to look like a more expensive or high-quality product—that undermine the 'real' luxury brands.[88] Luxury credit cards have also had to change their operations. While, in the past, membership of a luxury credit card scheme was by invitation only, some of today's most exclusive cards are open to anyone with a high enough credit score. These cards charge high annual fees and offer generous benefits, such as annual travel credits, elite status, and airport lounge memberships.[89] As younger generations shift away from credit cards, driven away by high fees and interest rates towards using a debit card or BNPL options, luxury brands have had to rethink their credit offers. When one Italian luxury brand partnered with a BNPL platform, its online sales increased by 24% in one quarter.[90]

When BNPL was launched, analysts predicted that it would be 'a wallet stretcher' for cash-strapped customers.[91] Commonsense suggests that wealthy shoppers would have no need of BNPL schemes, given they can readily access credit or have sufficient cash to pay up front. However, in a discourse that reveals the resilience of the credit hierarchy, the aspiring luxury shopper is advised to emulate the behaviour of the wealthy and wield BNPL as an intelligent money management strategy. High-end consumers, it is argued, are more critical shoppers than other cohorts, because they conduct lengthy research before they buy and avoid impulse buys.[92] Using BNPL means they can hold onto their cash for longer, invest it rather than spend it, and thus avoid credit card interest. The wealthy know that BNPL is 'a smarter, more thoughtful way to pay' and, if you want to join their ranks, you should use it, too.[93]

Those aspiring to luxury without the necessary funds have an additional avenue through which to assuage their status anxiety: the numerous websites offering luxury loans, a counterpoint to the pay-day and fast loan websites that target vulnerable customers. While these websites promise retailers improved customer loyalty, higher sales, higher average order values, and competitive advantage,[94] the consumer is assured of greater accessibility to luxury goods and the chance to 'Elevate Your Lifestyle'.[95] Customers are encouraged to borrow so they can buy luxury handbags and watches 'to add to your collection'.[96] With a luxury handbag loan, the consumer can fulfil their dream of owning 'an iconic Hermès Birkin, a Louis Vuitton Neverfull or a Chanel Classic Flap' without the burden of upfront costs.[97] Elsewhere, you can purchase 'Your Dream Watch' with a flexible payment plan.[98]

Once a consumer owns a luxury watch or bag, they can then utilise it to access ready cash, to pay for unexpected bills.[99] Luxury pawnbrokers (pitched as modern and flexible) allow consumers to leverage the value of their luxury assets, everything from fine art, jewellery, luxury handbags, watches, cars, boats, and antiques. These schemes use two appeals to attract customers: speed and discretion: 'Traditional lending can be rigid and slow, with numerous requirements and lengthy approval processes'.[100] Australia's first online loan exchange offering cash for luxury goods promises that its scheme is 'a fast, secure, simple, and confidential loan platform designed purely for clients to release the maximum amount of cash from their dormant luxury goods'.[101]

It is yet to be seen whether the shift to digital payments and the allure of luxury experiences will solve the high-end market's current fragility. For the past decade, it has relied on China's rising (and massive) middle class to maintain profits, but that nation's sluggish economy is affecting the profits of most of the luxury brands, which are now seeking new, more dynamic markets, including in the Middle East.[102] In 2024, luxury spending shifted from goods to experiences with the sales of personal luxury goods dipping for the first time in 15 years; luxury products declined by 2%, caused in part by inflationary pressures.[103] That said, some commentators are sanguine about the future of the luxury market.[104] According to a recent report, the profile of the luxury consumer has shifted from the older, well-heeled consumer to Gen Y and Gen Z consumers who are more 'digitally savvy, environmentally and socially conscious, and diverse' than previous generations.[105] However, younger generations are not necessarily more financially savvy than previous generations: a 2024 survey found that nearly 40% of Gen Z shoppers had gone into debt to buy a luxury item.[106] Luxury marketing is still aimed at aspirational shoppers rather than the wealthy and, through the recommendations of influencers, social media marketing has a significant impact on their purchasing intentions.[107] These influencers tap into a fundamental insight into luxury aspirants: that purchasing luxury goods signifies something beyond mere ownership and holds a deeper meaning for the consumer, often reflecting status anxiety, issues of self-worth and belonging, as well as FOMO (fear of missing out) (Fig. 8.1).[108]

> This Australian brand uses the name 'Status Anxiety' ironically: 'Status Anxiety is the feeling we get when we compare how we're doing to those around us. Instead we're for not taking ourselves too seriously, worrying a little less about how others perceive us and investing in things we really value and that last. #brand #ethos #statusanxiety.'[109]

The changing luxury customer has, of course, affected the luxury offering in what is left of the 'traditional' department store. A recent report found that luxury customers 'love the aura of buying directly from a

Fig. 8.1 'Status Anxiety' mid-range brand display in Myer department store. Photographed by the author

brand' and that 'For luxury items, the experience of purchasing within the brand's own castle walls is enchanting'.[110] In a study conducted by a high end watchmaker, researchers found that buying a prestigious timepiece on a multi-brand supersite was 'less pleasurable and enjoyable' than purchasing it from the brand's own website. Department stores such as David Jones in Melbourne have invested significantly in the presentation of in-store luxury concessions, as well as the types of payment and finance options that the luxury consumer now demands. Despite this investment, today's increasingly fragmented market has diminished the aura of the department store and its brightly lit windows now struggle to entice the Australian consumer with the promise of magical transformation.

Notes

1. https://www.finder.com.au/home-loans/mortgage-stress, accessed 20 July 2025.
2. Amy Bradney-George, 'Australian Household Debt Statistics', 24 March 2025, https://www.finder.com.au/credit-cards/australias-personal-

debt-reported-as-highest-in-the-world, accessed 17 July 2025; William Jolly, 'Australian Household Debt Statistics', 21 March 2024, https://www.jacarandafinance.com.au/general/average-household-debt-statistics/, accessed 17 July 2025; 'Credit Card Debt Statistics', https://www.money.com.au/credit-cards/credit-card-statistics, accessed 17 July 2025.

3. Shyam Gupta, 'BNPL Market: How New Tech Is Changing the Game', 10 March 2025, https://www.nextmsc.com/blogs/bnpl-market-how-new-tech-is-changing-the-game, accessed 17 July 2025.
4. Daniel Law, 'Buy Now Pay Later Statistics Australia (2024)', 19 September 2024, https://www.redsearch.com.au/resources/buy-now-pay-later-statistics-australia/, accessed 17 July 2025; Susannah Binsted, 'Buy Now Pay Later Statistics 2024', https://www.finder.com.au/buy-now-pay-later/buy-now-pay-later-statistics, accessed 17 July 2025; Airil Edly, 'The Impact of Buy Now, Pay Later (BNPL) on Millennials and Gen Z', https://trisilco.com/impact-of-bnpl-on-millennials-and-gen-z, accessed 17 July 2025; Gupta, 'BNPL Market'. A recent UK study shows this may be changing with increasing numbers of 55- to 64-year-olds using BNPL: 'Buy Now, Pay Later Use Exploding among Older Britons, Data Shows', *Guardian*, 1 October 2025.
5. Douglas J. Tigert, Lawrence J. Ring, Bert McCammon, 'Change the Strategy, Changes the Management: Do the Department Stores Risk Success', *Journal of Services Marketing*, 2 no. 2 Spring (1988): 5–18; David Rachman and Keith J. Fabes, 'The Decline of the Traditional American Department Store', *Journal of Marketing Channels* 1, no. 3 (1992): 39–60, 39.
6. Tigert, Ring, McCammon, 'Change the Strategy', 6; Rachman and Fabes, 'The Decline of the Traditional American Department Store', 39; Vicki Howard, *From Main Street to Mall: The Rise and Fall of the American Department Store* (Philadelphia: University of Pennsylvania Press, 2015), 6–7.
7. Tigert, Ring, McCammon, 'Change the Strategy', 6. Rachman and Fabes, 'The Decline of the Traditional American Department Store', 39.
8. Chris Isidore, 'How Department Stores Became a Dying Breed', *CNN Business*, 27 February 2024.
9. Wendy Weidenhoft Murphy, *Consumer Culture and Society* (Thousand Oaks, Calif., Sage, 2016), 161–62; Tigert, Ring, McCammon, 'Change the Strategy', 6; 'The Middle Class Isn't What it Used to Be', *Business Week*, 17 November 1986.
10. David Harvey, *A Brief History of Neoliberalism* (Oxford: Oxford University Press, 2005), 12, 20, 27; Richard, *The Bonds of Debt* (London, New York: Verso, 2011), 11–12, 24, 58.

11. Michael D. Sousa, 'Consumer Bankruptcy in the Neoliberal State'. *Emory Bankruptcy Development Journal* 39 (2023): 199.
12. Sousa, 'Consumer Bankruptcy in the Neoliberal State', 204.
13. Christopher Payne, *The Consumer, Credit and Neoliberalism: Governing the Modern Economy* (London and New York: Routledge, 2012), 184. https://doi.org/10.4324/9780203139066.
14. Payne, *The Consumer, Credit and Neoliberalism,* 45, 168, 182, 227–29.
15. Margaret Griffiths, 'The Sustainability of Consumer Credit Growth Late Twentieth Century Australia'. *Journal of Consumer Studies & Home Economics* 24, no. 1 (March 2000): 24; Fiona Guthrie, 'Debt is Our Drug and Credit Pushers Are To Blame, *Courier Mail,* 5 July 2004, 13.
16. Griffiths, 'The Sustainability of Consumer Credit Growth', 30.
17. Rachman and Fabes, 'The Decline of the Traditional American Department Store', 40–41.
18. Rachman and Fabes, 'The Decline of the Traditional American Department Store', 40–41; Isidore, 'How Department Stores Became a Dying Breed'.
19. Isidore, 'How Department Stores Became a Dying Breed'.
20. Isidore, 'How Department Stores Became a Dying Breed'.
21. Parliament of Australia, Chapter 2, 'The Extent of Income Inequality in Australia', https://www.aph.gov.au/Parliamentary_Business/Committees/Senate/Community_Affairs/Income_Inequality/Report/c02; 'Inequality in Australia', https://povertyandinequality.acoss.org.au/inequality/, accessed 26 June 2025.
22. Peter Spearitt, 'Suburban Cathedrals: The Rise of the Drive-In Shopping Centre', in *The Cream Brick Frontier: Histories of Australian Suburbia,* ed. Graeme Davison, Tony Dingle, and Seamus O'Hanlon (Melbourne: Monash Publications in History, 1995).
23. Sue Mitchell, 'The Pitch for Your Hearts, Minds and Wallets', *The Australian Financial Review,* 7 October 2004, 4.
24. Mitchell, 'The Pitch for Your Hearts, Minds and Wallets'.
25. Anthony Marx, 'Card Hits Use-by-date', *Herald Sun,* 31 July 2004, 87.
26. 'Shopper Confusion over New Myer Card', *The Australian,* 3 October 2017, 19; Margaret Griffiths, 'The Sustainability of Consumer Credit Growth in Late Twentieth Century Australia', *Journal of Consumer Studies & Home Economics* 24, no. 1 (March 2000): 23–33. https://www.wemoney.com.au/blog/fashion-retailers-memberships; https://www.pointhacks.com.au/myer-one-rewards-program/.
27. Dawn Burton, *Credit and Consumer Society* (New York: Routledge, 2008), 92–93.
28. Carrie LaFrenz, 'What's in Store Next?' *Australian Financial Review,* 14 March 2022, 14.

29. 'Always Rewarding', https://www.myer.com.au/c/myer-one, accessed 17 July 2025.
30. 'Fashion Retailers' Memberships', https://www.wemoney.com.au/blog/fashion-retailers-memberships, accessed 17 July 2025.
31. Rob M.A. Nelissen and Marijn H.C. Meijers, 'Social Benefits of Luxury Brands as Costly Signals of Wealth and Status', *Evolution and Human Behavior* 32 (2011) 343–55.
32. LaFrenz, 'What's in Store Next?'
33. https://www.myer.com.au/content/myer-one-vip-event Myer Mural Hall.
34. LaFrenz, 'What's in Store Next?' https://www.wemoney.com.au/blog/fashion-retailers-memberships.
35. Claudia D'Arpizio et al, 'Luxury in Transition: Securing Future Growth', https://www.bain.com/insights/luxury-in-transition-securing-future-growth/.
36. 9News, 'New Report Reveals Australia's Most Popular Loyalty Programs', 4 June 2025, https://www.9news.com.au/national/new-report-from-consultancy-company-the-point-of-loyalty-reveals-australias-most-popular-loyalty-programs/bf6139bb-0e38-4f6d-8828-7e51763d4266, accessed 22 July 2025.
37. 'Dr Peter Langkamp', https://www.vic.gov.au/dr-peter-langkamp, accessed 17 July 2025; https://www.canstar.com.au/credit-cards/flybuys-credit-cards/.
38. Thomas Nguyen, 'Top 10 Loyalty Programs In Australia: Why They're So Successful', https://joy.so/australian-loyalty-programs, accessed 27 June 2025; 'Get More Out of Your Everyday', https://experience.flybuys.com.au, accessed 17 July 2025; 'Myer Reveals 'Biggest Expansion' of Loyalty Program', *Ragtrader*, 20 October 2025, https://www.ragtrader.com.au/news/myer-reveals-biggest-expansion-of-loyalty-program.
39. Katherine Fleming and Kate Bastians, 'Loyalty Cards Face Invasion of Privacy Test', *The West Australian*, 19 May 2012, 20.
40. Chenzi Zu and Jeffrey Repucci, 'The Dirty Little Secret of Credit Card Rewards Programs', *New York Times*, 4 March 2023.
41. Zu and Repucci, 'The Dirty Little Secret of Credit Card Rewards Programs'.
42. 'David Jones Ltd: New Instant Rewards Customer Loyalty Programme', *ASX Feed*, 2 February 1998; Carrie LaFrenz and Ayesha de Kretser, 'David Jones, Qantas Loyalty Tie-up will Challenge Wirth's Myer Reboot', 5 June 2025, https://www.afr.com/companies/retail/david-jones-qantas-loyalty-tie-up-will-challenge-wirth-s-myer-reboot-20250602-p5m49e, accessed 3 August 2025.

43. Anna Patty, 'AMEX Targeted Over David Jones Credit Card Taken for Loyalty Card', *Sydney Morning Herald*, 6 December 2022.
44. Naomi Neilson, 'Amex Hit with $8 m Penalty for David Jones Credit Cards', *Lawyers Weekly*, 23 July 2024.
45. Pauline Hatch, 'David Jones Launches Mastercard Partnership', 28 May 2025, https://www.creditcard.com.au/latitude-creditcards/, accessed 15 June 2025.
46. Australian Bureau of Statistics, https://www.abs.gov.au/statistics/industry/retail-and-wholesale-trade/retail-trade-australia/latest-release, accessed 24 July 2025.
47. Will Webster, 'What is Market Fragmentation', https://www.qualtrics.com/experience-management/brand/market fragmentation/#:~:text=Market%20fragmentation%20is%20the%20concept, accessed 17 July 2025.
48. Kimberlé Crenshaw, 'Mapping the Margins: Intersectionality, Identity Politics, and Violence against Women of Color', *Stanford Law Review*, 43, no. 6 (July 1991): 1241–299; Elizabeth Parsons et al., 'Marketing Inequalities: Feminisms and Intersectionalities', in *Contemporary Issues in Marketing and Consumer Behaviour* (London: Routledge, 2023), 89–112, 89, 97.
49. David Jacobs and Vanessa Ryan, 'The Role of Credit Supply in the Australian Economy', Research Discussion Paper, Reserve Bank of Australia, February 2012, 34.
50. Jacobs and Ryan, 'The Role of Credit Supply in the Australian Economy'.
51. Mustafa Yuksel, 'A Decade of Post-crisis G20 Financial Sector Reforms', *Bulletin*, June 2019, 53, https://www.rba.gov.au/publications/bulletin/2019/jun/pdf/a-decade-of-post-crisis-g20-financial-sector-reforms.pdf, accessed 17 July 2025; 'The Global Financial Crisis, 20 November 2020', https://www.rba.gov.au/education/resources/explainers/the-global-financial-crisis.html#:~:text=In%20response%20to%20the%20crisis,prevent%20the%20spreading%20of%20risk.
52. 'National Consumer Credit Protection Bill 2009, Second Reading', *Parliament of Australia: House Hansard*, 25 June 2009, 7147.
53. 'Credit, Finance and Loan. Complaints', https://www.afca.org.au/make-a-complaint/credit-finance-and-loan-complaints, accessed 17 July 2025.
54. 'Phil Hawkins, 'Loyalty Blinks: Flybuys at 30 – Loyalty Lessons', *Australian Loyalty Association*, 15 February 2024, https://australianloyaltyassociation.com/flybuys-at-30-loyalty-lessons/, 17 July 2025.
55. 'Loyalty Blinks'.
56. 'About Us', https://www.loyaltymagazine.com/about-us/, accessed 9 June 2025.

57. Anna Bligh, 'Efficient and Responsible: Getting the Lending Right', 25 November 2020, https://www.ausbanking.org.au/efficient-and-responsible-getting-the-lending-balance-right, accessed 27 June 2025.
58. Reserve Bank of Australia, 'RDP 2023-08: The Evolution of Consumer Payments in Australia: Results from the 2022 Consumer Payments Survey, Table 1: Consumer Payment Methods', 5, accessed 31 July 2025; 'The RBA Wants to Ban Debit and Credit Card Surcharges. Banks are Fighting Back, *The Guardian* 14 September 2025.
59. Nassim Khadem, 'Australians Ditch Credit Cards As Millennials Turn to "Buy Now, Pay Later" Players Like Afterpay, Zip', *ABC News*, 17 August 2020.
60. 'What is Buy Now Pay, Later for Business', https://gocardless.com/en-au/guides/posts/what-is-buy-now-pay-later-for-business/, accessed 6 October 2024.
61. Scott Phillips, 'Afterpay a Fantastic Retail Innovation', *Sydney Morning Herald*,25 July 2018; Jonathan Shapiro and James Eyers, *Buy Now, Pay Later: the Extraordinary Story of Afterpay* (Sydney: Allen & Unwin, 2021).
62. Clancy Yeates, 'Bad Debts Force Zip to Tighten Loans', *Sydney Morning Herald*, 22 April 2022.
63. Phillips, 'Afterpay a Fantastic Retail Innovation'; Georgia Wilkins, 'Afterpay Attracts Interest of ASIC and Hit with Stop Order', *Sydney Morning Herald*, 12 April 2016.
64. Phillips, 'Afterpay a Fantastic Retail Innovation'.
65. 'Buy Now Pay Later: Fastest Growing Payment Method', 3 December 2021, https://www.morganstanley.com.au/ideas/buy-now-pay-later-fastest-growing-payment-method.html, accessed 21 July 2025.
66. Phillips, 'Afterpay a Fantastic Retail Innovation'.
67. Phillips, 'Afterpay a Fantastic Retail Innovation'.
68. Dean Blake, 'Myer Implementing New Payment Options In-store', *Inside Retail*, 7 June 2019, https://insideretail.com.au/news/myer-implementing-new-payment-options-201906; https://www.davidjones.com/afterpay#:~:text=Afterpay%20can%20be%20used%20online,Google%20Pay%20or%20Samsung%20Pa, accessed 17 July 2025.
69. Dean Blake, 'Credit Cards Decline Amid Buy Now Pay Later Boom', *Inside Retail*, 23 July 2019, https://insideretail.com.au/news/credit-cards-decline-amid-buy-now-pay-later-boom-201907, accessed 14 July 2025.
70. John Collet, 'Afterpay, Zip not Fearful of Regulation', *Sydney Morning Herald*, 19 October 2018; Phillips, 'Afterpay a Fantastic Retail Innovation'.
71. Emma Koehn, 'Afterpay Dismisses "Warnings"', *Sydney Morning Herald*, 17 October 2019.

72. Koehn, 'Afterpay Dismisses "Warnings"'.
73. Eyers, 'UBS expects "significant drop"'.
74. Eyers, 'UBS expects "significant drop"'.
75. 'Uplift, "Buy Now, Pay Later at Checkout" Now the New Must-have Logo Amongst Luxury Shoppers', https://www.uplift.com/buy-now-pay-later-at-checkout-luxury-shopping/#:~:text=With%2060%25%20of%20shoppers%20opting,from%20the%20brand's%20own%20website, accessed 23 July 2024.
76. 'Buy Now, Pay Later at Checkout'.
77. Jolly, 'Australian Household Debt Statistics'.
78. 'National Debt Helpline', https://ndh.org.au/debt-problems/moneysmart.gov.au, accessed 17 July 2025; Noel Towell, 'Rising Costs Push Families into Debt-Pay Traps, *Age*, 26 March 2022, 5; https://www.cashconverters.com.au/loans.
79. Dean Blake, 'One in Five Consumers Are Missing Buy Now Pay Later Payments: ASIC', *Inside Retail*, 16 November 2020.
80. James Eyers and James Frost, *Time for BNPL Regulation Has Arrived: Matt Comyn*, *AFR Online*, 15 April 2021.
81. Yeates, 'Bad Debts Force Zip to Tighten Loans'; Alex Turner-Cohen, 'Entire Industry on the Brink of Collapse', news.com.au, 13 June 2022.
82. Benedict Guttman-Kenney, Chris Firth, and John Gathergood, 'Buy Now, Pay Later (BNPL) ... On Your Credit Card', *Journal of Behavioral and Experimental Finance* 37 (2023): 1–7.
83. Guttman Kenney, Firth, and Gathergood, 'Buy Now, Pay Later (BNPL)'
84. Yeates, 'Bad Debts Force Zip to Tighten Loans'.
85. Dean Blake, 'Myer Implementing New Payment Options In-store'; 'Now Accepted Online and In-store; Afterpay', https://www.davidjones.com/afterpay, accessed 17 July 2025.
86. 'Australia Buy Now Pay Later Business Report 2025–2030', 17 February 2025, https://www.fintechfutures.com/press-releases/australia-buy-now pay later business-report-2025-2030-expansion-into-diverse-retail-sectors-key-players-and-new-entrants-current-state-of-the-bnpl-market-strategic-partnerships-with-major-retailers, accessed 17 July 2025.
87. The Real Difference between Premium and Luxury Brands', Designtastemaker.com, accessed 25 July 2025.
88. Carrie Le Frenz and Ayesha de Ketser, 'David Jones, Qantas Loyalty Tie-up Will Challenge Wirth's Myer Reboot, https://www.afr.com/companies/retail/david-jones-qantas-loyalty-tie-up-will-challenge-wirth-s-myer-reboot-20250602-p5m49e, accessed 17 July 2025; Gareth Friesen, 'Can Luxury Compete With Fast Fashion's Imitation Game?', https://www.forbes.com/sites/garthf, accessed 11 July 2025; 'Luxury Dupes', https://luxurydupes.co.uk, accessed 25 July 2025; 'Vogue

Business', https://news.law.fordham.edu/blog/2025/03/19/vogue-business-prof-susanscafidi-the-fashion-and-beauty-executives-guide-to-dupes/, accessed 25 July 2025; 'How An Aldi Court Case Could Impact Dupe Culture in Australia', https://halfords.com.au/aldi-case-impact-on-dupe-culture-australia, accessed 23 July 2025; George Arnett, 'What Happens to Luxury during a Recession? *Vogue Business*, 16 August 2019, https://www.voguebusiness.com/companies/luxury-recession-saks-bond-yield, accessed 25 July 2025; Mark Tungate, *Luxury World: the Past, Present, and Future of Luxury Brands* (Philadelphia: Kogan Page, 2009) 62; Cornelia Staritz, *Making the Cut? Low-income Countries and the Global Clothing Value Chain in a Post-quota and Post-crisis World* (Washington, DC: The World Bank, 2011); 'Retail Sales are Weakest in 35 years', *New York Times*. Retrieved March 18, 2013, from http://www.nytimes.com/2008/12/05/business/economy/05shop.html?_r=1&; Rachel Sanderson, 'Ferragamo to Raise Prices in Europe', *Financial Times,* 14 January 2013, http://www.ft.com/intl/cms/s/0/52e412b2-5593-11e2-bdd2-00144feab49a.html#axzz2QqDJbPeG, accessed 13 July 2025.
89. Holly D. Johnson, 'A Guide to Luxury Credit Cards', *Bankrate*,17 June 2025, https://www.bankrate.com/credit-cards/advice/guide-to-luxury-credit-cards/, accessed 25 July 2025.
90. 'Orders and Payments', https://www.gucci.com/au/en_au/st/faq#payment, accessed 25 July 2025.
91. 'Buy Now, Pay Later at Checkout'.
92. 'Buy Now Pay Later at Checkout'.
93. 'Buy Now Pay Later at Checkout'.
94. 'Offer Finance for Luxury Goods', https://www.kandoo.co.uk/guides/offer-finance-for-luxury-goods-handbags-designer-items, accessed 25 July 2025.
95. 'Offer Finance for Luxury Goods'; 'Luxury Goods Financing Elevate Your Lifestyle with Fundingo's Loan Solutions', https://www.fundingo.com/luxury-goods-financing-elevate-your-lifestyle-with-fundingo-s-loan-solutions/, accessed 21 July 2025.
96. 'Luxury Handbag Loans and Lending Solutions, https://australianequipmentfinance.com.au/personal-loans/luxury-handbag-loans, accessed 25 July 2025.
97. 'Luxury Handbag Loans'.
98. 'Luxury Watches', https://proloans.au/loans/luxury-watches/, accessed 25 July 2025.
99. 'Online Lending Using Your Luxury Items As Security', https://pledg.com.au, accessed 25 July 2025.

100. 'How the High Street Works', https://www.thehighstreet.com.au/how-it-works, accessed 25 July 2025.
101. 'Online Lending'.
102. Joelle de Montgolfier, *Luxury in Transition: Securing Future Growth*, Report on the Luxury Goods Worldwide Market Study 2024, Bain & Company, 2024.
103. Montgolfier, *Luxury in Transition*, 7, 11; 'A Luxury Experience in China: Global High-end Brands Bet on Conceptual Stores to Revive Sales', *Fashion Network*, 30 June 2025, https://ca.fashionnetwork.com/news/A-luxury-experience-in-china-global-high-end-brands-bet-on-conceptualstores-to-revive-sales,1744822.html, accessed 17 July 2025.
104. KPMG, 'The Market of Luxury Goods', January 2024, 31, https://assets.kpmg.com/content/dam/kpmg/gr/pdf/2024/02/gr-kpmg-future-of-consumer-goods-the-market-of-luxury-goods.pdf, accessed 25 July 2025.
105. 'The Market of Luxury Goods', 31; Michele Gargiulo, 'Why We're Bankrolling Luxury Brands: The Spending Habits No One Talks About', blogpost, 6 May 2025 https://www.michelegargiulo.com/blog/middle-class-luxury-spending, accessed 20 July 2025.
106. 'The Market of Luxury Goods', 31.
107. Gargiulo, 'Why We're Bankrolling Luxury Brands'.
108. 'The Market of Luxury Goods', 31.
109. https://www.facebook.com/StatusAnxiety/posts/whats-with-the-brand-namestatus-anxiety-is-the-feeling-we-get-when-we-compare-ho/1194179242751587/, accessed 20 September 2025.
110. 'Buy Now Pay Later at Checkout'.

References

Crenshaw, Kimberlé. 'Mapping the Margins: Intersectionality, Identity Politics, and Violence against Women of Color'. *Stanford Law Review*, 43, no. 6 (July 1991): 1241–299. https://doi.org/10.2307/1229039

Burton, Dawn. *Credit and Consumer Society*. New York: Routledge, 2008.

Davison, Graeme, Tony Dingle and Seamus O'Hanlon, eds. *The Cream Brick Frontier: Histories of Australian Suburbia*. Melbourne: Monash Publications in History, 1995.

Dickenson, Jackie. 'Luxury and the Labour Press, 1890–1918'. *Labour History* 134 (May 2023): 1–29. https://doi.org/10.3828/labourhistory.2023.2

Diest, Richard. *The Bonds of Debt*. London, New York: Verso, 2011.

Griffiths, Margaret. 'The Sustainability of Consumer Credit Growth in Late Twentieth Century Australia'. *Journal of Consumer Studies & Home Economics* 24, no. 1 (March 2000): 23–33. https://doi.org/10.1046/j.1365-2737.2000.00117.x

Guttman-Kenney, Benedict, Chris Firth and John Gathergood. 'Buy Now, Pay Later (BNPL) ... On Your Credit Card'. *Journal of Behavioral and Experimental Finance* 37 (2023): 1–7. https://doi.org/10.1016/j.jbef.2023.100788

Harvey, David. *A Brief History of Neoliberalism*. Oxford: Oxford University Press, 2005.

Howard, Vicki. *From Main Street to Mall: The Rise and Fall of the American Department Store*. Philadelphia: University of Pennsylvania Press, 2015.

Lazaretto, Maurizio. *The Making of the Indebted Man: An Essay on the Neoliberal Condition*. Los Angeles: Semiotexte: 2012.

Marx, Karl. 'Comments on James Mill'. Economic and Philosophical Manuscripts of 1844, in Marx/Engels, *Gesamtausgabe*. Berlin: Erste Abteilung, Band 3, 1932, trans. Clemens Dutt. https://www.marxists.org/archive/marx/works/1844/james-mill/

Montgolfier, Joelle de. *Luxury in Transition: Securing Future Growth*. Report on the Luxury Goods Worldwide Market Study 2024, Bain & Company, 2024.

Murphy, Wendy Weidenhoft. *Consumer Culture and Society*. Thousand Oaks, Calif.: Sage, 2016.

Nelissen, Rob M.A. and Marijn H.C. Meijers. 'Social Benefits of Luxury Brands As Costly Signals of Wealth and Status'. *Evolution and Human Behavior* 32 (2011) 343–55. https://doi.org/10.1016/j.evolhumbehav.2010.12.002

Parsons, Elizabeth et al. *Contemporary Issues in Marketing and Consumer Behaviour*. London: Routledge, 2023.

Payne, Christopher. *The Consumer, Credit and Neoliberalism: Governing the Modern Economy*. London and New York: Routledge, 2012.

Rachman, David and Keith J. Fabes. 'The Decline of the Traditional American Department Store', *Journal of Marketing Channels* 1, no. 3 (1992): 39–60. https://doi.org/10.1300/J049v01n03_03

Retail Trader. Sydney: The Journal of the Retail Traders' Association of NSW, 1921–1963.

Sousa, Michael D. 'Consumer Bankruptcy in the Neoliberal State', *Emory Bankruptcy Development Journal* 39, no. 2 (2023): 199–283. https://scholarlycommons.law.emory.edu/ebdj/vol39/iss2/1

Staritz, Cornelia. *Making the Cut? Low-income Countries and the Global Clothing Value Chain in a Post-quota and Post-crisis World*. Washington, DC: The World Bank, 2011.

Tigert, Douglas J., Lawrence J. Ring and Bert McCammon. 'Change the Strategy, Change the Management: Do the Department Stores Risk Success?' *Journal of Services Marketing*, 2 no. 2 (1988): 5–18. https://doi.org/10.1108/eb024720

Tungate, Mark. *Luxury World: the Past, Present, and Future of Luxury Brands*. Philadelphia: Kogan Page, 2009.

CHAPTER 9

Conclusion

Abstract Australians embraced credit culture enthusiastically, encouraged by governments that recognised the importance of consumer credit to the country's economic success. Australian consumers' use of credit in retail locations depended on their position in the class and social hierarchies and department stores leveraged these distinctions to encourage the use of credit in their stores and maximise their profits. Technological change has reduced the social stigma associated with credit use for the majority of consumers, but for many low-income Australians its capacity to draw them into unmanageable debt remains a significant problem. The hierarchy of retail credit in Australia remains firmly in place.

Keywords Credit • Retail • Australian History • Class • Hierarchy • Status Anxiety • Indebtedness • Women • Technology

Retail credit has a mixed history in Australia. For department stores, the expansion of retail credit offered numerous opportunities. Credit expanded a department store's customer base by drawing in those with limited access to ready cash. It also increased the amount customers were prepared and able to spend and, thus, improved the store's bottom line. Arguably of

J. Dickenson, *Credit and the Australian Department Store Since 1900*, https://doi.org/10.1007/978-3-032-16612-8_9

most value to retail stores, credit helped build customer loyalty, locking consumers into a store and thereby ensuring future sales. As credit expanded and technology evolved to manage it, credit would become a means of capturing names, thus providing a valuable database for promotions. But these opportunities all came at a significant cost. The schemes were expensive to manage, involving significant time and expenditure, especially in staff wages. Technological changes required considerable investment in order to stay ahead of competitors, and department stores had, of course, to live with the risk of non-payment and the expense of chasing unpaid debts.

For the consumer, the retail credit schemes offered the emotional high of instant gratification and provided more flexibility and convenience in their economic lives by extending their spending ability. On the other hand, this flexibility could become a loss of control if their economic circumstances changed, through sickness or redundancy, for example, with the resulting loss of income. There was also the threat of increasing interest charges and the pressure to repay the debt. However, consumer experiences with retail credit varied greatly depending on the class and/or gender of the debtor. Social classes used credit in different ways. Middle-class consumers took advantage of available credit facilities to purchase items they desired but did not always need. Working-class consumers had a more complex relationship with credit: for many working-class women, the shrewd use of credit facilities such as cash orders enabled them to stretch their budget in order to provide their family with goods that middle-class Australians might have considered necessities.

Examining emerging forms of retail credit and the efforts that department stores put into promoting them recasts the history of Australian credit. It is commonplace to pin the expansion of consumer credit in Australia to the decades immediately after the Second World War, as employment stabilised and wages improved, but, as we have seen, Australians were already familiar with consumer credit in a variety of forms, with and without interest charges—they bought goods on 'the slate', used hire purchase and the cash order, and, from the 1930s, embraced department store charge cards. The form of credit they used to complete their purchases was contingent on a range of factors, not least their position in society, that is, where they sat in the economic and social hierarchies. Linked to this, the study also reveals consumers' use of a much broader range of credit forms than is usually discussed in histories of post-war Australia. Finally, women's role on the frontline in retail credit's mixed history complicates the history of consumption in Australia, bringing into question, for example, the commonly held belief that consumption in the 1950s supported a pervasive ideology of domesticity. The marketing of retail credit did not always promote the requirements of domesticity. Rather, advertisements often encouraged women to buy items for personal use on credit, utilising appeals based on notions of US modernity and targeting a woman's desire for individual expression.

Consumer credit has been a crucial factor in Australia's economic success since the 1950s. As we have seen, governments have been reluctant to act on increasing indebtedness, moving to regulate only after intense pressure from consumer advocates. Fulfilling their responsibilities to owners, shareholders, and capitalism, department stores exploited Australians' anxieties about social status to maximise their profits, constantly remaking systems to keep aspiration at the front of the consumer's mind, maintaining the credit hierarchy and its inherent status anxiety so their customers would keep spending. The stores were helped in this task by the marketing of retail credit, as advertising appeals became evermore targeted, aided by technological advances such as data processing. More efficient direct marketing, and the relationship marketing that developed in the 1990s, helped stores reach their key target—women—more effectively than ever before. By giving consumers permission to use credit, marketing transformed accessing consumer credit from a dubious if not shameful undertaking to one that was acceptable, if not quite respectable.

This book has shown that Australian consumers' entanglement with credit was not inevitable. Before the Second World War, insecure, undervalued employment and a lack of government support drove working-class women to resort to credit in the form of cash orders. After the war, increasingly targeted retail strategies made possible by technological change drove more consumers (again, mostly women) to embrace credit. Department stores rebadged and reconfigured the hierarchies of retail credit that had existed before the war in order to sustain the aspirations of consumers and thus boost retailers' profits. In short, the costs and benefits of using credit varied significantly across the spectrum of Australian society.

Department store credit encouraged the expansion of consumption to the Australian 'masses' by simultaneously emphasising and subsuming class differences, in the broader context of a gradual shift away from class allegiances to the prioritisation of individual identities. On the one hand, it allowed more cash-strapped Australians than ever before to participate in the ever-expanding consumer market, retail credit, and the mass consumption it facilitated, and thus played a crucial role in subsuming the performance of class difference in Australia. On the other hand, by harnessing a store's existing market position and emulating the significant market diversification modelled by the US charge/credit card industry, credit forms such as department store charge and revolving credit cards (facilitated by technological changes) helped make class hierarchy and status more visible, defined, and entrenched.

The urban shopping experience remains polarised, in Melbourne at least. A stroll along Collins Street reveals that the upmarket 'Universal Providers' and artisan boutiques of the early twentieth century have been replaced by a string of global luxury brands: Hermès, Prada, Fendi, YSL, Cartier, Jimmy Choo, Bulgari, Giorgio Armani, Louis Vuitton, Loewe, Gucci, Max Mara, Balenciaga, Dior, and Tiffany all call Collins Street home; Chanel is just around the corner in Flinders Lane. What is left of the 'traditional' department stores operate their own brand of spatial hierarchy. With its intimidating plethora of glitzy, high-end concessions (some needlessly replicating those in Collins Street), the Little Bourke Street entrance of David Jones is destination shopping for the wealthy and the wannabes. The less-well-heeled shopper is better advised to enter the store via Bourke Street to avoid being overwhelmed by status anxiety.

Amidst concerns about the social implications of bad debt and debilitating interest rates, the feelings of shame and embarrassment attached to using retail credit were fuelled by decades of critical commentary, aimed primarily at women. Now, in part because of its ubiquity, credit no longer attracts the same level of opprobrium. Technological advances also helped undermine this criticism and shaming. They led to smoother operations, which, in turn, meant consumers of all classes faced fewer moments of embarrassment in-store; the rise of online shopping has further detached consumers from public shaming. However, for many vulnerable Australians, little has changed. With limited income and few options, they turn now to BNPL platforms or extortionate payday and fast loan schemes to help them through the month, much as working-class women once turned to the cash-order system. Far from conferring status on these Australians, their use of these credit forms can lead to mounting debt for which they are then vilified as profligate and undisciplined, just as working-class women were once vilified. Schemes might change as technology evolves but the hierarchy of retail credit in Australia remains firmly in place.

Correction to: Fragmentation

Correction to:
Chapter 8 in: J. Dickenson, *Credit and the Australian Department Store Since 1900*,
https://doi.org/10.1007/978-3-032-16612-8_8

The original version of the chapter [8: Fragmentation] was inadvertently published before incorporation of the final correction. The chapter has been updated with the following change:

Fig 8.1: The caption was changed to read "Figure 8.1. 'Status Anxiety' mid-range brand display in Myer department store. Photographed by the author"

The updated version of this chapter can be found at
https://doi.org/10.1007/978-3-032-16612-8_8

J. Dickenson, *Credit and the Australian Department Store Since 1900*, https://doi.org/10.1007/978-3-032-16612-8_10

Index[1]

[1] Note: Page numbers followed by 'n' refer to notes.

J. Dickenson, *Credit and the Australian Department Store Since 1900*, https://doi.org/10.1007/978-3-032-16612-8

The manufacturer's authorised representative in the EU is Springer Nature Customer Service Centre GmbH, Europaplatz 3, 69115 Heidelberg, Germany. If you have any concerns regarding our products, please contact ProductSafety@springernature.com

Printed and bound by CPI Group (UK) Ltd, Croydon, CR0 4YY
16/09/2026
02217786-0004